DOCTRINE OF TERROR

MAHBOOB ILLAHI

Copyright © 2020 by Mahboob Illahi.

ISBN   Softcover   978-1-950596-84-3

This is abridged version of the book which was first published in October 2018 by Friesenpress.

All rights reserved. No part of this book may be reproduced or transmitted in any form or by any means, electronic or mechanical, including photocopying, recording, or by any information storage and retrieval system without express written permission from the author, except in the case of brief quotations embodied in critical reviews and certain other non-commercial uses permitted by copyright law.

Printed in the United States of America.

To order additional copies of this book, contact:
Bookwhip
1-855-339-3589
https://www.bookwhip.com

CONTENTS

Introduction 1

Chapter 1 Islam and the Prophet (pbuh) 5

Chapter 2 Fundamentalism 53

Chapter 3 Islamic Fundamentalist Movements outside Arabia 71

Chapter 4 House of Saud 88

Chapter 5 Persecution of the Prophet and Followers 112

Chapter 6 Spread of Saudi Salafism 161

Chapter 7 Islamic Terrorism and Terrorist Groups 186

Chapter 8 Saudi-inspired Conflicts in the World 216

Conclusion 239

Addendum 242

Abstract of Study 243

Further Reading 244

A Fervent Appeal to the King of Saudi Arabia 245

INTRODUCTION

During Islamic history, spanning 14 centuries, tolerant and inclusive teachings of Islam resulted in mass conversions of Christians and Jews to the Islamic faith, without coercion or intimidation, by the caliphs and generals of the time. According to Mark Weston in his 'Prophets and Princes,' the Prophet (PBUH) and his descendants propagated a way of life that had more fairness and justice than other religions. This resulted in spreading the faith from Spain to India. Muslim civilization became the most advanced in the world until the European Renaissance in 1300. As an example of Muslim advancement, an Arab scientist ibn AL Haytham carefully saw the twilight and correctly concluded that the air peters out, and space begins, about 60 miles above the earth.[1] This was about 900 years before Western scientists discovered the ionosphere and reached a similar conclusion. Misconceptions and ignorance of Islam are widespread among Europeans and Americans. Few Americans realize that Muslims revere the Genesis, Exodus, Psalms and parts of the Bible, as holy scriptures, and honor Noah, Abraham, Moses, and Jesus as the prophets of God. Few Westerners know that Muslims believe in the virgin birth, miracles, and the resurrection of Jesus. Of course, Muslims do not believe in the Trinity or that Jesus was the son of God. To them, this is a deviation from the belief in One God. Few Americans know that the prophet of Islam was a reformer who loved the company of women and improved their lives. The Quran forbids the killing of girls at birth and commands that a woman inherits half of what a man does, a

---

[1] Al-Haytham (965-1040)- Malaspina Great Books, archived from on September 27, 2007, retrieved 2008-01-23

revolutionary idea until the 19th century. It was also the prophet (PBUH)'s opinion that a woman should be educated and have a say in choosing her husband. Some famous Americans show a surprising ignorance about Islam. In 2003, General Boykin, undersecretary of defense for intelligence, said that the Muslims he fought in Somalia, worshipped an idol. Similarly, Franklin Graham, son of Billy Graham said in NBC News in 2002 that "the God of Muslims is a different God and Islam is an evil religion." Jerry Vines said in a Baptist Convention in 2001 that "Allah is not Jehovah" although Allah is the Arabic word for God and Jehovah and God are just words meaning the same God. Bill O'Reilly, the famous ex. Icon of Fox News asked why Americans should study "our enemy's religion."[2] Answer to his question is that terrorism is America's enemy, and not Islam which teaches regard for the sanctity of human life, peace, and tolerance, as given in Chapter 1, and opposes all kinds of violence against those who differ from its message. Terrorists, therefore, do not represent Islam. As the Qur'an does not spell out precisely many aspects of the religion, such as the prayer rituals in each prayer, a study of the Prophet's life is necessary, to get the right perspective on various issues of the religion. Chapter 2 deals with Islamic Fundamentalism which, today, is the root cause of Islamic terrorism, due to its intolerant ideology of Takfir, which calls for the killing of those who disagree with it. This chapter gives detail of its origins and modern-day application which, really, has had political motives, of defeating the Ottoman Empire, confronting the Soviet expansionism, and to counter the nationalist movements in the Muslim countries, like the Nasserism of Egypt. Chapter 3 describes other Islamic Fundamentalist movements, outside the Arabian Peninsula, whose ideology was like the Saudi Salafism, and whose followers played a vital role in the Afghan Jihad against the Soviets. Chapter 4 details the House of Saud, which has been a dominant power in the world for over 3 centuries. It describes, the upheavals, resulting from the devastation of World Wars 1 and 2, during which the Saudi Kingdom was unaffected, due to its founder King ibn Saud's firm policy of impartiality. Saudi Arabia allied itself with whoever served its political interests and enhanced its finances. This chapter also hints at what the Saudis need to do, to ensure their continued survival and progress in the future, which is really the tolerance and accommodation of

---

[2] O'Reilly—on Fox news - August 27, 2002

others, and abandoning its current policy of forced replacement of other beliefs with its Saudi/Salafi ideology. Chapter 5 deals with the persecution of Shia Muslims who have been a marginalized and oppressed minority sect of Muslims, who have been under oppression for centuries, ever since the demise of the Prophet (PBUH) of Islam, simply because they opposed repression and tyranny of the Sunni Rulers, and voiced their criticisms of the oppressive governments. More space has been given to this topic, in the book, because the main target of modern Islamic terrorism, is the Shia community of Muslims. According to scholars, Islamic Terrorism today is rooted in Saudi Salafism, the religion of Saudi Arabia, which considers only its own interpretation of Islam, to be the true Islam, and considers all others, to be apostates who need to be killed, in contravention of the clear injunctions of Islam, as described in chapter 1. Chapter 6, is devoted to Saudi Salafism, detailing how its worldwide propagation had resulted in Global Terrorism, particularly, in the Muslim majority countries. Saudi-sponsored entities set up for propagation, within the kingdom and abroad, at a cost of billions of dollars, had fueled intolerance of other faiths of Islam, disrupting the peaceful societies of other countries, especially the Muslim majority ones. Country-wise detail has been given so that the reader can see the documented incidents. Chapter 7 describes Islamic Terrorism, its motivations, and tactics used by the terrorists. It also discusses the terrorist groups, their start, logistical and financial support, and activities in different countries of the world. Covert support of these terrorist groups, by donors in the Arab countries, has been described, along with references, so that the reader can comprehend the illicit connections. Chapter 8 details the Saudi-sponsored or supported conflicts in the world, which had resulted in thousands of deaths of security personnel and civilians of the US and their coalition partners, from Europe, Australia, New Zealand, without direct involvement of Saudi forces except for Yemen. Thousands of people had been killed in these conflicts in Iran, Iraq, Syria, Yemen, Afghanistan, Pakistan, and other countries. In conclusion, solution to the terrorism problem has been suggested, hoping that the King of Saudi Arabia, will adopt a path which will strengthen his kingdom, instead of weakening it. The present King Salman, and the Crown Prince Mohammad bin Salman have, already, expressed their resolve to return Saudi Arabia to Moderate Islam, which is excellent news for the world.

CHAPTER 1

Islam and the Prophet (pbuh)

To understand Islamic terrorism, we need to study Islam, and the Prophet of Islam, described briefly in this Chapter, to decide if the religion itself or the Sunnah [sayings and example of the Prophet (pbuh)] encourage or incite terrorist acts, or promote intolerance of other faiths. If not, then, the ideology behind terrorism, is a clear deviation from the teachings of Islam.

Concepts of Faith: God is described in chapter 112 of the Quran: O' Prophet proclaim that "God is only one, eternal, and absolute. He neither gave birth to anyone like humans, nor anyone gave birth to Him" (Quran 112: 1-4). God is beyond all comprehension and is beyond human imagination. He is known by certain names and attributes like" the compassionate and the Merciful". Muslims believe that everything in the Universe was created by God's sheer command, and that the purpose of existence is to worship God who responds whenever a person in need or distress, calls him. There are no intermediaries, such as the clergy, to contact God who states, "I am nearer to you than your Jugular Vein. (Quran: 50:16)[3]

---

[3] Bentley, David (September 1999). The 99 Beautiful Names for God for All the People of the Book.

Afterlife and the Day of Judgment: The human body decays after death but the soul exists for ever. After death, another phase of life starts, in the grave, known as Barzakh which continues until physical resurrection for the day of Judgement when God will judge how each one of us fared on earth. Resurrection will be physical and is explained by suggesting that Allah will re-create the decayed body like He created the first human (Quran; 17;100) Entry into hell or heaven will depend on the deeds on earth except that Warriors who die fighting in the cause of God, are ushered at once to God's presence (Surah 2:159 and Surah 3:169); and - "Enemies of Islam" are immediately sentenced to Hell, upon death.

Islam's Message is the same as Christianity and Judaism: Quran emphasizes the fact that the Prophet Muhammad's message is the same as conveyed by Abraham, Moses and Jesus during their times, evident from (Qur'an 42:13) which says: "Allah has ordained for you a religion He gave Abraham, Noah, Moses and Jesus and which He revealed to you, [O Muhammad], and not be divided therein. It is difficult for those who associate others with Allah who chooses for Himself whom He wills and guides to Himself whoever turns back [to Him]." In the following ayahs, the Quran reiterates that followers of the above prophets should really be united on the basic concepts of the religion. The division among the followers took place due to Jealousy, and after full knowledge of religion was imparted to them, as stated in the following ayahs which say that division was due to jealousy and animosity among them. And that penalty has been postponed to the next life. (Qur'an 42:14). God instructs the prophet to follow the right course as commanded and not to follow their inclinations and say "Our deeds are for us and yours are for you, and there is no need to argue. Allah will judge both of us." (Qur'an 42:15)

Virgin Birth of Mary and Oneness of God: Quran is explicit in the virgin birth of Mary(pbuh), narrated in the following ayahs: "My Lord, how will I have a child when no man has touched me?" [The angel] said, "Such is Allah; He creates what He wills. When He decrees a matter, He only says to it, 'Be,' and it is." (Quran 3:47). Regarding oneness of God, the Quran says: Allah will ask Jesus whether he told people to take Jesus and Mary as deities besides Allah? Jesus will respond in the negative saying:

"You know if I had said anything like that" (Qur'an 5:116) According to the Quran, the prophets of Judaism and Christianity were the true messengers of God, Muhammad being the last prophet.

Crucifixion of Jesus and resurrection: According to the Qur'an, Jesus escaped the crucifixion and ascended directly to heaven. According to the Quran, Jesus (pbuh) did not die on the cross, although the person on the cross resembled Jesus. Quran says: "People say; Indeed, we have killed the Messiah, Jesus, the son of Mary, the messenger of God, but they crucified someone resembling Jesus who was taken to Heavens by Allah. "(Qur'an 4:157) And "Jesus will be a witness to all the People of the Scripture who did not believe in him." (Qur'an 4:159)

Status of Non-Muslims in Islam: The Qur'an distinguishes between those who believe in one God (the monotheistic) like the Jews, Christians, Sabeans and others, and the Idolaters (polytheists). Muslim males can marry a Christian or Jew, but not a polytheist. According to the Quran:" Indeed, the believers, Jews, Christians, and Sabeans—whoever truly believes in God, and day of judgement, and has virtuous deeds need not have any fear.' (Quran 22;17). According to Historian al-Biruni (writing at the beginning of the eleventh century CE), the real Sabeans were Jewish tribes who had remained in Babylonia, in the days of Cyrus. They adopted an ideology based on Zoroastrianism and Judaism. The Quran suggests that Jews, Christians, and people of other faiths will be judged according to "their own book": (Qur'an 2:62, 45:30) (Qur'an; 45:28)

Punishment for Disbelief: Quran says: "For sins of the Jews, we made certain good foods unlawful, as a punishment." (Qur'an :160) The Jews of Medina wanted the Prophet of Islam to bring a book, in written form from heaven like Prophet Moses had done, to prove his prophethood. In response to this demand, the Quran says that the Jews had demanded Moses show them God. So, lightening struck them. Then they started worshipping a calf, after clear evidences had come to them, but We still pardoned them, and We cursed them for slandering Mary (Qur'an 4:156)

Islam and Non-Muslims: Christians and Jews who had accepted the Muslim rule, could worship in their own way, follow their own family law, and govern their territories themselves. However, the non-Muslims were subject to taxation (Jizya), at a different rate than the Muslims. Some Jews rejected the status of the prophet (pbuh). According to historian Watt, "Jews were normally unwilling to admit that a non-Jew could be a prophet." In the, Constitution of Medina, the prophet (pbuh) demanded the Jews' political loyalty, in return for religious and cultural autonomy. In every major battle with the Muslims of Medina, two local Jewish tribes were treacherous (see Qur'an 2; 100). After the battles of Badr and Uhud, Banu Qaynuqa and Banu Nadir, took up arms against the Muslims, and, as a result, were expelled from Medina, with their families and possessions, according to Muslim Historian al-Ya'qubi.[4] However, this incident does not mean that, Jews in general, rejected Muhammad's constitution. One Yemenite Jewish document was found in the Cairo Genizah (which is a collection of about 300,000 manuscript fragments) that were found in the storeroom of the Ben Ezra Synagogue, in Old Cairo, Egypt. The manuscripts found, outline a 1,000-year (870 CE to 19th century) history of Jews in the Middle East and North Africa and make up the largest collection of medieval manuscripts in the world. Genizah texts were in Hebrew, Arabic and Aramaic, on vellum and paper, and on papyrus and cloth. The documents claim that many Jews had not only accepted Muhammad as a prophet, but even desecrated Sabbat, to join Muhammad in his struggle. However, it is an established fact that most Yemeni Jews considered Muhammad to be a true prophet, including Nathaniel al-Bayoumi, a major 12th century rabbi who incorporated various Shia doctrines into his view of Judaism.[5] The Syriac Patriarch Ishoyahb III wrote to Simeon of Rewardashir that "Muslims praise our faith and give donations and aid to the churches and monasteries."[6] After Muhammad's death in 632, Islamic rule grew rapidly, extending to, what

---

[4] Esposito, John. 1998. Islam: the Straight Path, extended edition. Oxford university press, p.17

[5] Yakov Rabkin—perspectives on the muslims in Jewish tradition—(PDF). Archived—(PDF) on 2012-03-27. (126 KB)

[6] Sidney H. Griffith:—Disputing with Islam in Syriac—archived—2006-07-16 at the wayback machine.

is now the Middle East, Egypt, North Africa, and Iran, where, most of the new subjects were Christian or Jewish, and, were considered People of the Book. After some argument, the Zoroastrians were also considered People of the Book. Christians, Jews, and Zoroastrians were called dhimmi, the protected persons. As noted above, they could worship in their own way, implement their own laws and possess property. They were not subjected to certain Islamic laws about alcohol and pork. They were not required to pay Zakat or serve in the military but had to pay Jizya, in return for protection under the Islamic government.[7]

Befriending Jews and Christians: According to the Quran, righteousness is the criteria for superiority regardless of religious affiliation or social and financial status. Regarding the Jews and Christians, the Quran says that there are righteous Jews and Christians, just like people of other faiths. So, Muslims may befriend people of good character whatever their religion might be. It further states that among the people of Moses, some do justice in the light of faith. (Quran 7:159). It says that "among the people of the book, some pray all night and enjoin right and forbid what is evil. Such people are the good ones." (Quran 3:113-115)

Exceptions to Friendship: The Quran does not discriminate human beings, based on their faith, as to who can be befriended and who cannot. As noted above, the criterion is righteousness, and this rule applies to all, including the Jews and Christians. In Medina, the Prophet was at war with Meccans and some Jews and Christians secretly allied with Meccans against the Muslims, breaking their agreements with the Prophet. Ayah (Quran 5:51) refers to those people. Quran specifically encourages us to study all the ayahs concerning an issue before making a judgment. Different ayahs revealed according to the difficulties of the time, may have discussed a topic. All such ayahs should be studied to get the right perspective. (Quran 2:85) "Quran forbids friendship with people who drive you out of your homes and fight you due to your faith". (Quran 60:8,9):

---

[7] Zoroaster and Zoroastrians in Iran—2005-11-22 at the wayback machine—, by Massoume Price, Iran Chamber Society, retrieved March 24, 2006

Sanctity of Human Life in Islam: We heard about the Terrorist Groups like ISIS and Al-Qaeda, killing innocent civilians in Iraq and Syria, and in other countries. Their actions violate the very clear injunctions of Islam, about the sanctity of human life. The Quran says: "do not kill the soul which Allah has forbidden (to be executed), except by legal right" (i.e., for the requirements of justice)- (Quran—6: 151). Another ayah of the Quran says: "Whoever kills a person unjustly, it is as though he has killed all humankind. And whoever saves a life, saves the entire human race ". (Qur'an 5: 32). These ayahs emphasize regard for the survival of all human beings, regardless of their faiths or beliefs. The ideology of intolerance and extremism is in fact from the Saudi/ Salafi religion, founded by Imam ibn Abd al-Wahhab in 1741, following the Khawarij of the seventh century, and later the Muslim Scholar of the 14th-century ibn-Taymiyyah. This deviant ideology considers all those who do not agree with it, to be apostates who deserve to be killed. The ISIS and other terrorist groups follow this ideology in killing the Shia Muslims, Jews, and Christians, considering such killing to be a Holy War. This ideology and the terrorist groups have been discussed in detail, in chapters 6 and 7.

Islam is a Religion of Peace: Many scholars, church leaders, and politicians say that Islam is a religion of peace. George Bush said this on September 17, 2001, and Barack Obama, in November 2010, in Mumbai, India said: "ISIS is not Islamic. No religion condones the killing of innocents. The religion of Islam teaches justice, fairness, and tolerance". Tony Blair also said, "Those of us who have studied Islam have no doubt about its peaceful and tolerant nature." Pope Francis made similar comments. He said: "Hearing about violent fundamentalism of Jihadi groups such as ISIS, we must remember the tolerance of all faiths taught by Islam, which is opposed to every form of violence." He pointed out that "organizations such as the Islamic State are evil, and they do not represent Islam. They are a perversion of Islam". –Pope's statements are on the Catholic Online (www.catholic.org) dated 8/3/2016.

Teachings of Islam: The Quran is considered the "sourcebook of Islamic principles and values." Muslim jurists consult the Hadith or the written record of Prophet Muhammad (PBUH) 's life, to both supplement the

Quran and assist with its interpretation. Islam says that all of God's messengers preached the message of Islam, which was submission to the will of God. The Quran mentions the names of several Prophets namely, Adam, Noah, Abraham, Moses, Jesus, Jacob, David, Joseph, Jonah, Elisha, Solomon, Aaron, Job, John, Zechariah, and Elijah. The names in the Quran are, however, not biblical names. [8] During his lifetime, the Prophet of Islam (pbuh) taught equality of human beings, regardless of social status, financial resources, race, and color of skin. He regarded slaves to be equal to their masters and personally regarded some with high esteem like Bilal and many others. The only criteria for dignity, in Islam, is who fears God more, and is more righteous. The Prophet's message transformed society and moral orders of life in the Arabian Peninsula. Economics was an issue at that time. The Quran needs payment of an obligatory alms tax (Zakat) for the benefit of the poor. As the Prophet (PBUH) 's power grew, he insisted that tribes who wished to ally with him, implement the zakat. [9] Quran promotes the principle of religious freedom, saying: "There is no compulsion in religion." (Quran- 2; 256) Conversion to the Muslim faith by Coercion is, therefore, not permissible, according to the quoted ayah of the Quran.

Economics and Welfare State: Interest-bearing loans and hoarding of food for speculation is discouraged in Islam. During the time of the prophet (PBUH), money received in the treasury was immediately distributed among the poor. In 634, Umar (r.a), the 2nd caliph, formally set up the Bayt al-mal (welfare state) which was for the Muslim and Non-Muslim poor, needy, elderly, orphans, widows, and the disabled. He also introduced Child benefits and Pensions for the children and the elderly. The system continued for hundreds of years, through the Umayyad and Abbasid caliphates.[10]

---

[8] Momin 1987,(p. 176), "Islam" Encyclopædia Britannica Online.
[9] Medani Ahmed and Sebastian Gianci, Zakat, Encyclopedia of Taxation and Tax Policy, p. 479
[10] Karim, Shafiel A. (2010). The Islamic Moral Economy: A Study of Islamic Money and Financial Instruments. Boca Raton, FL: Brown Walker Press

Social Welfare: A Muslim's religious life is seen incomplete if not used in serving human beings. Islam advanced the rare concept of social services, stressing on the care of relatives, orphans, the needy, those seeking help, freeing slaves, and the travelers as detailed in Quran; 2:177. Also emphasized are service to the parents in their old age, the neighbors, the sick, the elderly, and the minorities, regardless of their religious affiliation. Quran forbids admonishing the weak, the orphaned children and the destitute, and preaches justice and equality among the human beings. (Qur'an 89: 17-18.)[11]

Morality in Islam: The Quran and the Sunnah of the prophet (PBUH) prescribe righteousness, good deeds, forgiveness, honesty, kindness, and justice as the basic requirement for a Muslim, the moral values which Jesus (PBUH) also preached. The imposition of a penalty for an offense is permissible, but forgiving the offender, is better, and, offering a favor to the offender, is considered superior. (Quran 41: 34) says evil should be countered with the best manners. Other emphasized moral virtues include, charitable activities, the fulfillment of a promise, modesty and humility, decency in speech, tolerance, trustworthiness, patience, truthfulness, controlling one's temper, and sincerity of intention. As a religion, Islam emphasizes the idea of having a good character as the prophet (PBUH) said: 'The best among you are those who have the best manners and character'. Sahih Bukhari (8: 73: 56). As a virtue, forgiveness is considered commendable in Islam and is regarded as a critical Muslim practice. About modesty, the prophet (PBUH) is reported as saying: 'Every religion has its characteristic, and the characteristic of Islam is modesty'. The teachings of the Islamic faith, described above, are very much like Christianity and Judaism, except that Islam considers Jesus (PBUH) to be a human, like other prophets, such as Abraham, David, and Moses.[12]

---

[11] Ibn Majah Vol 3 Hadith 2289—International Business Success in a Strange Cultural Environment By Mamarinta P. Mababaya Page 202 Islamic Capital Markets: Theory and Practice By Noureddine Krichene Page 119.

[12] Khadduri, Majid (1984). islamic concept of justice.The Johns Hopkins University Press. p. 10.

Freedom of Worship: Qur'an 2:256, says: "There is no compulsion in religion". This ayah of the Quran emphasizes freedom of worship and religion.

The Prophet of Islam (610–632): To fully understand the teachings of Islam, the sayings and example of the Prophet (PBUH) are of vital importance because the Qur'an does not exactly specify many of its tenets. For example, prayer ritual which is the first requirement from a Muslim is not spelled out exactly in the Qur'an, about how exactly it should be performed, and the exact timings of the prayers. The Prophet (PBUH) performed Noon (Zuhr) and afternoon (Asr) prayers together, one after the other, and Sunset (Maghreb) and Evening (Isha) rituals together, one after the other, although he was not pressed for time. This, he did at Arafat, during the Hajj. So, if the prayers are performed like the Prophet, as he did during the Hajj, described later in the section on Farewell Pilgrimage, they cannot be wrong. This further means that if Shia Muslims combine Zuhr and Asr prayers, and Maghreb and Isha prayers, performing them one after the other, they are not wrong. There are many such tenets of Islam that are not specified in the Qur'an but were explained and demonstrated by the Prophet (PBUH). Therefore, the study of the Sunnah of the Prophet (PBUH) is very important for the correct understanding of Islam, except things that are clearly defined and specified in the Qur'an and are not ambiguous.

Early Life of the Prophet: He was born in 570. His father Abdullah died before his birth and his mother Amna sent him to live with a Bedouin family in the desert, according to Arab tradition which considered desert life to be healthier for infants. He stayed with his foster-mother Halima until the age of two. Amna also died, when he was about 6 years old, and he went under his grandfather Abd al-Muttalib's supervision. After the death of Abd al-Muttalib, young Muhammad (PBUH), came under the care of his uncle Abu Talib, the new leader of Banu Hashem. In his teens, he used to go with his uncle on Syrian trading journeys, to gain experience in commercial trade.[13]

---

[13] Watt, "Halima bin Dhuab, Encyclopedia of Islam.

Meeting Bahira-A Christian Monk: At the age of nine or twelve, while accompanying the Meccans, he came across a Christian monk or hermit named Bahira, cited by Armand Abel in Encyclopedia of Islam. [14]The monk was looking outside when he saw an approaching caravan which seemed to be unusual. He offered his hospitality to the caravan members. He studied the faces of the guests and asked if anyone was left behind. They answered that they had left a young lad to look after the camels. Bahira asked for the boy to be brought also. When Bahira saw Muhammad (PBUH), he was delighted, because he had read in the holy scriptures about the coming of a Prophet. He asked Muhammad many questions as to what he dreams about and what he sees during his sleep. The answers convinced Bahira about Muhammad's identity. He asked Abu Talib about his relationship with the boy. Abu Talib first said he was his son but Bahira rejected his claim. Abu Talib finally told him he was his nephew. Bahira disclosed to Abu Talib that Muhammad is going to be a Prophet of God and he should be returned to Mecca because his life could be endangered if the Jews saw him during their trip. He told Abu Talib that he had noticed a cloud shading the caravan, and trees and stones prostrating to Muhammad (PBUH). He also looked at the oval-shaped seal of prophets on Muhammad (PBUH)'s back. Abu Talib accepted advice of the monk and sent Muhammad back to Mecca with some guides. Young Abu Bakr and Bilal accompanied Muhammad (PBUH) on this trip, forming a bond of friendship which lasted during their adult life.

The setting of the Black Stone (605 CE): According to historian Ibn Ishaq, there was a controversy in Mecca in 605 about setting the black stone of the Kaaba after renovations. The leaders quarreled over which clan should return the black stone to its place. They finally decided to ask the next man entering the Kaaba to decide. That man was the 35 years old Muhammad (PBUH) who asked for a cloth and put the black stone in the center and asked clan leaders to hold the corners, and they all carried the black stone to its place, satisfying the honor of all. [15] This event took place five years before the first revelation by Gabriel in 610.

---

[14] Armand Abel, Bahira, Encyclopedia of Islam
[15] Dairesi, Hırka-i Saadet; Aydin, Hilmi (2004).

Prophethood and Beginnings of the Qur'an (610 CE): Muhammad (PBUH) began to pray alone in a cave near Mecca, called Hira when in 610, Surah 96.1 was revealed to him by angel Gabriel. Muhammad (PBUH) was deeply distressed upon receiving his first revelation. After returning home, he was consoled and reassured by Khadijah and her Christian cousin, Waraqah ibn Nawfal. The first revelation was followed by a three-year pause during which Muhammad (PBUH) felt deeply depressed. Then (Qur'an 93.3) was revealed in which God assured him that he was not abandoned and that he should start preaching to the people of Mecca to worship ONE God, abandoning idol worship.[16] Muhammad (PBUH)'s wife Khadija was the first to believe he was a prophet. She was followed by Muhammad (PBUH)'s ten-year-old cousin Ali (a.s). Ibn Abi Talib, followed by close friend Abu Bakr (r.a) and adopted son Zaid. He preached his message in Mecca for 12 years, attracting many followers, but facing severe persecution from the leading Meccans. The Meccan élite felt that Muhammad (PBUH) was destabilizing their social order by preaching about one God and about racial equality, giving ideas to the poor who were their slaves.

Summoning the Family: Muhammad declared his prophethood at the age of forty but kept his mission secret for the first three years, after which he was instructed to preach his message openly, starting with his near relatives of Banu Hashim clan. "Warn your nearest relations."[17] Muhammad (PBUH) organized a feast, known as Da 'wat dhul- 'Ashīra (Summoning the Family). He invited about forty men from his clan, the Banu Hashim and asked Ali to plan a feast. When he stood up to speak, his uncle Abu Lahab interrupted him and said: "Your host has long since bewitched you". The guests left before Muhammad (PBUH) could present his message to them, but he invited them again the following day. After the feast, he said to them: 'O Sons of 'Abdul-Muttalib! By Allah, I have brought you the good of this world and the next. Who among you will support me in this task, becoming my successor and my caliph? Ali was the only one who responded in the affirmative, saying:" I will be your helper O Prophet of God." The Prophet (PBUH) then put his hand on the back

---

[16] Brown (2003), pp. 72–73
[17] Quran 26;214.

of Ali's neck and said, "Ali is my brother and successor. I ask everyone to obey him."[18]

The Hadith of the Cloak: Ayesha (r.a) reported that Muhammad (PBUH) put Fatima (r.a), Ali (a.s)., Hassan (a.s), and Husayn (a.s) under his cloak and prayed to God to keep uncleanliness away from the people under his cloak. In response, God sent Gabriel to reveal the Quran;33:33, called the "Verse of Purification". Although the ayah addresses wives of the Prophet in the first part, where the verbs and pronouns are in feminine plural, meaning the wives only, in the second part they are masculine plural, meaning a group consisting of males and a female, according to Laura Veccia Vaglieri in Encyclopedia of Islam. Therefore, the second part is referring to the group having males and not only a group of females. People of the house means, Ahle Bayt, meaning, Muhammad (PBUH), Fatima (r.a), Ali (a.s), Hassan (a.s), and Husayn (a.s), as narrated above.—(Sunan al-Tirmizi vol.2 Sahih 902).

Conversion of Umar (r.a) to Islam (616 CE): It is said that one day Umar (r.a) resolved, in sheer exasperation, to kill Muhammad (PBUH), and thereby to extinguish the flame of Islam itself. He left his home with this intention. In those days, the Muslims used to pray at Arqam's house. They were alarmed to see Umar, with a drawn sword, approaching the house. Hamza (r.a), who was also present, reassured them and said that he would confront Umar if required. On his way, toward Dar-ul-Arqam with the intention of killing the prophet (PBUH), someone told him to put his own house in order as his sister and her husband had become Muslims. Umar (r.a) came to the door of his sister as Khabbab, a companion of the prophet (PBUH) was reciting the Surah Taha. Umar's sister hid the paper from which they were reading while Khabbab hid himself in the house. Umar (r.a) asked what was being read to which she answered that it was merely a conversation between them. Umar (r.a) exploded in wrath and struck his sister in her face. The blow caused her mouth to bleed. Umar (r.a) was going to strike again but the sight of blood made him pause. He suddenly appeared to calm down. His sister asked him to clean up before she would allow him to touch the words of God. Umar went home, washed

---

[18] Ibn al-Athír, al-Kāmil, vol. 5 (Beirut, 1965) pp. 62-63.

up, and returned. Quran was recited to him and he was so impressed that he went straight to the Prophet and became Muslim.[19] Historian, Sir William Muir in (The Life of Muhammad (PBUH), London, 1877), says that Umar (r.a)'s conversion to Islam took place at the close of the sixth year of Muhammad (PBUH) 's mission, in Dhul Hajj. Umar (r.a) was in his thirties when he became a Muslim. The believers at that time were, in all, were 40 men and ten women; or by other accounts, 45 men and eleven women.

Opposition and Persecution by Meccans (610-622): As his followers increased, Muhammad (PBUH) became a threat to the elite of Mecca whose wealth depended on the Kaaba and the trade it created. Denouncing the Meccan religion irked the Quraysh who offered to admit him to the group of powerful merchants and a helpful marriage. He refused both offers. Sumayya, a slave of Abu Jahl, was killed by her master when she refused to give up her faith. Bilal, a Muslim slave, was tortured by his master Umayya who placed a heavy rock on his chest to force his conversion. The influence of his family protected the prophet, but not entirely, as his uncle Abu Lahab's wife Umm Jamil regularly dumped filth outside his door and spread thorns and nails outside his door to hurt him.[20]

Migration to Abyssinia (614-615): The first group of emigrants, including eleven men and four women, was granted asylum in Abyssinia in the year 615.The group included Usman (r.a). bin Affan. After a year they heard rumours that the Quraysh had accepted Islam, resulting in their return to Mecca where they found that nothing had changed. This caused them to return to Abyssinia, in 616, along with others, 83 men and 18 women in all. When the Quraysh learned that Muhammad (PBUH)'s companions could safely practice their religion in Abyssinia, they decided to send envoys to the king of Abyssinia, to ask for their return. They sent expensive gifts made of fine skin leather, for the king and his generals. They told the king that the fugitives had invented a new religion unlike the Abyssinian and the Meccan religions, and that their relatives wanted

---

[19] Al Mubarakpuri, Safi ur Rahman (2002). Ar-Raheeq al-Makhtum- Darussalam. pp. 130–131.
[20] Watt, The Cambridge History of Islam (1977), p. 36

their return. The king received the envoys but refused to hand over the emigrants without hearing them. Jaffar bin Abi Talib who acted as the leader of the exiles, spoke in their defense. He described to the king how they lived before Islam, and Prophet Muhammad (PBUH)'s teachings. The king asked them to read if they had anything that had come from God. Jaffar recited a passage from Surah Maryam. On hearing, the king wept and said: "This and what Jesus brought came from the same source". He refused to give up the Muslims. The next day, the envoy Amr ibn al-As, thought of another tactic.[21] He told the king that the Muslims had said a dreadful thing about Jesus. So the king summoned the Muslims again who, decided to speak according to the revelation. Jaffar said the Muslims held Jesus to be God's servant, his prophet, his spirit, and his word that was cast on the Virgin Mary. On hearing these words, the King declared that Jesus was indeed no more than that, and dismissed the envoys, returning their gifts. He said to the Muslims that they were welcome in his country. Many of the exiles returned to Mecca in 622 and migrated to Medina with the Prophet (PBUH), while a second batch came to Medina from Ethiopia in 628, about 6 years later.[22]

Boycott of Banu Hashem (617-619): In 617, Meccans imposed a public boycott against the prophet's clan Banu Hashem so that they withdraw their protection from the Prophet. The terms included a complete boycott of all kinds of dealings with members of Banu Hashim. The boycott however failed because it created a lot of sympathy for Banu Hashim who had nothing to eat and some fed themselves on leaves of trees. They finally decided to annul the agreement. Abu Lahab, prophet's uncle supported the boycott and sided with Quraysh. The boycott included even those who had not accepted Islam. The boycott was ended in 619.[23]

---

[21] Buhl, F.; Welch, A.T. (1993). "Muḥammad". Encyclopedia of Islam (2nd ed.). Brill. pp. 360–376.

[22] William Montgomery Watt (1961). Muhammad:. Oxford University Press. p. 66.

[23] Daniel W. Brown, A New Introduction to Islam, Blackwell Publishing, p.76, 2004,

Last years in Mecca before Hijra (Migration): Prophet Muhammad (PBUH) 's wife Khadija and uncle Abu Talib died in 619, and leadership of Banu Hashem clan passed to Abu Lahab, a tenacious enemy of Muhammad (PBUH). Soon afterward, he withdrew the clan's protection over Muhammad (PBUH). This placed the Prophet (PBUH) in great danger as there will be no retribution if he is killed.

Visit to Taif (619): Now, not just the elite of Mecca attacked Muhammad (PBUH), but even young children threw stones and shouted insults at him. Muhammad (PBUH) lost hope in the people of Mecca and proceeded to Taif, accompanied by his adopted son, Zaid ibn Haritha, for the preaching of Islam. Fearful of the Meccans, the chiefs of the local tribes, left them at the mercy of the street gangs who threw rocks and stones at them to make them leave the city. Muhammad (PBUH) and Zayd ibn Haritha were finally turned out by the mocking and jeering crowds. The rocks injured the Prophet (PBUH) and he bled so profusely from the stoning that his feet became clotted to his shoes. Once Muhammad (PBUH) and Zayd ibn Haritha were outside the city walls, Muhammad (PBUH) almost fainted. They stopped at an orchard which belonged to two Meccans who sent their slave to care for them until they could resume their journey. The owners of the orchard told their slave Addas to offer a tray of grapes to the visitors. Addis became curious and inquired about the identity of Muhammad (PBUH) who presented himself. The conversation that ensued led Addis to declare his acceptance of Islam, so that Muhammad (PBUH)'s journey to Taif proved to be fruitful.[24]

Return to Mecca from Taif: Muhammad (PBUH) sent Zayd to seek asylum for him among 4 nobles in the city. Three of them refused but the fourth one, Mut'im ibn Adi responded. Mut'im ordered his sons, nephews and other young men of his clan to put on their battledress and then brought Muhammad (pbuh) to the Kaaba where he prayed. They then escorted him to his home. Many people visited Mecca on business or as pilgrims to the Kaaba. During his search for a new home Muhammad (pbuh) found hope with some men from Yathrib (later called Medina) where the people were familiar with monotheism due to Jewish population

---

[24] Hazrat Muhammad pbuh's Visit to Ta'if - on al-islam.org

who expected appearance of a Prophet. They also hoped, by Muhammad (pbuh) and the new faith, to gain supremacy over Mecca. Converts to Islam came from all Arab tribes in Medina.

Pledges of al-Aqaba (620-621): In Mecca, at the pilgrimage season of 620, Muhammad (pbuh) met six men of the Banu Khazraj from Medina, presented to them the doctrines of Islam and recited portions of the Qur'an. Impressed, all six accepted Islam and brought seven others with them. They informed the Prophet about gradual propagation of Islam in Medina and took a formal allegiance at the Prophet's hand to accept him as a Prophet and worship one God and refrain from sins such as theft, adultery, and murder. This was the first pledge of Aqaba. At their request, Muhammad (pbuh) sent Mus'ab ibn Umair to teach them about Islam. Mus'ab's efforts caused 73 men and 2 women to come to Mecca the following year for pilgrimage and to meet the Prophet (pbuh) who came to the meeting in the middle of night, accompanied by his uncle Abbas. Ansar (Muslims of Medina) pledged to defend and support the prophet (pbuh) and his followers even at the risk of their lives. Following the pledges at Aqaba, Muhammad (pbuh) encouraged his followers to emigrate to Medina. The Quraysh tried to stop the emigration. However, all Muslims managed to leave, within 2 months.[25]

Prophet's Migration to Medina (622): After receiving divine direction to leave Mecca, Muhammad (pbuh) began preparations and informed Abu Bakr (r.a) of his plan. On the night of his departure, Muhammad (pbuh)'s house was surrounded by Quraysh who planned to kill him in the morning. He had some Quraysh properties with him in trust, which he handed over to Ali, and asked him to sleep on his bed, saying God will protect him. When the Prophet (pbuh) left his house, he recited the ninth verse of Surah Yasin and threw handful of dust at the besiegers, making them unable to see him. Soon Muhammad (pbuh) joined Abu Bakr (r.a) and the two left the city and in the morning, the Quraysh were surprised to see Ali on Muhammad (pbuh)'s bed. Fooled and thwarted by Muhammad (pbuh)'s plan, they looked for him all over the city and some of them eventually reached the front of the cave but did not bother to

---

[25] 1= Watt (1974), p. 83   2= Peterson (2006), pp. 86–89

enter the cave as its front was covered with a spider's web and assumed no human could be inside. When the Quraysh came to know of Muhammad (pbuh)'s escape, they announced heavy reward for bringing him back alive or dead. After three days in the cave, Muhammad (pbuh) and Abu Bakr (r.a) headed toward Medina. Suraqa bin Malik chased them but when he neared them, his horse stopped, forcing him to give up the chase. After eight days' journey, they reached the outskirts of Medina around June 622, and stopped at Quba where the Prophet set up a mosque. After four days at Quba, they continued their journey to Medina, offering Friday prayers on the way. On arrival, they were received by a big crowd of the people of Medina.[26]

Constitution of Medina (622): In Medina, the prophet (pbuh) formulated the constitution of Medina, establishing a religious and political authority, with several rights and responsibilities for the Muslims, and non-Muslims, forming a single community. The constitution included guidelines for: the security of community, religious freedom, barring violence and weapons in Medina, rights of women, tribal relations within Medina, a tax system for supporting the community in time of conflict, parameters for political alliance with outsiders, a system for granting protection of individuals, and a legal system to resolve disputes, in which non-Muslims could use their own laws and judges. All tribes signed the agreement to defend Medina against invaders and live peacefully themselves.[27]

Aftermath of Constitution of Medina: Muhammad (pbuh)'s followers suffered from poverty, after leaving Mecca and migrating with Muhammad (pbuh), because Meccans had seized their wealth and belongings. Following nomadic tradition of Arabs, some of them started raiding Meccan caravans to and from Syria, in order to survive. Arab tribes were either nomadic or sedentary, the former moving constantly in search of water and pastures for their flocks while the latter settled in one place and carried out trade and

---

[26] Buhl, F.; Welch, A.T. (1993). "Muhammad". Encyclopedia of Islam (2nd ed.). Brill. pp. 360–376.

[27] Watt, The Cambridge History of Islam, p. 39.

agriculture. The survival of nomads was partially dependent on raiding caravans or oases, which, by tradition, was not considered a crime.[28]

The First Battle (624 AD): The prophet (pbuh)'s battles were all either defensive or in response to his enemy's treacheries or breach of pacts. None of them were aggressive. They were neither to win territory nor to plunder, or to subdue peaceful populations or to convert them to Islam by force. The first battle of Badr was a defensive battle. A trade caravan which had gone to Syria that year, headed by Abu Sufyan, was on its way back to Mecca. Abu Sufyan feared that his caravan might be intercepted by the Muslims. He informed Quraysh about his fears, and they readied a well-armed force of 1000 warriors led by Abu Jahl and sent it to Medina. When they reached Badr, 80 miles from Medina, news came that the caravan had not been attacked. But Meccans had one thousand well-equipped warriors, eager to fight the Muslims. So, they continued their advance towards Medina. They camped at the stream of Badr. Quraysh sent three warriors for individual combats. Ansar volunteers confronted them, but the Quraysh shouted them back, insisting on fighting men from Muhammad's clan. The Prophet sent Hamza, Ali, and Ubaidah of Banu Hashim to fight Utba, Shaibah, and Walid bin Utba of the Meccan side. Ali killed his adversary Walid, and Hamza killed Utba, but Ubaidah was mortally wounded by Shayba who was then jointly killed by Ali and Hamza who carried Ubaidah back to the Muslim lines where he died. An intense battle started after that. The Prophet prayed for Almighty's help in this first encounter between the pagans and the Muslims. Quran, 8:9-10 depicts Almighty's response to the Prophet's prayers saying: "I will assist you with a thousand angels, to ease your hearts and victory is from Allah, the Mighty, and Wise."[29] Seventy Meccans were killed, including several notable chiefs, including their leader Abu Jahl. Out of 70, thirty-five were

---

[28] Fazlur Rahman—(1979), p. 21 2=John Kelsey—(1993), p. 21

[29] Quran: Al-Imran 3: 123-125 "Allah helped you at Badr, when ye were a contemptible little force; then fear Allah; thus, May ye show your gratitude. Remember thou said to the Faithful: "Is it not enough for you that Allah should help you with three thousand angels (Specially) sent down? "Yea, – if ye remain firm, and act right, even if the enemy should rush here on you in hot haste, your Lord would help you with five thousand angels Making a terrific onslaught."

killed by Ali (a.s). Ibn Abi Talib alone. It was his first war. The Muslims won the battle. Seventy Meccans were taken prisoners. 14 Muslims were martyred. The prisoners were treated with exceptional kindness. The critic William Muir says: "In pursuance of Mahomet's commands, the citizens of Medina and the refugees gave exceptional hospitality to the prisoners. One of them later said: they made us ride while they walked and gave us wheat bread when there was little available and eating dates themselves. The well-off prisoners paid ransom and were freed. Others were employed on teaching to read and write. Entire 1400 years of history has no record of better treatment of the prisoners than the Prophet's, after his first encounter which aimed at annihilating the Muslims.[30]

Aftermath of Badr: This victory dealt a severe blow to the prestige of the Quraysh. Some of their chiefs, such as Abu Jahl, 'Utbah, Shaibah, Zam'ah, 'Aas ibn Hisham, and Umayya ibn Khalaf had been killed and, so, Abu Sufyan became their undisputed chieftain. 'Abdullah ibn Ubayy and his followers professed Islam, though in name only, and as munafiq (hypocrites), they were always a source of danger. Writer Paul K Davis sums up: "Muhammad (pbuh)'s victory confirmed his authority as leader of Islam; by impressing local tribes that joined him, and the expansion of Islam began."[31]

The Battle of Uhud (624 AD): To exact revenge for their defeat at Badr, an army of three thousand well-equipped soldiers, under the command of Abu Sufyan, gathered at Uhud, 3 miles from Medina. The Prophet's army numbered only a thousand men. On the way, 'Abdullah ibn Ubayy, with three hundred of his followers, deserted the believers, leaving the prophet (pbuh) with seven hundred only, who had only a hundred coats of mail and two horses. The prophet (pbuh) took up his position below the hill. The army was arranged in fighting formations and fifty archers were posted, under the command of 'Abdullah ibn Zubair, between the

---

[30] Muir, William (1861). The Life of Mahomet (Volume 3 ed.). London: Smith, Elder and Co. p. 122. Retrieved 26 February 2015.
[31] Paul K. Davis, 100 Decisive Battles from Ancient Times to the Present: The World's Major Battles and How They Shaped History—Oxford University Press, 1999), 95–96.

hills, to protect against an attack from there. They had orders not to leave their posts under any circumstances. Talha challenged the Muslims to individual combat, accepted by 'Ali ibn Abi-Talib (a.s). who killed Talha, the standard bearer, which was taken by his brother who was also killed by Ali (a.s). A general engagement then started. [32]An Abyssinian slave, Wahshi, had been commissioned by Hind, wife of Abu Sufyan, to kill either Muhammad (pbuh), Ali (a.s), or Hamza (r.a), to avenge the death of her father 'Utbah ibn Rabiah, her brother al-Walid as well as that of Hatzalah, son of Abu Sufyan, at Badr. He singled Hamza (r.a) out and threw a spear at him, which pierced Hamza's abdomen and killed him. After a heavy toll, the Meccans started retreating, and the Muslims started collecting the booty. The soldiers at the pass thought the battle was over left their posts against the orders of their leader Abdullah ibn Zubair, to collect their share of the booty. Noticing the unguarded pass, Khalid bin Walid, leading a Meccan group, attacked the Muslims from the rear.[33] The retreating Meccan forces returned and launched a fresh attack from the front. The Muslim standard-bearer, Mus'ab ibn 'Umayr, who resembled the prophet (pbuh), was killed. Up went the cry that the prophet (pbuh) was killed. This rumour caused utter dismay and confusion among the Muslims, including stalwarts like Umar (r.a) who threw away his sword saying fighting was useless without the Prophet. He ran to the mountain to take refuge. In his own words:": I was jumping from one boulder to another, like mountain goats." Abu Bakr (r.a). and 'Usman (r.a). also ran away, the latter returning to Medina. The confusion continued till Ka'b ibn Malik saw the prophet (pbuh) and shouted at the top of his voice that the Prophet (pbuh) was alive. The Prophet (PBUH) then became the main target of the Meccan forces. Abdullah ibn Qama of the Quraysh forcefully struck the prophet (pbuh) on the head with his sword. Utbah ibn Abi Waqas threw a stone at the prophet (pbuh), further injuring his face and dislodging his two upper teeth. The prophet (pbuh) now had fallen in a pit where 'Ali ibn Abi Talib (a.s), along with the brave lady Umm Ammarah protected him against a rain of arrows. Other Muslims soon arrived and took the Prophet to a cave in the heights of Uhud. The

---

[32] Watt (1974) p. 137-139.
[33] "Uhud", *Encyclopedia of Islam Online*

Prophet was in much pain and prayed to God: "O'God forgive my people, for their ignorance." There was no bitterness or ill-will in his heart against his enemies. Meccan forces however ceased further attacks and resorted to violence against the wounded, and mutilation of the dead. Hamza was martyred and Hind, wife of Abu Sufyan, cut his nose and ears, and took out his liver and heart, and chewed them as vengeance for the killing of her father and brother in the battle of Badr.[34] Muslims lost 70 warriors in this battle against 30 from the Meccans, of whom 12 were killed by Ali(a.s) who received 16 serious wounds, in this battle.[35]

Aftermath of Uhud: Muslims had hoped for a victory like Badr, but in Uhud they just managed to hold off the enemy, with a much heavier death toll. Their setback, according to the Quran resulted from their disobedience of the Prophet and their lust for the spoils of the war. The Quran 3;152 describes the event: "Allah fulfilled his promise to you when you were about to annihilate the enemy until you disobeyed and got distracted by the sight of loot."[36]

Treacherous Tribes and Meccans after Uhud: The Meccans realized that on their own they could not crush the Islamic movement. They, therefore, started instigating other tribes to rally their support. The victory of the Muslims over the Quraysh in Badr scared the nomadic tribes but defeat of Uhud emboldened them and they started raiding Medina, resulting in several skirmishes. They also resorted to treacherous ways to harm the Muslims. Abu Bara of Banu Kalb approached the prophet (pbuh) to send teachers to preach to their members. Seventy Muslims were sent, out of which only one survived. All others were killed by the tribe. Another tribe did the same, killing all ten Muslims sent.[37]

Attitude of the Jews of Medina: The Jews were a prosperous people and they had a lot of prestige among the people of Medina. Their position of authority received a setback when Islam started spreading in Medina

---

[34] Ibn Ishaq (1955) 380—388, cited in Peters (1994) p. 218
[35] Nafziger; Walton (2000) pp. 16-18
[36] Quran 3;152
[37] Watt (1974) pp. 147-148

and they began plotting against the Muslims. They started distorting the words and verses of the Qur'an, and the Muslims. Nevertheless, the prophet (pbuh) was instructed by Qur'an, 3:186, to bear patiently, saying: "You will hear much annoying talk from the people of the book and others. Be patient and guard against evil. It will be a matter of great resolve". The Prophet tried hard to have good relations with the Jews. The Quran emphasized the unity of the two religions. Qur'an, 3:64 said:" say: O'people of the book come to a word common between us and you that we will worship only Allah and not associate any with Him, and not take others for lords besides Allah—" Qur'an, 3:72. Increasing power of the Muslims irked the Jews, and they redoubled their efforts to exterminate the new religion. The Quraysh were further instigating them to do so, sending a threatening epistle to them. Chief of Banu Nadhir, Kab bin Ashraf was a famous poet. He composed eulogies mourning the Meccan chiefs slain in the battle of Badr and recited them at each Meccan gathering inciting vengeance. He contacted Abu Sufyan for a joint effort to wipe out the Muslims. He openly recited several poems, derogatory to the prophet (pbuh). Ka'b ibn Ashraf had become not only a nuisance but a serious menace. We have it on the authority of al-Yaqubi and Hafiz ibn Hajar that Ka'b plotted to kill the prophet (pbuh). When the prophet (pbuh) knew this plot, he consulted his companions and it was decided that Ka'b should be silenced forever. Mohammad ibn Masalmeh undertook to carry out the job and, on getting an opportunity, he killed Ka'b ibn Ashraf.[38]

Banu Nadhir: Encouraged by the Meccans and by 'Abdullah ibn Ubayy, Banu Nadhir plotted to kill the prophet (pbuh). Once the Holy prophet (pbuh), together with some companions, visited them to arrange blood money of two persons from Banu Amir. They asked the Prophet to come inside their fortress, but the Prophet preferred to sit outside the walls. At that moment, a man went up to the fort wall and dropped a big boulder on the Prophet. At that instant, the Prophet came to know of this treacherous scheme by divine revelation and at once left the place. The Prophet, therefore, sent Banu Nadhir an ultimatum that, since they had broken their treaty, they should leave Medina in ten days. They wanted to

---

[38] Nadir, Banu—. Encyclopedia of Islam Online

migrate when 'Abdullah ibn Ubayy encouraged them not to leave Medina, promising them help with 2000 warriors. The Jews then refused to leave Medina. The following ayahs were revealed regarding the help Abdullah ibn Ubayy promised: "Allah knows that they will not be helped." (Qur'an, 59: 11-12). After 15 days of siege, they destroyed their houses and left Medina. They could take all their belongings with them. Some of them left for Syria, while others settled with the Jews of Khyber. (Quran, 59:2) depicts their plight.[39]

The Battle of the Trench: (Jan/Feb. 627 AD) Upon settling down at Khyber, Banu Nadhir gathered 20 Jewish leaders and 50 from Quraysh who swore at the Kaaba that if they lived, they would fight Muhammad (PBUH). Then the Jews and the Quraysh contacted their allies and sent emissaries to several tribes. Banu Ghatfan, Banu Asad, Banu Aslam, Banu Asha, Banu Kinanah and Banu Fazara who prepared 10,000 warriors and marched on Medina led by Abu Sufyan. When news of these preparations reached Medina, the Holy Prophet consulted his companions. Salman al-Farsi (r.a) recommended digging a wide and deep trench on the unprotected side of Medina. Muslims were divided into 10 groups, each required to dig 10 yards. The Prophet himself took part in digging. The trench was completed three days before the enemy arrived. The head of Banu Nadhir Huyayy ibn Akhtab instigated Banu Quraizah, and they tore down the treaty with the Prophet. [40]This treachery presented a danger from inside Medina, when Muslims were surrounded by the massive armies of the Quraysh and the Jews. The Prophet deputed 200 men led by Salima bin Aslam to guard against any attack inside Medina from Banu Quraizah. The enemy received a big shock on seeing the trench, which was something new to them. They camped at the other side of the trench for 24 days, and their numbers kept increasing, really terrifying the Muslims. The situation is depicted in (Qur'an, 33:10-11) which says: "Many started doubting the power of Allah when they saw armies all around them when the eyes turned dull, and the hearts rose up to the throats." At that crucial moment, many approached the Prophet saying: "our houses are exposed, and they were not exposed; they only desired to leave." (Qur'an, 33:13). The Muslim

---

[39] Stillman (1979), p. 14. 2=Watt (1956), p. 211-12.
[40] Watt (1956), pp. 36, 37, 167-174, 169, 170-72.

army, however, tolerated the freezing weather and lack of provisions, and the enemy hurled stones and arrows at the Muslims. Some warriors from Quraysh succeeded in crossing the moat. Amr challenged the Muslims for a fight. He was considered equal to a thousand warriors. The Prophet called on the Muslims three times, but no one responded except Ali (as). At this time, Ali had sore eyes, and could not see clearly. The Prophet spat in his eyes to cure him and let him go. Ali gave Amr three options: to accept Islam, return to Mecca, or dismount, as Ali was on foot. Amr came down from his horse, and the fight started. Amr managed to inflict a severe cut on Ali's head. But after a while Ali killed him. Amr's killing demoralized the enemy, and Amr's allies fled except his friend Nawfal, who was also killed by Ali.[41] Muslims had run out of food supplies such that the Prophet tied a stone on his stomach to lessen the pain of hunger. The besieging army was also in a desperate situation due to extreme cold, stormy winds, and rain. Its horses were perishing, and provisions were running out. The Holy Prophet (PBUH) went to the Al-Fath mosque and prayed for Almighty's help. A fierce storm erupted, tearing the enemy tents. Their belongings went flying in all directions, and the Meccan army fled. Abu Sufyan was so terrified that he tried to mount his camel without untying its rope. The situation is summarised in Ayah 25 of (Qur'an, 33:9) that said: "Allah sufficed the believers in fighting and turned back the invaders in defeat, and Allah is Strong and powerful."(Qur'an, 33:25) 'Abdullah ibn Masoud elaborated this ayah in Tafsir Durrell-Mansour saying: "And God sufficed the believers through 'Ali ibn Abi Talib (a.s) in their fight".

The aftermath of the battle of Trench: As a direct result of this defeat, influence of the Quraysh diminished and those tribes who were till then hesitating to accept Islam, out of their fear of Quraysh began to send, deputations to the prophet (PBUH). Many delegations came to accept Islam, including tribes of Mazinah, Ashja, and Juhainah.[42]

Banu Qurayza: The Confederates (Abu Sufyan and his allied forces) then tried several simultaneous attacks, by persuading Banu Qurayza

---

[41] Ramadan (2007), p. 141. 5=Meri, Medieval Islamic Civilization: An Encyclopedia, p. 754.

[42] Meri, Medieval Islamic Civilization: An Encyclopedia, p. 754.

who had a pact with the Prophet and had so far remained neutral, to attack the Muslims. The leader of Banu Nadhir instigated them further. Renunciation of the agreement with Muhammad (PBUH) leaked out. The prophet (PBUH) was alarmed at Banu Qurayza's betrayal because he had done nothing to defend against them. They had weaponry: 1,500 swords, 2,000 lances, 300 suits of armor, and 500 shields. The leaders, sent to investigate the conduct of Banu Qurayza found that they had really renounced the treaty, and tried to persuade them to revert, reminding them of the fate of Banu Nadir and Banu Qaynuqa.[43]

Crisis in Medina: Muhammad (PBUH) tried to conceal his knowledge of Banu Qurayza's activities, but news soon leaked out, about a massive assault from the Qurayza side, which severely demoralized the people of Medina. Muslims were hard pressed. They had nothing to eat, and nights were freezing cold. For the first time, the Muslim community neglected the daily prayers and only prayed at night in darkness. Quran describes the dire situation of the Muslims in Qur'an: 33.10-22, which may be consulted by the reader.[44]

Muslim Response: Immediately after hearing the rumors about the Qurayza, Muhammad (PBUH) sent 100 men to the inner city for its protection. Later, he sent 300 riders. The Prophet (PBUH) understood that his men had reached the limits of their endurance. He sent word to Ghatfan, trying to pay for their defection and offering them a third of Medina's date harvest if they withdrew. Although the Ghatfan demanded half, they eventually agreed to negotiate with Muhammad (PBUH) on those terms. Before Muhammad (PBUH) began the order of drafting the agreement, he consulted the Medina elders who rejected the terms saying the conditions were degrading. So, the negotiations were broken off. While the Ghatfan did not retreat, they had compromised themselves by entering a talk. At about that point, Nuaym ibn Masud, an Arab leader who was well respected by the entire Confederacy, visited Muhammad (PBUH). Nuaym had secretly become a Muslim-a fact unknown to others. The Prophet asked him to do something to end the siege, by creating discord

---

[43] Watt, "Qurayza, Banu" Encyclopedia of Islam.
[44] Peterson, Muhammad. Prophet of God, p. 123f.

amongst the Confederates. Nuaym then came up with an efficient strategy. He told Quraiza that if the siege fails, the Jews will be abandoned by the Confederacy. He told the Confederacy that Quraiza had defected and they intended to ask the Confederacy for hostages whom they intended to hand over to Muhammad (PBUH)[45]

The collapse of the Alliance: Nuaym 's plan worked. Ikrama was sent by Quraysh indicating a joint attack. Quraiza demanded hostages as a guarantee that the confederation will not desert them. The demand was refused, and messages were exchanged, each side sticking to its stand. Meanwhile, provisions of the invaders were running out, and camels and horses were dying of hunger and wounds. Violent winds blew out the campfires, taking away from the Confederate army their source of heat whereas the Muslim camp was sheltered and faced no such storm. The invaders were terrified by the calamity facing them and were completely demoralized. During the night the enemy forces withdrew.[46]

Aftermath: Following the retreat of the Confederate army, the Muslims besieged the Banu Qurayza, in revenge. After a 25-day siege of their neighborhood, the Banu Qurayza surrendered unconditionally. On the request of the Banu Aws, who were allied to the Qurayza, Muhammad (PBUH) chose one of them, Saad ibn Mu'adh, as an arbitrator to pronounce judgment upon them. Saad, an ex rabbi, who later died, pronounced that their men be killed, and women and children enslaved. The sentence was according to the Torah vide Deuteronomy 20: 10-14 which says: "When you march up to a city and offer them peace, and they do not accept and start a battle and God puts them into your hands, put to the sword all the men, and take everything else as plunder." Muhammad (PBUH) approved of this decision, and the next day, the sentence was carried out. 400-900 men were executed under the custody of Mohammad ibn Masalmeh, and the women and children were placed under Abdullah ibn Salam, an ex

---

[45] Watt, Muhammad: Prophet and Statesman, pp. 167–174 The whole was a battle of wits in which Muslims had the best of it; without cost to themselves they weakened the enemy and increased the dissension.

[46] Ramadan, In the Footsteps of the Prophet, pp. 137-145.

Rabbi who distributed them among the Muslims. The Prophet (PBUH) selected one of the women, Rehana, freed her, and later married her.[47]

The Agreement of Hudaybiyah (628 AD): In 628, the prophet (PBUH) decided to perform the 'Umrah (pilgrimage) to the Ka'ba which had been denied to the Muslims until then. Fourteen hundred Muhajir and Ansar showed readiness to go with him. The Prophet told them not to carry any arms except swords. The Prophet put on Ihram (the pilgrimage robe) and took camels for sacrifice. They camped at Hudaybiyah, ten miles from Mecca. An envoy was sent to Mecca to seek permission for pilgrimage. The Meccans refused and sent a force to prevent the Muslims from entering Mecca. Meccan force was captured but the Prophet (PBUH) showed great kindness and set the captives free. 'Usman (r.a). (who belonged to the same clan as Abu Sufyan) was sent to Mecca to negotiate permission for pilgrimage. Soon, the news came that 'Usman (r.a). had been killed by the Quraysh. The Muslims swore a pledge at the hands of the Prophet (PBUH), known as "Bait-ur-Rizwan," to stand by him to the last.[48] Referring to this pledge, the (Quran, 48:18) states: "God was pleased with the believers for swearing allegiance to you and will reward them with victory". Ultimately, a treaty was signed saying: "Muslims will not be allowed this year but may return the next year, with maximum stay of three days. Muslims may bring sheathed swords, and that there will be no war for ten years. Muslims living in Mecca will not be allowed to migrate to Medina and those leaving will be returned to Mecca. Muslims of Medina coming to Mecca will not be allowed to return. Any tribe of Arabia may join either party and will be bound by this treaty." Although these terms were unfavorable to the Muslims, the Prophet (PBUH) agreed with them. At that time, a critical situation developed. Abu Jundal of Mecca who had become a Muslim and had been tortured and imprisoned by his father, escaped and came to the Prophet in Hudaybiyah. Meccan envoy demanded his return according to the treaty although the treaty had not been signed yet. Abu Jundal showed his injuries inflicted by the Meccans and pleaded with the Muslims not to return him to the Meccan tyranny. The Muslims were greatly moved by his story, and Umar (r.a) made an impassioned appeal, but the prophet

---

47 Muir, A life of Mahomet and history of Islam- pp. 272–274.
48 Watt, al- Hudaibiya or al-Hudaibiya Encyclopedia of Islam.

(PBUH) refused to cancel the agreement. He consoled Abu Jundal by saying that God will find a way of his deliverance. Some Muslims were unhappy about the agreement, and Umar (r.a) was somewhat rude to the Prophet, and later said: "Never did I have doubt about the truth of Islam since my acceptance of the faith, except on that day (of Hudaybiyah)." The prophet (PBUH) sacrificed his animals, had his head shaved, removed Ihram, and ordered return to Medina. On the way back, Surah 48 of the Quran, titled "The Victory", was revealed to the Prophet, indicating the Treaty had been a victory for the Muslims, proved by the later events.[49]

Aftereffects of the Treaty: Till then, idolaters and Muslims had not been mixing with each other. By this treaty, they started doing so freely. During their visits to Medina for family reasons or trade, Meccans were being exposed to the teachings of Islam, and the righteous conduct and moral integrity of the Muslims. Historians have recorded that during the two years following the treaty of Hudaybiyah, more people accepted Islam than during the whole nineteen years since the start of the mission, proved by the fact that while only 1,400 Muslims had gone with the prophet (PBUH) to Hudaybiyah, 10,000 accompanied him two years later at the conquest of Mecca. The famous Muslim general Khalid bin Walid, along with 'Amr ibn al-'As and Uthman ibn Talha converted to Islam a year after the treaty of Hudaybiyah, in 629. There was quite a controversy at the time of the treaty. Originally the treaty referred to Muhammad (PBUH) as the Messenger of God but this was unacceptable to the Quraysh envoy Suhail ibn Amr. Muhammad (PBUH) compromised and told his cousin Ali (a.s). to strike out the wording. But Ali (a.s) said "I will not be the person to rub it out". So, the Prophet (PBUH) himself rubbed out the words. Sahih al-Bukhari,3:49:862 Sahih Muslim 19: 4404.[50]

Battle of Khyber: After exile from Medina, Banu Nadir settled in Khyber. They persuaded other Jewish tribes to join them, in the battle of trench, against the Muslims. Also, Jews of Khyber raised a coalition and joined in the fight against Muslims in the battle of trench. Banu Nadir persuaded Banu Qurayza to break their treaty with the Prophet, to join the coalition

---

[49] Hudaybiyah - Al-Islam.org. Retrieved 22 November 2015.
[50] Lewis (2002), p. 42

against the Muslims in the battle. According to Montgomery Watt, Banu Nadir used their wealth to incite tribes against the Muslims and left the prophet (pbuh) no choice but to attack them. Muslim army consisted of 1400-1800 men, and 100-200 horses against 10,000 of the enemy.[51] The Muslim contingent marched to Khyber swiftly and quietly in only three days, catching the city by surprise, so that they could not put up a joint defense against the Muslims. Muhammad (pbuh) conquered each fortress, one by one, with relative ease, claiming food, weapons, and land, as he went.[52] The siege of the last most heavily guarded fortress called al-Qamous, endured for 13-19 days. Several attempts by Muslims failed to conquer the fort. Abu Bakr (r.a) tried first, followed by Umar (r.a) but failed. That night, Muhammad (pbuh) proclaimed: "By God, tomorrow, I shall give the banner to someone whom God and the Prophet love, and who also loves them, and Allah will make him victorious. All wondered whose honor it will be, to carry the banner. In the morning, Muhammad (pbuh) called out for Ali (a.s) ibn Talib. At that time, Ali (a.s). was unwell and could not take part in the failed attempts. Ali (a.s) came to Muhammad (pbuh), who cured him of his ophthalmia, an inhibitive inflammation of the eyes, by spitting in Ali's eye. The Jewish soldiers came out of the fort and an intense battle ensued during which Ali lost his shield. Looking for a substitute, Ali pulled a door from the wall and used it as a shield. The door was so heavy that eight men were needed to put it back on the hinges.[53] The Jews met with Muhammad (pbuh) to discuss the terms of surrender. The people of the two forts gave in on the condition of leniency which the Prophet accepted and did not take any property of the two forts.[54]

---

[51] Haykal, Muhammad Husayn. Ch. "The Campaign of Khaybar and Missions to Kings". The Life of Muhammad. Shorouk International, 1983.

[52] al-Tabari (1997). The History of al-Tabari: The Victory of Islam. Albany : State University Of New York. p. 117.

[53] P. Bearman; Th. Bianquis; C.E. Bosworth; E. van Donzel; W.P. Heinrichs (eds.). Khaybar-*Encyclopaedia of Islam, Second Edition*. Brill Online. Retrieved April 18, 2012.

[54] Ibn Hisham—*Al-Sira al-Nabawiyya (The Life of Muhammad)*. English translation in Guillame (1955), pp. 145–146

Aftermath of Khyber: According to Veccia Vaglieri, L. in "Khyber, the Muslims agreed to cease warfare and not hurt any of the Jews. After the agreement, some Jews requested Muhammad (pbuh) to allow them to remain in the oasis, paying half of the produce to the Muslims. Jews of Fadak also made a similar pact.[52] The victory in Khyber raised the status of Muhammad (pbuh) among his followers and local Bedouin tribes, who, seeing his power, swore allegiance to Muhammad (pbuh) and converted to Islam. The captured booty and weapons strengthened his army, and he captured Mecca just 18 months after Khyber.[55]

Conquest of Mecca: (629 AD) In 628 CE, the Quraysh had signed a 10-year truce called the Treaty of Hudaybiyah with the Muslim community. The Arab tribes could join either of the parties, the Muslims, or Quraysh. Should any of these tribes' face aggression, the party to which it was allied with, would have the right to retaliate. Therefore, Banu Bakr joined Quraysh, and Khuza'ah joined Muhammad (pbuh). Due to tribal rivalry, Banu Bakr who were given men and arms by the Quraysh, attacked Khuza'ah. Members of Khuza'ah sought refuge in the Holy Kaaba, but men of Banu Bakr entered the Kaaba and killed them all. Khuza'ah informed Muhammad (pbuh) about breach of the agreement. Quraysh petitioned to Muhammad (pbuh) to keep the treaty, offering material compensation but the Muslim forces had already been mobilised by the Prophet to deal with the Quraysh.[56] The Muslim army set out for Mecca on Wednesday, 29 November 629, with a force of 10,000. Abu Sufyan made several trips to Medina but failed to persuade the Prophet (pbuh) to avoid conquest of Mecca.

Muhammad (pbuh) divided the Muslim army into four columns: led by Abu Ubaidah ibn Jarrah, his cousin Zubair, Ali, and Khalid bin Walid, advancing at the same time, to prevent enemy from concentrating on any one front. The Prophet instructed not to fight unless the Quraysh attacked. The Muslim army entered Mecca on Monday, 11 December 629. The entry was peaceful and bloodless on three sectors except for that of Khalid's

---

[55] Watt (1956), pg. 218.
[56] Peters, Francis E. (1994). muhammad and the origins of Islam. SUNY Press. p. 235 & 334.

column. The hardened anti-Muslims, like Ikrimah and Safwan, gathered a band of Quraysh fighters and faced Khalid's column. The Quraysh attacked the Muslims with swords and bows, and the Muslims charged the Quraysh positions. After a short combat, the Quraysh gave in, losing 12 while only 2 Muslims were killed.[57]

Aftermath: Abu Sufyan accepted Islam saying that the Meccan Gods had not helped, and that there was no god but one God, the first part of the Islamic confession of faith. At this, the prophet (pbuh) declared Abu Sufyan's house as a sanctuary and that "whoever enters his house will be safe and whoever lays down arms, and who locks his door will be safe. Then the prophet (pbuh) entered the Kaaba and broke the idols and recited: "say, the truth has come, and falsehood gone. Verily falsehood is bound to vanish "- Quran 17:81. Then, he turned to the Quraysh and asked: "What treatment should I give you?" People replied: We expect only good from you. The prophet (pbuh) declared: I speak to you in the same words as Yusuf did to his brothers. Today, there is no reproof against you. Go your way as you are free. However, out of these, Ikrimah accepted Islam; Ibn Sarh took refuge with Usman (r.a) bin Affan; out of the two singing girls condemned by the prophet (pbuh), one accepted Islam and the other was killed.[58]

Battle of Hunayn: (630 AD) All Arab tribes were shocked by the Muslims conquest of mecca. A staunch adversary of the Meccans, al-hawazin, saw Muhammad (pbuh) as another powerful Qurayshi chieftain. Hawazin and Thaqif formed a coalition, in which other tribes also joined in, to fight the Muslims. The prophet (pbuh) had 12,000 soldiers. The Muslims prided in their considerable number, ignoring military tactics and principles of war. When Muslims started setting up camp, the enemy suddenly attacked showering arrows from all directions. The Muslims fled in disarray except a few who continued fighting such as Ali (a.s). bin Abi Talib, the standard bearer, Abbas bin Abdullah, Abu Fadl Al-Abbas, Usama, and Abu Sufyan ibn Harith ibn Abd al-Muttalib (a cousin of the prophet (pbuh). The prophet (pbuh) said: "Come on, people! I am the Messenger of Allah.

---

[57] Akram 2007- p.60,61.
[58] Sahih Bukhari, Volume 5, Book 59, Number 603

I am Muhammad (pbuh), the son of Abdullah." Then he prayed: "O, Allah, send down Your Help!" The Muslims' returned to the battlefield. Muhammad (pbuh), then picking up a handful of earth, hurled at the enemy blinding them, and making them retreat.[59] About seventy men of Thaqif were killed, and the Muslims captured all their riding camels, weapons, and cattle. The Quran verse 9:25 was revealed at this event, according to Muslim scholars: "God helped you in Hunayn when your numbers elated you, but Allah calmed the Prophet and believers and sent down forces to punish the non-believers".

Aftermath: Muslims captured the leader of Hawazin, his 6000 men, 24,000 camels. The Bedouins fled and split into two groups-one resulted in the battle of Autas later, the other larger group took shelter in Taif where the prophet (pbuh) besieged them.[60]

Conquest of Arabia: After defeating the Hawazin, Muhammad (pbuh) organized an attack against northern Arabia because of their earlier defeat at the Battle of Mut'ah for which an army of 30,000 was set up out of which half of them led by Abd Allah ibn Ubayy, came back. Although Muhammad (pbuh) did not engage with hostile forces at Tabuk, he received the submission of some local chiefs of the region.[61]

Siege of Taif (630): The last city to hold out against the Muslims in Western Arabia was Taif. Muhammad (pbuh) did not accept surrender of the city unless they converted to Islam and allowed them to destroy the statue of Goddess Allat. Abu Sufyan lost his eye during the siege of Taif and complained to the Prophet who asked him:" Would you like God to restore your eye now or you prefer restoration in the hereafter?[62] "The siege of Taif continued for 15 days. The Prophet wanted to bring the chief of

---

[59] Akramulla Syed. the battle of hunayn'. Retrieved 17 December 2014.
[60] Lammens.H and Abd al-Hafez Kamal. "Hunayn". In P.J. Bearman; Th. Bianquis; CE Bosworth E. van Donzel; W.P. Heinrichs.Encyclopedia of Islam,Online Edition. Brill Academic Publishers
[61] the year of deputations and Abu Bakr's leadership 2=the life of mahomet and history of islam, vol.4 by Sir William Muir, p.145,155,433,434.
[62] sahaba.net—stories of the companions—an eye now or an eye in heaven

Hawazin to his side and promised to return his family and belongings if he converted to Islam, the offer he accepted, and aided the Prophet in the siege of Taif.[63]

Farewell pilgrimage (Feb.632): The Prophet went to Mecca, in the tenth year of his migration to Medina, for the last and only Hajj. He was accompanied by all his wives. The Muslims saw every move, every act, and every gesture of the Prophet (pbuh), and became Hajj precedents for Muslims all over the world. Before leaving Medina, he appointed Abu Dujana Ansari, as the Governor for the duration of his absence.[64]

Wearing Ihram: Before arriving in Mecca, he taught how to wear Ihram at Miqat. He did Wuzu and put on Ihram which consisted of two unsewn pieces of white cloth which later became his coffin. He moved to Shajara Mosque and offered Zuhr prayers.

Tawaf and Prayers: The next day, the prophet (pbuh) entered Masjid al-Haram from Dar al-Salam, went to the Kaaba and touched the sacred stone of Hajr-e-Aswad. He circled around the Kaaba and touched the stone again and cried. He, then, offered two Rakat behind the Station of Abraham[65]

Sa'ay: After prayer, he drank Zamzam water. After that he ran back and forth between Safa and Marwah, starting from the al-Safa because God mentioned it in Qur'an first. When he arrived there, he turned towards Kaaba and prayed to God, and jog-trotted part of the way. When he arrived at Mount Al-Marwah, he stopped and prayed.[66] **On eighth Dihu al-Hijjah**, Muhammad (pbuh) went to Mina and stayed the night there.

---

[63] Muir, William (August 1878)—life of Hazrat muhammad pbuh—Kessinger Publishing Co (10 August 2003), p. 155,433,434
[64] Buhl, F.; Welch, A. T. (1993). "Muḥammad". Encyclopaedia of Islam. 7 (2nd ed.). Brill Academic Publishers. pp. 360–376
[65] Muḥammad Ḥusayn Haykal (1 May 1994). The Life of Muhammad. The Other Press.
[66] Hosseini Tehrani, Muhammad Husayn. Imamology (امام شناسی). Mashhad: Allama Tabatabaie. p. 47. Retrieved 2015-10-18.

On his camel, he went to Mount Arafat and had a tent erected at Nimrah where he delivered a sermon.

Farewell Sermon at Arafat: On the 9th of Dhu al-Hijjah he delivered his Farewell Sermon. Main points of the sermon were as follows: God is one like your father is one.—all humans are equal regardless of color, creed, ethnicity—the criteria of superiority being who fears God the most—usury is abolished—be righteous and do not wrong others—bloodshed of pre-Islamic days not to be avenged. I set the example by forgiving the killing of Ibn Rabī ah b.al-Ḥārith b. 'Abd al-Muttalib slain by the Banu Hudhayl of 'Abbas b. 'Abd al-Muttalib is abolished, all of it—the number of the months with God is twelve. Four of them, Rajab, Dhu al-Qa'dah, Dhu al-Hijjah, and Moharram, are sacred, during which fighting, and blood-letting is prohibited—a deliberate murder deserves retribution in kind—your women have been given to you in God's trust, treat them well—Hold on to the book of God and the Sunnah of the Prophet for guidance—Indemnity for unintended murder is one hundred camels: whoever asks for more is a person of the Era of Ignorance. After the sermon, the prophet (pbuh) led Zuhr Prayer followed by afternoon prayers (Asr). At sunset, Muhammad (pbuh) rode on his camel towards Masher al-Haram (Muzdalifa) and recommended pilgrims to slowly pass the way. Islamic prophet (pbuh) did his Maghrib followed by Isha Prayers in Masher al-Haram then took a rest. After Fajr prayers, he went to Jamara and stoned the devil.

Sacrifice: The Prophet sacrificed 63 camels, equal to the number of years he was alive. The remaining 37 camels were also slaughtered. Some of their meat was eaten and the rest given to charity. Then, he went back to Mecca, circled around the Kaaba, and offered Zuhr Prayer in Masjid al-Haram. He then drank Zamzam water, and returned to Mina the same day, and spent 11th, 12th and 13th of Dhul Hijjah (days of tashriq) there. On the last day, he did Stoning of the Devil and left Mina.[67]

---

[67] IslamKotob. the biography of the Prophet, IslamKotob. pp. 154-. Retrieved 2015-10-18.

Event of Mubahala: (October 632): In the ninth year of Hijri, Muhammad (pbuh) sent a letter to Abdul Harris ibn AL qama, Grand Bishop of Najran, inviting them to accept Islam. A delegation from Najran came, between 22-26 March 632, and discussions of religion and theology began, with the subject eventually turning to Jesus, as to what and who Jesus is understood to be. The Christians insisted on their explanations of Christ being divine and refused denying their beliefs. Muhammad (pbuh) demanded the two sides engage in Mubahala and recited the verses of Mubahala to them: "the case of Jesus is like Adam who was created from dust, and God said to him 'be' and he was. If anyone disagrees with you, say to him: let us call our sons and daughters and yours, ourselves and yourselves, and pray fervently to God to invoke curse on those who lie? "Qur'an 3; 59-61. The Christian leader Sayyid, al-'Aqib said to his people:" if he had challenged us with his people, we would have accepted the challenge knowing he is not a Prophet. But he is challenging us with his family, so we do not accept because it means he is a prophet." The Prophet (pbuh) brought only selected members of his family, Husayn (a.s), Hassan (a.s), Fatima, and Ali (a.s). The Christians consulted each other and Abdul Harris ibn AL qama, the greatest scholar among them, declined the Prophet's offer, who then, gave them two choices, to become Muslims or pay Jizya (a tax on non-Muslims). The Christians agreed to pay Jizya and asked the Prophet to send someone to judge their disputes. Among many contenders, the Prophet sent Abu 'Obadiah bin Al-Jarrah.[68]

Ghadir Khumm: Returning from Mecca after pilgrimage, when Muslims arrived at Ghadir Khumm (a pond by a spring, located 4-6 km from Al-Johfa- modern day -Rabigh -180 km from both Mecca and Medina), the following verse of the Quran was revealed: "Announce what has been revealed to you by your Lord. If you do not, you have not fulfilled your mission. God will defend you from men who mean mischief. Allah does not guide the unbelievers." (Quran 5:67) According to the verse, Muhammad (pbuh) was bound to proclaim an important message. The verse emphasizes the importance of the message that if he does not

---

[68] Griffith Sidney H—(4 April 2010). *The Church in the Shadow of the Mosque: Christians and Muslims in the World of Islam*. Princeton University Press. pp. 160–162

announce it, he did not perform his mission. After revelation of the verse, Muhammad (pbuh) ordered the caravan to stop and ordered those who had passed Ghadir Khumm to return and wait until those who had not yet arrived there, to join them.[69]

The Prophet's Sermon: There were about 10 thousand pilgrims. By the order of Muhammad (pbuh), a rostrum of camel saddles, was installed. After performing Zuhr (Noon) Prayer, Muhammad (pbuh) delivered a speech known as Ghadir Sermon. It was a long speech. He recited many verses from the Quran and reminded and warned people of their deeds and future. However, while raising Ali (a.s)'s hand, the prophet (pbuh) said: "whoever I am his Master, this Ali (a.s). is his Master (Mawla)." Immediately after the speech, Quran-Surah Maidah-ayah 3 was revealed: "Today I have perfected your religion and chosen Islam for you, completing my favor on you. Those who reject the faith, have given up hope, do not fear them, but fear me."[70]

Oath of allegiance and Narrators of Ghadir Khumm: After leaving the rostrum, the Prophet (pbuh) ordered setting up a tent in which Ali (a.s). sat to receive oath of allegiance from Muslims who congratulated him, as the commander of the faithful. According to Musnad, Ahmad ibn Hanbal, p.281, Umar (r.a). was the first to congratulate Ali (a.s). Ibn Abi Talib. Also, Umar (r.a), later was quoted as saying: "After the pledge of allegiance, there was a handsome young man, sitting next to me, said "the Prophet has taken a firm pledge which only a hypocrite will break. So, Umar-avoid breaking it". Umar (r.a) described the incident to the Prophet who said the youth was not from Adam's progeny, it was Gabriel stressing the point about Ali. The event of Ghadir Khumm has been quoted by many Muslim sources. However, some do not believe in the interpretation.[71]

---

[69] Al-Shahrastani (1984). *Kitab al–Milal wa al-Nihal.* London: Kegan Paul. pp. 139–140

[70] al-Bahrani, Seyyed Hashim—pp. 434–437

[71] Ahmad ibn Hanbal, Ahmad. Musnad—4. Beirut: Dar al-Ihya al-Torath al-Arabia. p. 281

Narrators of this Hadith: are many including: -110 companions of Muhammad (pbuh) including: Umar (r.a), Usman (r.a)., Abu Dhar al-Ghifari, Salman Farsi (r.a), Zubayr ibn Awwam etc. who were all present in Ghadir Khumm and narrated the event directly.—83 of the followers include Omar bin Abdul Aziz, Tawus ibn Kayson—etc.—360 Sunni scholars of 2nd to 4th century AH including Abu Abdullah of Shafi'i school and Ahmad bin Hanbal of Hanbali school, Shia Hadith scholars: ibn Kulayni, Sheikh Mufid, Sharif al-Murtaza-etc.[72]—Shia scholar Sheikh Abdul Hossein Amini collected all the references for the event of Ghadir Khumm, from Sunni sources and compiled them in 11 volumes, known as "Al-Ghadir".[73]

Eid al-Ghadir: Shia Muslims celebrate the occasion of Muhammad (pbuh) declaring Ali (a.s) as his successor. Fasting and reciting the Dua Nudba and giving food to believers is among recommended practice of Eid al-Ghadir. It is a public holiday in Iran.[74]

Hadith of the Two Weighty Things: In this hadith, Muhammad (pbuh) referred to the Quran and Ahl al-Bayt, as the two weighty things. All Muslims accept the Hadith. The Prophet (pbuh) said, "I leave for you two weighty things: one is the book of Allah, the Quran, and the other is the members of my family, the Ahl-e-Bayt. If you cling to them, you will not go astray. "People asked him who the members of his family were. Are your wives included in your family? He replied: No. a woman lives with a man for a certain period and if he divorces her, she returns to her family. My family are my kith and kin (who are related to me by blood) and for whom, the acceptance of Zakat is prohibited.—Sahih Muslim—031 ;5920 and 5923.[75] Prophet's wife Umm Salama asked him if she was included

---

[72] Sahih Muslim, Chapter of Virtues of Companions, Section of Virtues of 'Ali, Arabic, v4, p1871, Tradition #32. For the English version of Sahih Muslim, see Chapter CMXCVI, p1284, Tradition #5916.

[73] Amini, Abdul Hosein. Ghadir Khumm. 1. Qom: Dar al-Kotob al-Islamia. pp. 9–30.

[74] Veccia Vaglieri Laura-Ghadir Khumm—*Encyclopedia of Islam, Second Edition.* Brill Online. Retrieved 28 March 2013

[75] Sahih Muslim v.31—hadith 5932, 031:5915.

in his family. The Prophet replied: 'you remain in your position'.[76] Quran 42;23 says: "Say, O Muhammad—I do not ask you for any payment for the message delivered, except for goodwill to my kinship (relatives). And whoever commits a good deed, we will increase for him the good. Indeed, Allah is forgiving and appreciative."[77]

Verse of Wilayah or Leadership: Someone gave his ring, in alms, to a beggar while he was in the state of raku (bending) in prayer. The prophet (pbuh) asked the beggar, "Who gave you this ring?" He replied, "That man during raku" Then Allah sent down the verse, Quran 5:55 "Your master and guardian is that who establishes salat and pays zakat while bowing in raku ". On that ring was written, "Glory be to He who honored me by making me His slave."[78]

Hadith of the Pen and Paper: Ibn Abbas narrated "the prophet (pbuh) was on his deathbed and said on a Thursday, three days before his demise (the prophet (pbuh) passed away on Monday): "Come, let me write for you a statement after which you will never go astray." Umar (r.a) replied, addressing the people in the room: "The Prophet (pbuh) is seriously ill and in a state of unconsciousness [yagura, literal translation: "talking nonsense."] Obviously, the prophet (pbuh) was conscious since he was speaking. Umar (r.a) continued: "We have the Qur'an; so, the Book of Allah is enough for us." When the people present started quarreling and caused a lot of noise before the prophet (pbuh), Allah's Apostle said, "Go away!" Obaidullah ibn Abbas used to say, "It was very unfortunate that Allah's Apostle was prevented from dictating his Will because of their disagreement and noise "Sunni view this as Sahih and have included it in Sahih al-Bukhari and Sahih Muslim.[79]

Shia View of this Hadith: Shias point out that obedience to Muhammad (pbuh) was mandatory for every Muslim under all circumstances. The Quran orders Muslims about Muhammad (pbuh), "So take what the

---

[76] Sahih al-Tirmidhi, v5, pp 351,663
[77] Quran—42;23
[78] shah kazemi 2010—p.124
[79] Sahih Bukhari—7.70.573.

Messenger assigns to you." Therefore, it was not the place of anyone to take matters into his own hands. The idea that Umar (r.a) disobeyed Muhammad (pbuh) out of love is an unproven assumption and conjecture. They refer to the Events of Ghadir which show that Muhammad (pbuh) had already nominated Ali (a.s.) as his successor. On the day of Ghadir, after Muhammad (pbuh) had announced, "Whomsoever master I am, this Ali (a.s.) is his Mawla', after which the ayah declaring perfection of Islam was revealed, as described above. Umar (r.a) ibn Al-Khattab claimed the Quran was enough guidance, despite the well-known tradition that Muhammad (pbuh) would be leaving two weighty things, not one. These being the Quran, and the Ahl- al-Bayt (the progeny of Muhammad (pbuh). Muhammad (pbuh)'s own words were that if they followed what he wished to write down, no one would go astray. So, it was a matter of grave importance. Sunni Muslims see this as a minor event and a test by Muhammad (pbuh) of the Sahaba (his companions). They believe the companions did the right thing and passed the test, having remained free from criticism by Muhammad (pbuh) for the rest of the days he remained with them. Furthermore, Sunnis say it was not a matter of disobedience but rather it was Umar (r.a)'s Ijtihad (independent reasoning) in that situation.[80] It is also known as event of a black Thursday when the Prophet was not provided with a means to dictate his will. Verse 7 of Surah Hashr and Verse 65 of Surah Nisa command obedience to Muhammad, and they are verses that have been mentioned considering Umar's actions at this event. They state that someone who does not listen to Muhammad's decisions, is not a believer.[81]

Wills of the First and Second Caliphs: Both the first and second Caliphs were able to dictate their wills despite acute illness.[82] Abu Bakr (r.a) had fainted during dictating his will; and Umar (r.a) ibn Khattab had several stab wounds, yet both considered it necessary to give details about their successor [83]. Shias do not claim that all Sahaba were part of a

---

[80] Muhammad al-Tijani al-Samawi, *Black Thursday*, trans. S. Athar (Qum: Ansarian, n.d.).
[81] Abdullah. A brief analysis of the incident of the paper—*Umar ibn Khattab*.
[82] Umar ibn Khattab—his life and times—vol.2—*archive.org*.
[83] *khalifa abu bakr-death—Alim.org*.

conspiracy. The fact that there were mixed views on Muhammad (pbuh)'s deathbed regarding writing his will, shows that Ibn al-Khattab spoke about Muhammad (pbuh) in an irreverent manner, when he said, "He is delirious" (yagura)

Demise of the prophet (pbuh): A few months after the farewell pilgrimage, Muhammad (pbuh) fell ill, with fever, pain, and weakness. He expired on Monday, 8 June,632 in Medina, in Aisha's house. He was 63 years old. His final words were: O'Allah, AR-Rafiq Al-A 'la (exalted friend in heaven). He was buried where he died in Aisha's house. [84]During the reign of the Umayyad caliph al-Walid, the Mosque of the prophet (pbuh) was expanded to include the site of Muhammad (pbuh)'s tomb. The green dome was built by the Mamluk sultan Al- Mansur Qalawun, in the 13th century, and green color added, in the 16th century, under the reign of Ottoman sultan Suleiman the magnificent. Among tombs next to that of Muhammad (pbuh) are those of his companions, the first two Muslim caliphs Abu Bakr (r.a) and Umar (r.a), and an empty one that is believed to be for Jesus.[85] When Ibn Saud conquered Medina in 1805, Muhammad (pbuh)'s tomb was stripped of its gold and jewel ornaments. Adherents to Saudi Salafism, ibn Saud's followers destroyed every tomb in Medina, to prevent their veneration, and the one of Muhammad (pbuh) is said to have narrowly escaped.[86]

Family Life of the Prophet (pbuh): At the age of 25, Muhammad (pbuh) married the wealthy Khadija bent Khuwaylid who was 40 years old. Muhammad (pbuh) did not marry another woman during this marriage which lasted for 25 years. After Khadija's death, other marriages were contracted mostly for political or humanitarian reasons. The women were

---

[84] Fethullah Gülen.—Muhammad.—the messenger of God—The Light, Inc. p. 24.
[85] Ariffin, Syed Ahmad Iskandar Syed (2005). *Architectural Conservation in Islam: Case Study of the Prophet's Mosque.* Penerbit UTM. p. 88.
[86] Doris Behrens-Abouseif; Stephen Vernoit (2006).—islamic art in 19th century—Brill. p. 22.

mostly widows of Muslim martyrs or from clans it was necessary to honor and strengthen alliances with.[87]

Succession Controversy: Disagreement over succession, broke out after the prophet's demise, as to who should succeed him, and it caused the Muslim community to split into two factions. The people who supported Abu Bakr (r.a) for the caliphate, became Sunni Muslims, and those who were in favor of Ali (a.s) succeeding the Prophet, were later termed as the Shia (means 'followers of Ali (a.s). Almost all the Meccans favored Abu Bakr (r.a) as the successor to the prophet. They all ignored the Prophet's sermon at Ghadir Khumm, in which he nominated his cousin and son-in-law, Ali (a.s) ibn Abi Talib, as his successor. While Banu Hashmi were busy in burial arrangements of the Prophet, Umar (r.a) nominated Abu Bakr (r.a), as the successor, in a gathering of the Ansar (the people of Medina). Some Muslims offered their oaths of allegiance to Abu Bakr (r.a) and he was confirmed as the first Caliph, after the prophet. Twelvers Shia believe that Ali (a.s) was convinced of the legitimacy of his claim, due to his nomination by the Prophet(pbuh), and his knowledge of, and service to Islam. He told Abu Bakr (r.a) that his delay in pledging allegiance (bay 'at) was based on his belief, in his own title. Ali (a.s). pledged allegiance to Abu Bakr (r.a), Umar (r.a) and Usman (r.a) in order to keep unity among the Muslims.[88]

Shia Islam: Shia Muslims have always been a minority Sect among Muslims, being 10-15 % of over 1.6 billion Muslims in the world today. In the middle east, there are 443 million Sunni Muslims and 144 million Shia. In Iran, the majority are Shia, at 93%; in Iraq 68%; in Bahrain 70%; and in Oman 75% are Shia Muslims. Shia Islam is the second-largest branch of Islam, Sunnis being the majority. Shia Islam consists of three main branches: Twelvers, Ismailis and Zaydis, with Twelver Shia, being the largest and most influential group. Like Sunnis, Shia Islam is also based on the Quran but accept only those Hadiths of the Prophet(pbuh), which are attested by their Imams. The Shia also extend this "Imamate" doctrine

---

[87] Karen Armstrong, *Muhammad: A Biography of the Prophet*, Harper San Francisco, 1992, p. 145.
[88] *Madelung 1997—p. 43*

to Muhammad (pbuh)'s family—to some men, in the lineage of Ali (a.s). bin Abi Talib, known as Imams, who they believe, have special spiritual and political authority over the community.[89]

Imamate: According to Twelver Shia (sect of 12 Imams), divine wisdom, is the source of guidance for the Prophets and Shia Imams. The difference is that prophets receive revelations through angel Gabriel whereas Imams do not see the angels but are guided through divine inspiration which gives them esoteric knowledge.[90] Although the Imam is not the recipient of a divine revelation, he is guided by secret texts called al-jafr and al-Jamia which have been passed on by the Imams to their descendants. Al-Jafr is composed of two skin boxes which contain a mystical Shia holy book, compiled by Ali (a.s), under guidance of the Prophet(pbuh), various books of the past Prophets, and the weapons of the Prophet (pbuh). Al-Jafr was inherited by Ali (a.s) and Fatima (r.a), from the Prophet(pbuh). Each new Imam inherited al-jafr, from his predecessor. Al-Jamia is a scroll made from ram skin measuring 70 cubit long,[91] and width of a sheepskin. Al-Jamia has details about permitted and sinful things, and legal verdicts. The Shia believe that Al-Jamia and Al-Jafr are currently in the possession of the 12th Imam Muhammad al-Mahdi, after he inherited them from his predecessors, and if needed he will reveal them when he reappears. Imamate or belief in the divine guidance is a fundamental belief in the Twelver Shia ideology that God would not leave humanity without access to divine guidance.[92] According to Twelvers, there is, always, an Imam of the era who is the divinely appointed to guide the followers in the Muslim community. Ali (a.s). was the 1st Imam in the Twelvers and Sufis' view, the rightful successor to Muhammad (pbuh), followed by male

---

[89] *Holt 1997—p. 57*
[90] Gleave, Robert. "Imamate". Encyclopaedia of Islam and the Muslim world; vol.1. MacMillan.
[91] Cubit-an ancient measure of length, approximately equal to the length of a forearm. It was typically about 18 inches or 44 cm, though there was a long cubit of about 21 inches or 52 cm.
[92] Imamreza.net-origins of knowledge of Ah al-Bayt—Ayatollah Rayshahri-Retrieved 2010-02-11 Nasr, Seyyed Hossein; Dabashi, Hamid; Nasr, Seyyed Vali Reza (1988). Shi'ism.

descendants, through his daughter Fatima (r.a). Each Imam was the son of the earlier Imam, except for Imam Husayn ibn Ali (a.s). who was the brother of the 2nd Imam, Hassan (a.s) ibn Ali (a.s). The twelfth and final Imam is Imam Mohammad al Mahdi (a.s) who is believed to be alive but hidden from public view until he returns to bring justice to the world, in collaboration with Jesus Christ (pbuh) at End Times.[93] Sufi orders also believe in the Imams as the spiritual heads of Islam, because most of the spiritual chains of Sufi orders lead to one of the Twelve Imams. All the historians and authors who have written about Shia Imams, agree that they had extraordinary personalities. They were all extremely pious, kind-hearted, and benevolent.

Jihad, the Holy War, in Shia Islam: In Shia theology, "armed activism" by Shia is limited to a person's immediate geography. Full-scale Jihad, by Shia can only be carried out under the 12th Imam when he returns from occultation in order to bring absolute justice into the world. However, struggles to defend Islam may be carried out. One important exception has been Ayatollah Ruhollah Khomeini's declaration of Jihad in 1980 when Iraq invaded Iran.[94]

Shias Tolerance of Other Religions: Shia Muslims are more tolerant of non-Muslims compared to Sunnis. For instance, all religions are protected by law in Iran where minority groups have seats in the government. However, in Saudi Salafi dominated Saudi Arabia, there is no religious freedom for Christians and Jews. Also, members of all Jihadist groups have been Sunni Muslims. The Prophet and Imam Ali (a.s). taught to be tolerant and open-minded to other human beings. Being a follower of the family of the prophet (pbuh) is following the prophet (pbuh) and Allah. Ali (a.s) said, 'Reprimand your brother by being kind to him, and react to his wrongdoing by being generous.' He also said, "Know that people are

---

[93] Sahih Muslim, bab nuzul 'Isa, Vol. 2; Sahih Bukhari, kitab bad' al-khalq wa nuzul 'Isa, Vol. 4.
[94] Kohlberg, Etan, "The Development of the Imami Shi'i Doctrine of Jihad." Zeitschrift der Deutschen Morgenländischen Gesellschaft, 126 (1976), pp.64–86, esp. pp.78–86

of two types: they are either your brothers in religion or your equals in creation." (Nahjul Balagha, Sermon 53)[95]

Pillars of Shia Islam: Twelver Shia Islam has five Usul al-Din and ten Furu al-Din. Five pillars are: 1-belief in the Oneness of God 2-belief in the Almighty's justice 3-Prophethood 4-Succession to the Muhammad (pbuh) 5-The Day of Judgment and the Resurrection. In addition to these Five Pillars, Shias perform: 1- Prayer 2- Fasting during Ramadan 3- Zakat like Sunnis. 4- Khums- an annual taxation of one-fifth (20%) of the gains or net income after deducting related expenses, is paid to the Imams; indirectly to the poor and needy people 5- Hajj 6- Jihad 7-Enjoining Good 8- Forbidding Wrong 9- Tawalla: expressing love towards Good. 10- Tabarra: expressing disassociation and hatred towards Evil.[96]

Khums and Ghanima: are revealed in the Quran 8:41 "And know that anything you obtain of war booty - then indeed, for Allah is one fifth of it and for the Messenger and for [his] near relatives and the orphans, the needy, and the [stranded] traveler." (Quran 8:38-41) and (Quran 8:1): "They (the believers) ask you about the war-gains. Say: "The war-gains belong to God and the Messenger (and they distribute them as they will). "So, keep from disobedience to God in reverence for Him and piety, and set things right among yourselves to allow no discord; and obey God and His Messenger if you are true believers." (Quran 8:1)[97]

Khums: It is a 20% tax paid on business profit and on minerals extracted and is different from Zakat or Jizya. The descendants of Muhammad (pbuh) and the Imams, in the lineage of Ali (a.s). and Fatima, receive Khums.[95] Sunni scholars have confined the Khums, 20% tax, to apply on only two items: a)-Booty seized during a raid and the spoils of war. b) Mines ad mineral of the state. After paying khums of 20%, the remaining 80% of the booty seized, spoils of war were distributed among the soldiers

---

[95] forums.catholic.com/t/is-shia-isla
[96] "Islamic Beliefs (the Pillars of Islam)" in Invitation to Islam by Sayed Moustafa al-Qazwini. www.al islam.org
[97] Abdulaziz Sachedina (1980), Al-Khums: The Faith in the Imāmī Shī'ī Legal System, Journal of Near Eastern Studies, Vol. 39, No. 4, 275-289.

and commanders, as a reward for their going to war against non-Muslims. The origins of the Khums, according to scholar, Abdelaziz Sachedina, go back to "the pre-Islamic Arab custom when one-fifth of the ghanima (booty), in addition to the part of the booty which especially attracted him, was given to the clan leader, the rest distributed among the raiders.[95]

Khums and the 1979 Islamic Revolution of Iran: For centuries, Khums has contributed towards financial independence of the Shia Imams who received Khums from their followers. This put considerable human and financial resources, at the disposal of the Imams who, being descendants of the Prophet (pbuh), considered themselves as the rightful leaders of the Muslim community, even when they did not assert their rights to the caliphates of their time. This was the main reason, the caliphs of the Umayyad, and Abbasid Dynasties, were always suspicious and apprehensive of the Imams, and subjected them to untold persecution, as described in Chapter 5. Of course, the rightful Imams of the Twelvers, had a peaceful and non-aggressive nature, and they preached tolerance and reconciliation in the community. In Shia doctrine, the 12th Imam is alive, but in occultation, destined to reappear at End times, to set up an Islamic state, based on justice and tolerance, in collaboration with Jesus (pbuh). According to the Shia doctrine, no armed uprising, to form an Islamic state, is permissible when Imam Mahdi (a.s), the 12th Imam, is in occultation. The Shia Muslims have, therefore, been in political inactivity for centuries, tolerating injustice and marginalization by the aggressive Sunni rulers. All this changed when Imam Khomeini challenged the aggressive Shah of Iran who had brutalized the populace of Iran, with his tyrannical policies of curbing the basic human rights of expression, assembly, and worship, through his Gestapo-style secret service, the SAVAK. He further alienated the Shia Clergy of Iran by opposing the religious edicts on Gender Segregation in society, consumption of alcohol, and other profanities. The shah was portrayed as the brutal Umayyad Caliph Yazid of the seventh century who was opposed by Imam Husayn (a.s), the exalted 3rd Shia Imam. Khums empowered the Shia clergy of Iran who used the funds collected to support the needy, and to fund public welfare projects. Khomeini (r.a) and his teacher Ayatollah Haeri paid for sanitation and water supply projects in Qom, Iran. When Khomeini (r.a) was arrested by the Shah in 1962, for his pronouncements against the Shah, the Shah gave him a blank check, to write his desired amount, in return for his conciliatory remarks in public about the shah. The Imam countered the proposal with his own blank check to the Shah if he left Iran for good. Such was the power of the Shia Clergy in Iran. During the occultation period of Imam Mahdi (a.s) Khums has been paid to the Shia Clergy who are the descendants of Muhammad (pbuh) and the Imams, in the lineage of Ali (a.s). and Fatima (those wearing a black turban). The Shia clergy were therefore able to develop closer relations with the populace who paid them Khums. The Shia clergy in Iran, when needed, were able to mobilize the masses, in protesting against the government policies. Modern day example of the power of Shia Ulama, is the 1979 Islamic Revolution of Iran, which was led by a religious figure, Imam Khomeini (r.a). Public support of the Imam and his supportive clergy was so overwhelming that they were able to mobilize millions in street demonstrations against the Shah. Another aspect of the power of Shia Ulama in Iran, which the outsiders do not know, was that even the Government Officials of the Shah of Iran, preferred to obey the Ulama rather than their superiors in the government. When Imam Khomeini declared the Shah's regime as illegitimate and called on the army personnel to defect, more than half of the Shah's soldiers abandoned their posts and went home, carrying their arms with them. Sunni Ulama, on the other hand, have always been under government control, being recipients of government sustenance allowances and stipends, and therefore, devoid of impartial opinions and fatwas on religious issues, and never had any say in the political matters. Many religious figures in Pakistan asked me, in the 1970's, why the Ulama in Pakistan have not been able to mobilize the masses for political purposes. I gave them the reasons mentioned above. In addition, I cited the theological difference between the Sunni and the Shia, due to which the Shia follow Imam Husayn (a.s)'s example of resistance to an unjust ruler, and an unparalleled fervor of martyrdom.

Five Pillars of Sunni Islam: Without strong pillars, a building is destined to collapse, eventually. The five pillars of Islam, therefore, are the foundation of Islam, on which the religion stands. They are as follows: 1) Recitation of the Shahada: a declaration: "there is no god but God and

Muhammad (pbuh) is the messenger of God ", is the basic requirement to become a Muslim. 2- Prayer - Salat: It consists of five daily prayers i.e. at dawn, noon, afternoon, evening and at night. All the prayers are performed facing the Kaaba in Mecca. Prayer may be performed anywhere but the mosque is preferable. 3- Charity - Zakat. A portion of wealth needs to be paid, for the benefit of the poor or needy, like debtors or travelers. 4-Fasting: It is obligatory for Muslims to fast during Ramadan for 30 days from dawn to dusk. It is necessary for all adults unless there is a medical reason which prevents them from doing so, such as those on medication, pregnant or breastfeeding, and menstruating women. 5-Hajj - Pilgrimage to Mecca: Every able-bodied Muslim is obliged to make the pilgrimage to Mecca, at least once in his/ her life, if financially feasible. [98]

Jihad in Sunni Islam: In the early era of Islam that lasted less than a century, jihad spread the realm of Islam from the borders of India and China to the Pyrenees and the Atlantic. Many modern historians question whether hunger and desertification, rather than jihad, was a motivating force in the conquests. The famous historian William Montgomery Watt thinks that "Most of the participants in the [early Islamic] expeditions probably thought of nothing more than the spoils of the war. Edward J, Jurji also believes that the motivations of the Arab conquests were certainly not for the propagation of Islam but mainly to enhance the state sovereignty. Some recent explanations cite both, the material and the religious causes in the conquests. When the Ottoman caliph called for jihad against the allied powers in world war 1, the appeal failed to mobilise the Muslims and the Muslims did not turn on their non-Muslim commanders. World war 1 ended in the end of the Ottoman caliphate as the empire sided with the losers and had to accept punitive measures imposed by the allies who won the war.[99]

Views on the prophet (pbuh) of Islam: Guillaume Pastel said that Muhammad (pbuh) should be esteemed by Christians as a valid prophet. Gottfried Leibniz praised Muhammad (pbuh) because "he did not

---

[98] Matthew S.Gordon and Martin Palmer 'Islam'. Infobase publishing 2009. p. 87
[99] Ahmed Al-Dawoody (2011), The Islamic Law of War: Justifications and Regulations, p. 87. Palgrave Macmillan.

deviate from the natural religion". Henri de Boulainvilliers, in his Vie de Mohamed, which was published posthumously in 1730, described Muhammad (pbuh) as a gifted political leader and a just lawmaker who was employed by God to free the Romans and Persians from the autocratic rulers and to spread the knowledge of the unity of God from India to Spain. Jean Jacques Rousseau, in his Social Contract (1762), "presents him as a sage legislator who wisely fused religious and political powers." Emmanuel Pastore, in his 'Zoroaster, Confucius and Muhammad (pbuh), published in 1787, says that the Quran presents the most sublime truths of cults and morals, and describes the unity of God admirably. Pastore writes that the Prophet's law preaches sobriety, compassion and generosity to his adherents, and thinks that the "legislator of Arabia" was "a great man.". Alford Welch holds that Muhammad (pbuh) was able to be so influential and successful because of his firm belief in his mission. Thomas Carlyle in his book 'Heroes and Hero Worship' (1840) describes Muhammad (pbuh) as a person who was sincere. Napoleon Bonaparte admired Muhammad (pbuh) and Islam and described him as a model lawmaker and a great man. Modern writers like William Montgomery Watt and Richard Bell believe that Muhammad (pbuh) "was absolutely sincere and acted in complete good faith" and Muhammad (pbuh)'s readiness to endure hardship for his cause, with what was no rational basis for hope, shows his sincerity.

CHAPTER 2

Fundamentalism

All religions have had their periods of fundamentalism which refers to the anti-modernist movements, based on a literal interpretation of religious scriptures. It, therefore, has a religious meaning, showing unwavering attachment to a set of religious beliefs—specific scriptures, dogmas, or ideologies, leading to an emphasis on purity and the desire to return to an earlier ideal, from which adherents believe, members have strayed. Fundamentalism has existed in all religions, including Buddhism, Christianity, and Judaism, but, over the passage of time, other religions have moved forward, managing to get over their fundamentalist trends, like the Christianity, and Judaism, but Muslims are still following the beaten track of the seventh century of Islam.[100]

Islamic Fundamentalism: In modern times, Islamic Fundamentalism is being spearheaded by Saudi Arabia through its most virulent and destructive interpretation of Islam which considers all those who disagree, as apostates and non-Muslims, who deserve to be killed. This interpretation had been the root cause of Global Terrorism, which had resulted in violence against the already marginalized Shia Community of Muslims, especially in the Muslim majority countries. If Islam or the Prophet of Islam's teachings did

---

[100] Hunsberger B—1995—Religion and Prejudice—Journal of Social Issues. 51 (2)—113-129.

not instigate intolerance of other beliefs, which we learned from Chapter 1 of the book, then, how did Islamic Fundamentalism evolve? In this chapter, we will explore the history of Islamic Fundamentalism, to show that it is a deviation and an affront to the teachings of Islam, and had been adopted in modern times, for political purposes. We will also discuss followers of this destructive ideology of terror, such as the Khawarij, Ibn-Taymiyyah, Imam Ibn Abd al-Wahhab, the Salafi Movement, Maulana Maududi, and Sayyid Qutb of Egypt who influenced extremists like Osama bin Laden.[101] Islamic Fundamentalists, like followers of other religions, aspire to return to the origins of the religion and live like the prophet Muhammad (pbuh) and his companions. They favor the literal interpretation of the Qur'an and Sunnah, rejecting later interpretations of scholars and theologians of Islam. Islamic fundamentalists believe that Islam is based on the Qur'an and Sunnah, and reject the traditions, commentaries, popular religious practices, like the visitation of the tombs of saints, as deviations and superstitions. This view is associated with Saudi Salafism today. As with the fundamentalists of other religions, Islamic fundamentalists believe that the problems of the world stem from secular influences.[102] In view of the worldwide terrorism prevalent in the 1970s and 1980s, Islamic Fundamentalism or radical Islam needs to be discussed and analyzed, to understand what it really is. Some people, especially, the Americans, demonize the Iranians, but knowledgeable scholars hold the intolerant ideology of the Saudi religion, responsible for world terrorism, particularly in Muslim majority countries. Whichever strand of Islam sanctions killings, for whatever reason, is the Radical Islam which should be rejected. Observation of terrorist acts shows that most acts are claimed by the Sunni Muslims and not the Shia. All terrorist acts, in the US and Europe have, so far, been attributed to Sunni Muslims of the intolerant ideology of Islam, namely, the Saudi Salafism. Some people blame Iran for its links to Hezbollah of Lebanon, but they forget who Hezbollah is. They are a legitimate political faction in Lebanon, with participation in the Lebanese government. Therefore, most countries do not consider them a terrorist organization. Iranians are Shia Muslims, and support Shias in

---

[101] DeLong-Bas, Natana J. (2004). wahhabi islam (First ed.). New York: oxford university press, USA. p. 228
[102] Roy -failure of political islam 1994- p. 215

other countries, only through rhetoric, and not politically or militarily. I know about Pakistan, where about 15 % of the population is Shia i.e., a total of about 30 Million Shias, in Pakistan, but they do not take up arms, to defend themselves against Sunni terrorist groups, such as the Lashkar-e-Jhangvi, Taliban, al-Qaeda, and ISIS, which have been funded by the Arab countries. These terrorist groups killed hundreds every month, and had killed thousands of security personnel and civilians, since the end of the anti-Soviet war in Afghanistan, in 1989. Islamic fundamentalism started with the Khawarij in the seventh century of Islam and has resurfaced in the modern world, in the form of the Saudi Salafi doctrine of Islam, which will be discussed in chapter 6.

Radical Islam: The British government defined Radical Islam as Islam that opposes democracy, freedom, and tolerance of other faiths and lifestyles.[103] We will compare Saudi Arabia and Iran, the modern-day adversaries, and let the reader decide which country's religion is more radical. Comparison is needed, due to the demonizing of Iran, by most people, including the media, top officials of the US government, and lawmakers. We will discuss various aspects of the two countries about democracy, and tolerance of other faiths.

Democracy: Saudi Arabia is an absolute monarchy, effectively a hereditary dictatorship. There is no public participation in government affairs. Iran, on the other hand, is the Islamic Republic, a political System in which there is a parliament elected by the people, with Islamic Jurists exercising overall control. [104]

Rule of Law: In both countries Sharia law, taken from the Quran, is enforced. Of course, the Saudi implementation is more repressive, due to its Saudi Salafi extremist doctrine which considers all other religions and other Muslim sects apostates who must be killed.

---

[103] Casciani, Dominic (10 June 2014).islamic extremism- BBC News. Retrieved 27 January 2016.
[104] Al Rasheed, Madawi (2010). A History of Saudi Arabia. pp. 180, 242–243, 248, 257–258

Women: As of November 2017, Women are allowed to drive and work, in Saudi Arabia, thanks to the Crown Prince Mohammad bin Salman and the current King Salman.[105] However, they are still, not allowed to mix with men in public places, such as mosques, shopping malls, eateries, hospitals, and schools. There was a fire in a girls school in Mecca, in 2002, in which many girls were burnt to death because the male rescue workers could not reach them as they were not wearing correct Islamic dress, and for not being escorted by a male, as reported by BBC. According to 'Human Rights Watch "Women and girls may have died unnecessarily because of the extreme implementation of dress code. The school building was overcrowded with 800 pupils. School staff and religious police pushed the girls back into the building when they tried to escape.[106]

Iranian Women: Before and after the 1979 Islamic revolution, women have held high posts in the Iranian parliament and government, and some have been ministers. In 1968, Farrukh Roo Parsa was appointed the minister of education and Mahnaz Afkhami became minister of women in 1976. Women took part in the Islamic revolution and their role was greatly commended by the leader Imam Khomeini. Many women joined government service in the Islamic government where 17 women are now in parliament. By 1999, there were 140 female publishers. As of 2005, 6 5% of Iran's university students and 43% of salaried workers were women. Before 1979, the literacy rate of women was 42.33 %, today it is 97.23 % for 1-24 years old. According to the current leader Ali Khamenei, "developing woman's talents in family and society is respecting the women".[107] There are also women in Iranian police to deal with crimes committed by women and children. By 2007, 70% of Iran's engineering students were women.[108]

---

[105] Shabrawi, Adnan—Girl gets a year in jail, 100 lashes for adultery—The Saudi Gazette. Archived on 13 January 2011. Retrieved 22 September 2010
[106] as reported by: Abou el Fadl, Khaled, The Great Theft, (2005), pp. 250-2.
[107] Leader speech in a meeting with women- english.khamenei.ir. 20 October 2009. Retrieved 12 March 2016.
[108] iran student enrolment- quandl.com.

Freedom of Worship: In Saudi Arabia, Public worship of all other religions is banned. There is discrimination against the Shia and Sufi Muslims.¹⁰⁹

Christianity in Saudi Arabia: Saudi Arabia allows Christians to enter the country as foreign workers who carry out religious practices in their homes. Converting from Islam to another faith is considered apostasy, punishable by death. Despite this, there are nearly 60,000 Christians with a Muslim background. Non-Muslim clergy are not allowed to enter Saudi Arabia. In 2001, 11 Christians were arrested for practising their religion in their homes. In 2004, 48 Christians were arrested after reports of desecration of a Quran at Guantanamo Bay Detention Camp.¹¹⁰ There was, however, a non-Muslim cemetery in Jeddah, in 1930.¹¹¹

Jews in Saudi Arabia: Census reports do not show any Jews living in Saudi Arabia. Jews entering the country must sign an affidavit saying that they were not Jewish. During the Gulf war, US Jewish service members were allowed but they had to perform their religious rituals in their homes or secretly at the base.¹¹²

Iran's Jews: In Iran, all religions and sects of Islam can worship in their own ways. There are 10 synagogues for Jews in Tehran only, and 25 in the whole of Iran. There is a Jewish member in the Iranian parliament. All financial enticements offered to Iranian Jews to immigrate were rejected by Iran's Jews in 2007.¹¹³ Moreh Sedgh, a Jewish member of Iranian Parliament, is a general surgeon who runs the Jewish charity hospital in Tehran, which takes in patients of all faiths. According to the lawmaker,

---

109   IRF- 2013 "Freedom of Religion is neither recognised nor protected under the law and government severely restricted its practice.
110   Johnstone, Patrick; Miller, Duane Alexander (2015). believers in christ from muslim background-a global census. Interdisciplinary Journal of Research on Religion. 11: 17. Retrieved 20 October 2015.
111   Saudi Arabia-friend or foe in war on terror- hearing of judiciary committee. November 8, 2005. Retrieved August 6, 2015.
112   The World Factbook. The Central Intelligence Agency. 2 =Saudi Arabia in 1970's- part-1-visitor impressions-. May 2005. Retrieved 12 May 2011.
113   Iran jews feel at home in Iran-The national-. Retrieved on 2011-05-29. 3=Iran jews reject cash offer to move to Israel. Guardian. Retrieved on 2011-05-09

Iran's Jews stay because it is their country where they can practice their faith freely and live comfortably. Moreh says he supports his country's policy, even about Israel. He says Judaism is different from Zionism, which is the project of building Israel. He thinks that people with good knowledge and a high degree of ability, from a religious minority, can help improve the country, and he hopes that Iran's Jews will one day be judges and ministers in the Iranian government, but he says: "it's best to seek improvements "little by little, step by step".[114]

Jewish Commitment to Stay in Iran: Regarding Iran's controversial former president, Mahmoud Ahmadinejad, who raised questions about the Holocaust, the Lawmaker says: "I think that the Ahmadinejad case must be viewed differently. He does not deny [the] Holocaust entirely. His opinion was that there is a question about the Holocaust, which is not the Iranian government's official position on the subject". Moreh Sedgh wrote a letter to the President objecting to his statement, telling him that denying the truth was not helpful for Iran.[115]

Iran's Christians: In 1976, the Christian population numbered 168,593 people, mostly Armenians. Due to the Iran/Iraq War in the 1980s, the number of Christians with Iranian citizenship was 109,415 in 2006, and 117,704 in 2011. According to the national Statistical center, Christianity was the fastest growing religion in Iran, during the 1996-2006 period (+38.9%), and second fastest during the 2006-2011 period (+7.6%, after Zoroastrianism). The government of Iran guarantees the recognized Christian minorities several rights, like the production and sale of non-halal foods, a seat in Parliament, special family law etc. Iranian Christians tend to be urban, with 50% living in Tehran. Bibles and religious material in Persian are freely available to Iranians.[116]

---

[114] Iran Jewish Mmn: "israel has anti-human behaviour" Reuters 8 May 2008. Retrieved 2008-10-31
[115] Pleitgen, Frederik. Iran jews in isfahan "we feel at home in Iran" CNN. March 11, 2015. Retrieved on March 11, 2015.
[116] RT: anyone can buy the new testament in iran.

The doctrine of Takfir: Takfir is a pronouncement to declare another Muslim an unbeliever, apostate (Murtad) who deserves extermination. It is the central ideology of terrorist groups such as al-Qaeda, ISIS, and the Taliban. Saudi Kings have used this ideology, promoted by the founder of their religion, Imam ibn Abd-al Wahhab, to declare war on other Muslim tribes and countries, to set up and strengthen their kingdom. [117] According to the 'Oxford Dictionary of Islam', the doctrine of Takfir has been derived from the ideas of Khawarij, Ibn Taymiyyah, Ibn Kathir, Imam ibn Wahhab and later, in the 1950s, from Sayyid Qutb of Egypt. Mainstream Muslims and Islamic groups reject the concept of 'Takfir' as a doctrinal deviation. Scholars Hassan Hudaybi and Yousef al–Qaradawi said:" 'Takfir' is un-Islamic, marked by bigotry and zealotry. Such narrow mindedness has worsened the evil of sectarianism and intolerance among the people".[118]

Origin of Takfir: Doctrine of "Takfir "was first adopted in the seventh century by Khawarij, a group of dissenters who disagreed with arbitration to decide the succession dispute between Ali (a.s) and Muawiya (r.a), declaring the leaders and their followers' apostates and unbelievers. They argued that Ali (a.s) was the rightful caliph and Muawiya was a rebel who must be fought and defeated in battle, as ordained by ayah 49.9 of the Quran. When efforts at reconciliation with the Khawarij failed, The Caliph Ali (a.s) fought against them, in the battle of Nahrawan, inflicting a crushing defeat on them. The Caliph, himself, was later assassinated by a member of the Khawarij, while praying in the mosque.[119]

Deviation from Teachings of Islam: The doctrine of Takfir is against the teachings of the Qur'an and the Sunnah of the prophet (pbuh), to declare another Muslim apostate, if he professes the faith by proclaiming Shahada i.e. "God is one and Muhammad (pbuh) is his messenger." This

---

[117] Mohamad Jebara More Mohamad Jebara.imam mohamad jebara—fruits of the tree of extremism-. Ottawa Citizen

[118] Oliveti, Vincenzo; Terror's Source: the Ideology of Wahhabi-Salafism and its Consequences,Birmingham: Amadeus Books, 2002.

[119] Stanley,, Trevor—definition of Kufr, takfir—. Perspectives on World History and Current Events. Retrieved 16 June 2016.

proclamation is enough to show one's faith. Islam forbids pronouncing a Muslim, professing the faith, as an unbeliever, based on suspicion or rumor. "In Qur'an 4:94, God forbids calling a Muslim infidel if he professes the faith by saying as-Salam-o-Alaikum. Incidents took place during the Holy Prophet's lifetime, when it was suspected by some Muslims that a person was not sincerely a Muslim. The Holy Prophet said to them:" Did you tear open his heart to see what was in it?"[120] [121]

Modern Day Application of Takfir: The armed groups al Qaeda, al Nusra, ISIS that had been fighting in Syria and Iraq to topple the Shia-led governments, followed this ideology. Similarly, the Taliban in Pakistan and Afghanistan, Al Shabab in East Africa, Boko Haram in Nigeria, and Jemaah Islamiyah in Indonesia have all been followers of this ideology. Members of these groups believe in this doctrine by which they justify their actions against those they consider infidels and apostates who deserve to be killed. They considered their acts to be completely justified and irreproachable and believed that they will be rewarded by God in the afterlife. The followers of this ideology had instigated devastating regional conflicts in the middle east and beyond, causing over 2,000,000 deaths worldwide, since 1979, including about 20,000 US and Allied soldiers, and resulting in widespread instability and lack of security in the Middle East and in other countries. These conflicts included:1980-89 Iran/Iraq War; 1990, and 2003 Iraq Wars, followed by Iraq/Syria Civil Wars; the Yemen War; the Afghan Jihad; the Afghan War of 2001, followed by Insurgency of Afghan / Pakistan Taliban. These conflicts are described in chapter 8.

Shia Genocide: The primary aim of all the terrorist groups, working in Pakistan, Afghanistan, Indonesia, Iraq, Syria, Africa, and Yemen, had been to kill all who were not like them, including followers of the Shia and the Sufi sects of Islam, and non-Muslims, such as the Jews, Christians, and people of other lifestyles. . They were all motivated by the Saudi Salafi ideology of Takfir which encouraged them to commit violence. All these

---

[120] Ethics; Book 78, Ch. 44) (Tabarani, reported from Ibn Umar)
[121] Commins, David (2006). Wahhabi Mission and Saudi Arabia (PDF). I.B.Tauris. p. vi.

groups had been funded by individuals and charities in Arab countries with the tacit approval and overt or covert support of their governments.

History of Takfir: This doctrine originated in the seventh century from a group of misguided Muslims called the Khawarij, described above, who concocted this ideology for declaring other Muslims unbelievers if they disagreed with their interpretation of Islam. They disregarded the Quranic injunctions or the Sunnah of the prophet (pbuh) for moderation. Takfir was later sanctioned, by a 14th century Jurist ibn Taymiyyah, against Mongols who were Muslims but who did not follow the Islamic Sharia. Takfir was part of the eighteenth-century leader of the Saudi Salafi Reform Movement, Imam ibn Wahhab, to legitimize raiding of neighboring Muslim tribes of Najd and Hijaz, by King ibn Saud, to expand and strengthen his kingdom. This Saudi Salafi Movement came to be known as Wahhabism by Western scholars, to differentiate it from other Salafis who are not as intolerant, and violent as the Saudis .Due to the Saudi Kingdom's unflinching financial and military backing, Saudi Salafism became a formidable destructive force worldwide, due to its intolerant ideology which calls for the annihilation of those who do not agree with it. An important follower of this ideology has been the late Maulana Maududi of Jamaat-e-Islami of Pakistan who advocated violent Jihad, to set up an Islamic State in Pakistan. His thinking had a profound effect on Sayyid Qutb of Egypt who declared leaders of Muslim governments who did not follow Sharia Law as apostates and called for their destruction and sanctioned the killing of innocent civilians, in the revolutionary process, if unavoidable. In the absence of the Secular Government backing, like Saudi Salafism of Saudi Arabia, Sayyid Qutb was imprisoned, and later executed by Gamal Nasser government of Egypt. Maulana Maududi also faced similar persecution by the Pakistan Government which sentenced him to death. The King of Saudi Arabia intervened and had him released from prison and exiled to Saudi Arabia. (More detail in another section on Maududi)[122]

---

[122] Glasse, Cyril (2001). The New Encyclopedia of Islam. California: Altamira Press. pp. 255–56.

Khawarij: After the death of the third Caliph, Usman (r. a), a struggle for succession started between Ali (a. s) and Muawiya (r. a), the governor of Syria, and cousin of Caliph Usman (r. a). In 657, Ali's forces met Muawiya (r.a)'s at the battle of Siffin. Initially, the battle went against Muawiya (r.a) but on the brink of defeat, Muawiya (r.a) directed his army to hoist Qurans on their lances. Muawiya proposed to Ali (a.s) arbitration to decide the issue which was opposed by the largest group in Ali (a.s)'s army which refused to accept arbitration because they said Muawiya was a rebel and should be fought until defeated and repents. They left Ali (a.s)'s army and declared the arbitrators, commanders, and their supporters, non-Muslims who deserved to be killed, including the Caliph himself. This group became known as the Khawarij, meaning Dissenters i.e. those who leave. Caliph Ali defeated them in the battle of Nahrawan. Later, a Kharijite member assassinated the Caliph, while he was praying in the mosque of Kufa.[123]

History of Khawarij: They were initially called the Qurra. They were all Quran Memorizers (reciters) and were famous as fierce fighters who longed to be killed in battle. They belonged to a tribal group, particularly strong in Kufa, Iraq who wanted to rule their own states. They were later known as the Khawarij. They took part in the Battle of Yamama, during caliph Abu Bakr (r.a)'s reign, but they never listened to orders and would start battles even when they were ordered not to and were heavily outnumbered. At Yamama, Khalid ibn al-Walid wrote to them and his commander Ikrimah, to just see the forces of Muslimah at Yamama, and told them not to start fighting until he had arrived. Still they started the fight, suffering heavy death toll. and did the same against Ali (a.s). in the Battles of Camel, Siffin, and Nahrawan, even though they were heavily outnumbered. Al-Masudi calls them 'the people of the village ', those who fought with Abu Bakr (r.a), against the desert tribes of Yamama when some of the tribes refused to pay Zakat. They received the highest stipend of the Muslim army, receiving 2000-3000 dirhams while the troops got only 250 to 300 dirhams each. The other Ridda tribe members in Kufa, in Iraq, resented the special position given to the Qurra. Policies of Usman (r.a),

---

[123] Higgins, Annie C. (2004). "Kharijites, Khawarij". In Martin, Richard C. Encyclopedia of Islam and the Muslim World v.1. Macmillan. p. 390.

of reducing their status, threatened their interests. The Qurra were based in Kufa, in Iraq. They had not been involved in Syria. The Caliph also removed the distinction between the Ridda and pre-Ridda tribe members which was not to their liking and lessened their prestige. In Medina they took an oath that they will not cause trouble and following the example of Muhammad (pbuh), Usman (r.a). accepted their word and let them go. [124]

Beliefs and Later history of the Khawarij: For hundreds of years, the Khawarij continued to be a source of insurrection against the Caliphate. The Khawarij considered the first two caliphs to be rightly guided but believed that Usman (r.a). had deviated from the path of justice. They also believed that Ali (a.s).committed a grave sin when he agreed on the arbitration with Muawiya (r.a).The Kharijites thus deemed the leaders Ali (a.s).and Muawiya who appointed the arbitrators Abu Musa Ashari and 'Amr ibn al-'As, and all those who supported arbitration as "disbelievers", and they also believed that all participants of the battle of Camel, including Zubair, Talha had committed a major sin.[125]

Assassination Attempts by Kharijites: Among the surviving Kharijites, three of them gathered in Mecca to plot a tripartite assassination tries on Muawiya (r.a), 'Amr ibn al-'As and Ali (a.s). The assassin was to come out of the prayer ranks and strike the target with a sword, dipped in poison. Muawiya (r.a) escaped the assassination try with only minor injuries. Amr was absent due to illness and his deputy was killed. However, the strike on Ali (a.s), by the assassin, Abdul-Rahman ibn-Muljam, proved to be fatal. Ali (a.s) died from injuries a few days later. All assassins were captured and put to death, in accordance with the Islamic laws.[126]

---

[124] Glasse, Cyril (2001). The New Encyclopedia of Islam. California: Altamira Press. pp. 255–56.

[125] Schultz, Joseph P. (1981). Judaism and the gentile paths and religions- Fairleigh Dickinson Univ Press. p. 175. bedouin nomads who resented the centralization of power in the new Islamic state that curtailed the freedom of their tribal society.

[126] Ali (a.s)'s Murder—. Islam Helpline. Retrieved 30 January 2014.

Khawarij Views on Muslim Governance and Other Doctrines: The Khawarij considered the caliphate of Abu Bakr (r.a) and Umar (r.a) to be rightly guided but believed that Usman (r.a) had deviated from justice in the last days of his caliphate and deserved to be killed. They also believed that Ali (a.s) committed a grave sin when he agreed on the arbitration with Muawiya (r. a). The Kharijites thus believed the arbitrators (Abu Musa Ashari and 'Amr ibn al-'As), the leaders who appointed these arbitrators, Ali (a.s). and Muawiya (r.a) and all those who agreed on the arbitration, all companions of Ali (a.s). and Muawiya (r.a), as Kuffar "disbelievers", as they had breached the rules of the Qur'an. They believed Talha, Zubair, and Ayesha (r.a) had committed a major sin. Kharijites differed with both Sunni and/or Shia on some points of doctrine.[127] According to Islamic scholar Abul A'la Maududi, using the argument of "sinners are unbelievers", Kharijites used abusive language against the sahaba.[128]

Groups Like the Khawarij: In the modern era, al-Qaeda, ISIS and Saudi/Salafi Jihadis have the same beliefs and actions, as the Khawarij. Ibadis, are like the Khawarij, with similar beliefs, and are a majority sect in Oman, and a smaller population of Ibadis are in Algeria, Tunisia, Libya, and Zanzibar. In the 18th century, the Hanafi scholar Abidin declared the Saudi Salafi Movement of Saudi Arabia as modern Khawarij.[129]

Ibadis: They are a group like Khawarij, but their views are more moderate. Their leader Ibn Ibad, the founder, broke off from the main Khawarij, during the reign of Caliph Abdul-Malik ibn Marwan. Initially, they opposed the rule of the third Caliph Usman (r.a). but rejected murder of the caliph, unlike the more extreme Kharijites. Due to their opposition to Umayyad Caliphate, Ibadis staged armed insurrection in 740. Caliph Marwan signed a peace accord and allowed them to keep a community in Shibam where they stayed for 4 centuries, paying taxes to Ibadi authorities in Oman. During the 8th century, Ibadis established an Imamate in Oman

---

[127] Goldziher, Ignaz. "Muslim Studies"(Transaction Publishers, 1971) Vol.1 p.130.
[128] Abul A'la Maududi Khilafat-o-Malookiat (Caliphate and kingship), (Urdu), p 214.
[129] Imam al-Albani-the prophet's description of dogs of hellfire and present Takfiri Kharijites. Islam Against Extremism. 2015. Archived on 2015-02-27.

which was chosen, unlike the Sunni dynasties where the rule is inherited. By 900, the sect had spread to Sindh, Khorasan, Muscat, parts of Africa and Spain. Ibadis prefer to resolve differences through reason rather than confrontation.[130]

Ibn Taymiyyah: (1263-1328) An important follower of the ideology of the seventh century Khawarij was an Islamic intellectual named Ibn Taymiyyah, a towering figure in the history of Muslim thought. He lived in Damascus in the 13th and 14th centuries when Syria was in danger of domination by the Mongols. Despite the formal Mongol conversion to Islam, the Mongols continued to follow the "Yasa code of laws of Genghis Khan, instead of the Islamic law" The failure of the Mongols to correctly implement the Sharia rendered the Mongols, in Ibn Taymiyya's juristic opinion, apostates and hence the lawful object of jihad, which entailed a "decisive fight against the disbelievers, thus being a righteous war.[131] Indeed, aspects of his teachings had a profound influence on the founder of the Hanbali reform movement practiced in Saudi Arabia, Mohammed ibn Abdul Wahhab. Moreover, Ibn Taymiyya's controversial fatwa allowing Jihad against other Muslims, is often quoted by al-Qaeda and other jihadi groups. In the contemporary world, he is considered the root of Saudi Salafism, the Senussi order, and other later reformist movements. Ibn Taymiyyah has also influenced Rashid Rida, Sayyid Qutb, Abul A 'la Maududi, Abdullah Azzam, Hassan Al Banna and Osama bin Laden. Taymiyya's views, on such widely accepted Sunni doctrines of the medieval period, such as the visitation of the tombs of saints, made him very unpopular with most of the Islamic jurists and scholars of his time, under whose orders he was imprisoned several times during his life.[132]

Views of Ibn Taymiyyah: On Existence of saints: Although ibn Taymiyyah was critical of some of the developments within Sufism but he never

---

[130] Hoffman, Valerie Jon (2012). Ibadi Islam.
[131] Makdisi, 'Ibn Taymiyya: a Sufi of the Qadiriyya order', American Journal of Arabic Studies 1, part 1 (1973), pp. 118–28.
[132] Halverson, Jeffry R. (2010). Theology and Creed in Sunni Islam: The Muslim Brotherhood, Ash'arism, and Political Sunnism. Palgrave Macmillan. pp. 48–49

rejected the practice outright and recognised many Islamic saints, including Bayezid Bastami, Junaid of Baghdad, Abdul Qadir Gilani, Hassan Basri, Karhi, Sirri, and Saqti, to be the leaders of humanity who called people to the right forbidding them from what is wrong. Ibn Taymiyya considered visiting the shrines of saints to be comparable to worshiping something besides God (shirk). Mainstream scholars vigorously rejected this view both during his life and after his death. Ibn Hajar Asqalani, a Shafi'i scholar, stated that "This is one of the ugliest positions that has been reported of Ibn Taymiyyah" and added that travelling to visit the tomb of the prophet (pbuh) was a noble and legitimate action.[133]

Intercession, Sufism, Extremist Doctrines: ibn Taymiyyah said that seeking the help of God through intercession is allowed if the other person is still alive.[134] However, he believed that those who ask help from the grave of the prophet (pbuh) or saints, are mushrikeen (polytheists). Mainstream Sunni scholars vigorously rejected this view. For example, the chief judge of Damascus, al Subki, said there is nothing improper about seeking intercession of the Prophet, and Ibn Taymiyya deviated from an established point of view. Historians Zarqani and ibn Ishaq also disagreed with ibn Taymiyya's views on intercession. Ibn Taymiyyah himself belonged to the Qadiriyya Order of Sufism of Abd al-Qadir al-Jilani and spoke highly of Abu Yazid al-Bastami and al-Junayd. ibn Taymiyyah is considered a forefather of al-Qaeda.[135]

Ibn Taymiyya's Works: Ibn Taymiyyah left a considerable body of work. Oliver Leeman says that Ibn Taymiyyah produced some 700 works in the field of Islamic sciences.[129]

Imam Ibn Abd al-Wahhab (1703-1792): Following the 14th century ideologue Ibn Taymiyyah, was an important religious leader, Imam ibn Wahhab, who was backed by an ambitious political leader, Ibn Saud of Arabia, in promoting the doctrine of takfir in the eighteenth century that

---

[133] Leaman, Oliver (2006). The Qur'an: An Encyclopedia. Taylor & Francis. pp. 280–282
[134] Ibn Taymiyyah, al-Mukhtasar al-Fatawa al- Masriya, 1980, p. 603.
[135] Kepel, Gilles, The Prophet and the Pharaoh, (2003), p.194.

has had a profound impact on the world scene, in terms of world security and stability, particularly since the 1979 Islamic Revolution of Iran. Imam Mohammad ibn Abd al-Wahhab was a preacher from Najd in Arabia who founded the movement known as Saudi Salafism (to differentiate it from Salafism). He belonged to a religious family of Sunni Muslims and studied jurisprudence of traditional Hanbali School of Law, in his hometown. Despite his first training in Sunni Muslim tradition, he gradually became opposed to the popular traditions of the veneration of saints and visitation of their tombs which he considered heretical or even idolatry. His ideas were opposed by notable Sunni scholars, including his own father and brother who were well-known religious figures of their area. His brother Sulayman b. Mohammad, was the Hanbali Jurist of Najd, and his father, Abd al-Wahhab, was a Judge of Hanbali law.[136] Ibn Wahhab travelled to Mecca for pilgrimage and later to medina where he met a Hanbali theologian from Najd named Abd Allah b. Ibrahim who supported views of Ibn Taymiyyah. Ibn 'Abd al-Wahhab's teacher Abdullah ibn Ibrahim ibn Sayf introduced him to Mohammad Hayyat Al-Sindi in Medina who belonged to the Naqshbandi order of Sufism and recommended him as a student. Imam Mohammad Ibn Abd-al-Wahhab and al-Sindhi became very close and Imam Mohammad Ibn Abd-al-Wahhab stayed with him for some time. Scholars have described Mohammad Hayyat, as having an important influence on Imam Mohammad Ibn Abd-al-Wahhab. Hayyat taught Ibn Abd al-Wahhab to use informed individual analysis Ijtihad. Mohammad Hayat also taught Imam Mohammad Ibn Abd al-Wahhab, to reject popular religious practices, associated with Walis and their tombs, which resembles later Saudi Salafi teachings. After his early education in Medina, Ibn Abdul Wahhab traveled outside of the peninsula, going first to Basra[137]

Friendship with Mr. Hempher in Basra: It is reported by Daniel Pipes, that a British agent named Mr. Hempher was tasked with finding ways

---

[136] Laoust, H., "Ibn Abd al-Wahhāb", in: Encyclopaedia of Islam, Second Edition, Edited by: P. Bearman, Th. Bianquis, C.E. Bosworth, E. van Donzel, W.P. Heinrichs.

[137] John L.Esposito-(edited by),—The Oxford Dictionary of Islam, oxford university press—(2004), p. 296.

and means of weakening the Ottoman caliphate. For this purpose, he was looking for a suitable person and during his search he got to know Ibn Wahhab who had ideas opposed to the traditional Sunni Islam, regarding visitation of the tombs of the saints and prophets, and their veneration. Hempher also noted that ibn Wahhab objected to the established Sunni and Shia doctrines, regarding Ijma (consensus of religious leaders on religious matters). "In Basra, I established a very intimate friendship with [him]. Mohammad of Najd was the sort I had been looking for". Disguised as a Muslim, Hempher, met ibn Wahhab who at the time was in his twenties, He convinced ibn Wahhab to start a new Muslim sect, opposed to traditional Sunni Islam which at the time accepted visitation of the tombs of saints and prophets and their veneration, to sow discord among Muslims. Hempher never left him alone and kept a close eye on his ward. They discussed theological and political subjects. Hempher joined up with ibn Wahhab in Najd and stayed there two more years with him, under the guise of being his slave. According to Hempher, the British government instructed him to ensure ibn Wahhab's safety because his preaching was expected to engender enmity towards him. The emergence of 11 other British officers who spoke Arabic, as reported by Daniel Pipes, was to aid Hempher in the much-needed security arrangements. These officers also introduced themselves as ibn Wahhab's slaves.[138]

Early Preaching and Pact with Ibn Saud: On return from Basra, Imam Ibn Wahhab started preaching and attracted many followers, including the ruler of his hometown Uyaynah, who helped him carry out his ideological reforms namely leveling of the grave of Zaid bin Khattab, a companion of the prophet (pbuh) and stoning of a woman who had committed adultery. When news of these actions spread, the ruler of Qatif and al-Hasa forced the ruler of Uyaynah to expel the Imam from his hometown. Upon expulsion from his hometown, the imam was invited to settle in neighboring Diriyah by its ruler Mohammad bin Saud. After some time, Imam Mohammad ibn Abd al-Wahhab concluded his second and more successful agreement with a ruler. Ibn Abd al-Wahhab and Mohammad agreed to wage Jihad against the unbelievers in Arabia who believed in

---

[138] Hempher- Daniel Pipes-Saga of Hempher.

the veneration of saints. Imam undertook to support the ruler with his Islamic legal dicta while ibn Saud promised to protect the Imam against enemies. [139] The agreement was confirmed with a mutual oath of loyalty in 1744. Ibn Abd al-Wahhab became responsible for religious matters and Ibn Saud in charge of political and military issues. This agreement became a "mutual support pact "and power-sharing arrangement between the Al Saud family, and the Al ash sheikh, the followers of Ibn Abd al-Wahhab, which remained in place for 300 years, giving the ideological impetus to Saudi expansion.[140]

Imam's Family: According to Encyclopedia Britannica, Ibn Abd al-Wahhab married an affluent woman when he was in Baghdad and inherited her wealth after her death. Imam Mohammad ibn 'Abd Al-Wahhab had six sons; Husain, Abdullah, Hassan, Ali and Ibrahim. Another son Abdul-Aziz died in his youth. All his surviving sons set up religious schools close to their homes and taught the young students from Diriyah and other places. The family is respected in Saudi Arabia like the Royal Family.[141]

Teachings: He preached unity of God and following the Qur'an and hadith of the prophet (pbuh) rejecting later interpretations and innovations by jurists and scholars of Islam. According to him, worship included the five daily prayers, fasting during Ramadan and seeking protection and help from God only. He preached that seeking intercession or protection or supplication (Dua) from anyone or anything except God was against tawhid (oneness of God) and therefore idolatry and shirk. He taught that visitations, supplications, and veneration of the tombs of prophets, Sahaba, Ahl Bayt, Shia Imams and saints were acts of idolatry and shirk. People performing such acts deserved to be killed, their properties confiscated, and women annihilated. Imam Mohammad ibn Abd al-Wahhab saw it as his mission to restore a more pure and original form of the faith of Islam. Anyone who did not adhere to this interpretation was considered

---

[139] DeLong Bas 2004, p.24, 34.
[140] Madawi al-Rasheed—a history of Saudi Arabia.
[141] Encyclopedia Britannica- Ibn Wahhab-Online. Retrieved 2016-12-12.

a polytheist worthy of death, including fellow Muslims (especially Shiite who venerate the family of Muhammad (pbuh).[142]

Views On Saints: Imam Ibn 'Abd-al-Wahhab did not deny the existence of saints but objected to their intercession after death. He acknowledged the miracles of saints. According to author Dore Gold, Imam in his Kitab al-Tawhid described followers of Christianity and Judaism as sorcerers who made graves of their prophets, places of worship. He said their punishment is 'that they be struck with the sword.[143] Historical accounts state that, Mohammad ibn Abd al-Wahhab saw it as his mission to restore a more pure and original form of the faith of Islam. Anyone who did not adhere to this interpretation was considered a polytheist, worthy of death, including fellow Muslims (especially Shiite who venerate the family of Muhammad (pbuh).[144]

Views about Imam ibn Wahhab: Imam Abd al-Wahhab's teachings were criticized by several scholars including his own brother Sulaimon ibn 'Abd al-Wahhab who wrote one of the first treatises' refuting Saudi Salafi doctrine, claiming he was ill-educated and intolerant, and classing Ibn Abd al-Wahhab's views as fringe and fanatical.[145]

Recognition: Despite Saudi Salafi destruction of many Islamic, non-Islamic, and historical sites associated with the first Muslims, the prophet (pbuh)'s family and companions, Saudi government renovated Imam's tomb, and has converted it into a tourist attraction.[146]

---

[142] Ibn Abd al-Wahhab, Kitab al-Tawhid
[143] Gold, Dore (2003). Hatred's Kingdom (First ed.). Washington, DC: Regnery Publishing. p. 25.
[144] DeLong-Bas, Natana J. (2004). Wahhabi Islam: From Revival and Reform to Global Jihad (First ed.). New York:oxford university press-, USA. p. 61
[145] Mannah, Buṭrus Abū; Weismann, Itzchak; Zachs, Fruma (2005-06-11)— Ottoman Reform and Muslim Regeneration—I.B.Tauris. p. 83, 87, 89, 91.
[146] Hubbard, Ben (31 May 2015).Birthplace of Imam Ibn Abdul-Wahhab turned into tourist spot.– via NYTimes.com.

CHAPTER 3

Islamic Fundamentalist Movements outside Arabia

Several Islamic fundamentalist movements akin to Saudi Salafism appeared in South Asia as a reaction to the British imperialism. Some of them are described below:

Syed Ahmad Barelvi (1786–1831): He is considered, by Edward Mortimer, to be a forerunner of Jihad in the Indian subcontinent to establish an Islamic state. He was influenced by Shah Wali Ullah's son Shah Abdul Aziz. Syed Ahmad toured India and developed a network of friends and followers in different parts of India. In 1821, he went for Hajj with many friends and spent two years there. The teachings of Saudi Salafism of Arabia influenced him, during his two years stay there. He returned from Hajj in 1823 and again toured all parts of India, collecting funds and volunteers for jihad against the expanding Sikh Empire. In 1826, he, along with one thousand disciples, arrived in Peshawar (now in Pakistan), to set up an Islamic state among Pashtun tribes in the area. They established a base at Charsadda, near Peshawar. He preached jihad amongst the local tribes, demanding they renounce their tribal customs and adopt the Sharia. Clerics and a system of Islamic taxes replaced the traditional Khans, to finance the jihad, which was declared but it failed, due to the "betrayal of the local khans." In December 1826, they clashed with the Sikh troops at Akora. The Peshawar governors initially pledged their allegiance but abandoned Syed Ahmed during the next clash with Sikh forces at Akora. The Pashtun initially supported him, but his interference in their social and economic matters displeased them. They rose against him and, around two hundred of his Mujahideen, were killed in Peshawar valley which compelled him to migrate. In 1831, at Balakot, Sayyid Ahmad and hundreds of his troops and followers were killed by the Sikh Army. [147]

Deobandi Movement in India (1867): Shah Waliullah Dehlavi (1703–1762), who fought against the British, in the 1857 mutiny in India, was the main inspiration of this Movement. Darul Uloom Deoband was founded in 1867, after the 1857 Sepoy Rebellion in Northern India. The Deobandi organization started in response to the British rule, which Muslim scholars believed was corrupting Islam. Anti-imperialist policy developed in the Deobandi school. Deobandi ideology was spread through Jamaat Ulema-e-Hind and Tablighi Jamaat. Deoband graduates belonging to different countries opened thousands of madrasas throughout the world. In 1967, there were 9000 madrasas in South Asia, and there are over 15000 now. Deobandis considered Hindus and Muslims of India to be one nation and asked them to implement a joint struggle against the British. In 1919, a group of Deobandis formed the political party Jamiat Ulema-e-Hind which opposed the Pakistan Movement, A minority group Jamiat Ulema-e-Islam (J.U.I.) however joined Mohammad Ali Jinnah's Muslim League in 1945. Deobandis followed the Saudi Salafi doctrine of Saudi Arabia. J.U.I. (an offshoot of the Deobandi Movement), in Pakistan propped up the Taliban. They received funding from Saudi Arabia from the 1980s to 2000s. Afterward, funding was diverted to the rival Ahl al-Hadith movement. About 600 of Britain's 1,500 mosques were under the control of Deobandis. They preached against the Jews, Christians, and Hindus. The militant organizations Lashkar-e-Jhangvi, the Taliban, and Sipah-e-Sahaba followed the Deobandi ideology, which is allied with the Saudi Salafism of Saudi Arabia. While many leading Muslims and Islamic scholars have been highly critical of the Taliban's interpretations of Islamic

---

[147] Abbott, Freeland (1962). "The Jihad of Sayyid Ahmad". The Muslim World. 52 (3): 216–222.

Law, the Darul Uloom Deoband has consistently supported the Taliban in Afghanistan, including their 2001 destruction of the Buddhas of Bamiyan and massacre of Shia Muslims in Mazar-Shariff. The Taliban follow the Deobandi fundamentalism.[148]

Barelvi Movement (1904): Ahmed Raza Khan (1856-1921) of Bareilly was the founder of this Movement. They followed the Sufi Muslim practices, such as the veneration of saints. They are opposed to the Deobandi Movement, which follows the Saudi Salafi religion of Arabia. They supported the Pakistan Movement.[149] Ahmed Raza Khan declared Mirza Ghulam Ahmad, the leader of Qadiani Sect, a heretic, an apostate. He called the Deobandis and Saudi Salafis unbelievers and collected scholarly opinions of 33 ulama of mecca and medina and compiled them into an Arabic work called 'Hussam al Haramain,' in support of his views. A clear majority of Muslims in India, adhere to the Barelvi Movement. They are funded by the barelvis of the U.K and are opposed to Saudi Salafi practices. Barelvis believe in the veneration of dead and alive saints, and visitation of their tombs. They follow the Hanafi Fiqh and the Sufi schools of Chishti, Quadria and Suhrawardy orders.[150]

Sectarian violence: Attack on a Barelvi gathering in Karachi, in Nishtar Park, on April 11, 2006, to celebrate the prophet's birthday, killed at least 70 people, including several central leaders of the Sunni Tehreek. In April 2007, Barelvi activists tried to gain control of a mosque in Karachi, firing on the mosque, killing one person, and injuring 3 others. On 27 Feb.2010, Taliban and Sipah-e-Sahaba affiliates attacked Barelvis celebrating the Prophet (pbuh) 's birthday in Faisalabad, creating tensions.[151]

---

[148] Darul Uloom Deoband. Retrieved 29 April 2013.
[149] John L. Esposito, ed. (2014)-ahle sunnat wal-jamaat- The Oxford Dictionary of Islam. Oxford: Oxford University Press.
[150] Roy, Oliver; Sfeir, Antoine (2007). Columbia world dictionary of Islamism-, page 92: "...as distinct from the reformist construction of Deoband."
[151] Ashok K. Behuria, Sects and within Sect-Deobandi/Barelvi Encounter in Pakistan. Strategic Analysis, vol. 32, no. 1- institute of defence studies- January 2008.

Conflicts with the Taliban: Barelvis oppose the Taliban, saying that suicide bombings, killing innocent people are not part of Islam, as declared by their leader Sarfraz Ahmed Naeemi, in 2009.[152] They declared that the Taliban were a product of global anti-Islam conspiracies and that they were tools in the hands of Saudi Salafism, backed by the United States, to divide Muslims and bring a bad name to Islam.[153]

Jamaat-e-Islami: Syed Abul A'la Maududi (1903 - 1979), a well-known philosopher and scholar of Islam, and founder of Jamaat-e-Islami, wrote about the role of Islam in South Asia. His thinking was deeply influenced by the defeat of the Ottoman Caliphate, Indian Nationalism, Hindus, and Muslims of India, and by the teachings of Imam ibn Abd al-Wahhab, the founder of Saudi/Salafi branch of Islam. He supported an Islamic state in which sovereignty would be exercised in the name of Allah, and Islamic Law (Sharia) would be implemented. Maududi believed politics was "an integral, inseparable part of the Islamic faith, and that the Islamic state, he envisioned, would not only be an act of piety but would also solve the many social and economic problems of the Muslims. Maududi opposed the establishment of Pakistan.[154] J.I. (short for Jamaat-e-Islami) was founded in Lahore in 1941. In 1947, after the partition of India, the Jamaat split into two organizations, Jamaat-e-Islami Pakistan and Jamaat-e-Islami Hind, the Indian wing. Other wings of Jamaat were in Kashmir and Bangladesh, founded in 1953 and 1975, respectively. Maududi and J.I.[155] migrated to Lahore, in Pakistan after the partition of India, and opened hospitals and medical clinics. In the 1951 elections, its candidates for office did not do well.[156]

Lahore riots of 1953: Sunni and Shia Muslims await the coming of the Mahdi (a.s) and the second coming of Jesus (pbuh). They rejected the claims of Mirza Ghulam Ahmad, leader of the Ahmadiyya Movement, as the Promised Messiah and the Mahdi (a.s). The Ahmadis were staunch

---

[152] Anti-Taliban views cost Mufti naeemi his life—Daily Times.
[153] Pakistani Sunnis unite against Talibanization-The Indian News. 9 May 2009.
[154] Nasr—vanguard of the revolution 1994. pp. 108
[155] Jamaat-e-Islami
[156] Haqqani-Pakistan between mosque and military-2005-p. 171

supporters of Pakistan and actively engaged, with the Muslim League for the establishment of Pakistan, and had cordial relations with many prominent members of the Muslim League. They had a higher literacy rate, and were, therefore, able to reach high Government, and Military posts in Pakistan, much to the annoyance of the religious coalition, which included the J.I. Mainstream Muslims considered Ahmadis to be apostates and non-Muslims and resented their hold in Pakistan's Government. An ultimatum was given to the Government by the religious coalition, to remove Zafarullah Khan (an Ahmadi) from the foreign ministry, dismiss all Ahmadis from government posts, and declare Ahmadis as non-Muslims.[157]

Disturbances and aftermath: The ultimatum was rejected, and disturbances began. Riots broke out in Lahore, in March 1953, leading to looting, arson and the killing of at least 200 Ahmadis. Martial Law was declared, on March 6, by the Governor General Ghulam Mohammad when the riots got out of control. The military leader, General Azzam Khan had Maulana Maududi, and Maulana Niazi arrested, and the military court, on May 11, sentenced them to death, for treason (writing anti-Ahmadiyya pamphlets). Maududi's unapologetic and impassive stance of not asking for clemency had an "immense" effect on his supporters. It was a "victory of Islam over un-Islam," proof of his leadership and strong faith. On May 13, Maududi and Niazi's death sentences were changed to life sentences. Many J.I. supporters were also imprisoned during this time.[158] The riots resulted in the first intrusion of the military into Pakistani politics. After that, Maududi endorsed the 1956 constitution which accommodated many of the demands of the J.I. and claimed it a victory for Islam. J.I. formed an alliance with the Muslim League and Nizam-e-Islami party. The alliance destabilized the presidency of Iskandar Mirza (1956 - 1958) and Pakistan returned to martial Law, declared by General Ayub Khan (1958 - 1964), who had a modernizing agenda and opposed the encroachment of religion into politics. He abolished the constitution, banned political parties, and warned Maududi, against continued religiopolitical activism. J.I. offices

---

[157] Ali Kadir. "Parliamentary Heretization of Ahmadiyya in Pakistan". In Gladys Ganiel (ed.). *Religion in Times of Crisis*. Brill. p. 139. Retrieved 30 October 2014.
[158] Court of inquiry report—*The persecution.org*. 10 April 1954. Retrieved 13 January 2014.

were closed, funds were confiscated, and Maududi was imprisoned in 1964 and 1967.

1964-1965 Pakistan Presidential Elections: J.I. supported the opposition leader, Fatima Jinnah, despite its opposition to women in politics. Ayub Khan won the elections securing 64% votes against Miss Jinnah's 36%. However, the opposition disagreed with the results, although the opposition leader accepted the results. J.I. resisted the socialist program of Zulfiqar Ali Bhutto and Maulana Bhashani, declaring it un-Islamic.[159]

1970 Elections and Reign of Zulfiqar Ali Bhutto: (1973 - 1977): J.I. took part in the 1970 elections running against the Pakistan people's party and Awami League, securing only four seats in provincial and national assemblies. Zulfiqar Ali Bhutto won the 1970 election campaign and was strongly opposed by JI. In early 1973, the J.I. even appealed to the army to overthrow Bhutto's Government because of "its inherent moral corruption." In 1977 elections, the Pakistan National Alliance won nine out of 36 seats, and P.P.P. secured 155 out of 200 seats. Maududi was arrested due to his anti-Bhutto campaign, and he called on Islamic parties to begin civil Disobedience. The Government of Saudi Arabia intervened to secure Maududi's release from prison, warning of revolution in Pakistan. J.I. helped the Pakistan National Alliance (PNA) to oust Bhutto. J.I. opposed the Awami League East Pakistan separatist movement. Students allied with Jamaat organized the Al-Badr to fight the Mukti Bahini (Bengali liberation forces). In 1971, J.I. members were alleged to have collaborated with the Pakistani army in the killing of Bengali civilians. In 1972, Maududi resigned citing poor health.[160]

Rule of General Zia-ul-Haq (1977 - 1987): When General Zia-ul-Haq overthrew Bhutto and came to power in 1977, he accorded Maududi, the status of a senior political leader. Zia-ul-Haq sat with Maududi for ninety minutes, on the night before Bhutto was hanged. Maududi supported Zia's decision to execute Bhutto. Maududi supported Zia and his Islamization program. In return, thousands of J.I. members were given government

---

[159] women in politics—a case study—H. Saiyid
[160] Ian Talbot (1998). -Pakistan-a modern history—St. Martin's Press. p. 193-196.

jobs. However, Zia did not hold elections, as promised, and distanced himself from the J.I. When Zia banned student unions, the J.I. protested. However, J.I. did not take part in the people's party movement for the restoration of democracy. J.I. also supported Zia's Jihad against the Soviet Union and supported Jamiat-e-Islami of Afghanistan, led by Burhanuddin Rabbani.[161]

J.I. Connections with Insurgents: When Pervez Musharraf assumed power in 1999 in a military coup, J.I. welcomed him first, but objected to his secular reforms and decision to join 'War on Terrorism', alleging Musharraf had betrayed the Taliban. J.I. condemned the 9/11 attacks but equally condemned the U.S. war in Afghanistan, against the Taliban Government. J.I. supported Sufi Mohammad who founded an offshoot of J.I., in 1992 called Tehreek Nifaz-e-Shariat -e-Mohammad which was a militant outfit allied with the Taliban.

Maududi and Sayyid Qutb: The Egyptian Ideologue Sayyid Qutb was a follower of Maududi. The only way, Qutb thought, the people of Egypt and the rest of the Muslim World could be saved was, through a revolution by radicals, the strict followers of Salafism, like the Saudis, who would alter the status quo. In Pakistan, Maududi's efforts to establish an Islamic state through the political process failed due to lack of support by the people and the military, shown by how many seats J.I. won in the various elections, described above. J.I. and the other religious parties, therefore, hated democracy, rulers, and the people. When all hopes faded away, J.I. and other religious parties of Pakistan took to the streets, to show their power. When General Zia-ul Haq took control, religious groups pinned their hopes on him, due to his religious rhetoric. But General Musharraf's coup in 1999, dashed all their hopes when he embarked on implementing secular reforms and joined the U.S. in a war against terror. Later they

---

[161] Jones, Owen Bennett (2002). Pakistan—eye of the storm—New Haven and London: Yale University Press. pp. 16–7. Zia rewarded the only political party to offer him consistent support, Jamaat-e-Islami. Tens of thousands of Jamaat activists and sympathisers were given jobs in the judiciary, the civil service and other state institutions. These appointments meant Zia's Islamic agenda lived on long after he died.

hoped their dream of enforcing Sharia will come true through the militant groups such as ISIS, al-Qaeda, and the Taliban, which were lavishly funded by the Saudis, and supported by the U.S., initially for the Afghan War against the Soviets. A new force, in the form of militant groups, appeared, waiting to strike for the real dream: enforcing Sharia in Pakistan, by destabilizing the political and military set-up, stripping the country of everything Western, serving the agenda of the Islamic parties.

The Tehreek-e-Taliban Pakistan (TTP). The TTP gave the religious parties that cover they needed to begin a push to enforce Sharia. Religious groups, especially the J.I., would not have to get their hands dirty this time. They would only capitalize on the TTP's lethal War on the Pakistani state and military. The religious groups never criticized the TTP's brutalities, allowing the state and the army to slowly bleed, which stood at odds with the religious groups. Therefore, the dream of Syed Qutb and Maududi of establishing an Islamic state is yet to come true.

Salafi Movement: This Movement appeared as a backlash against the influence of victorious allied Western Powers, in World War 1, followed by the fragmentation of the Ottoman Caliphate into smaller nation-states. Muslims worldwide considered themselves marginalized and weakened. The establishment of Israel in 1948, in the heartland of Islam, was another blow to the Muslim prestige. Muslim Ideologues like Hassan al-Banna (1906-1949) and Sayyid Qutb (1906-1966) blamed the Muslim rulers for their inaction and ineptitude, and envisioned the Muslim salvation and progress, in implementing the Sharia Law of Islam in their countries. They sought to return to a school of thought called the Salafi Movement that advocated bringing Islam back to its origin, i.e., the literal meaning of the sacred texts of Islam, rejecting later liberal interpretations by scholars. They rejected veneration and tawassul of religious figures, which were historically prevalent among the Sufis and Shia Muslims, whom they considered apostates who deserved to be killed. The Salafi movement also preached the ideology of takfir according to which non-Salafi Muslims were declared apostates. [162]Salafis followed Ibn Taymiyya rather than

---

[162] Stanley, Trevor. -kufr-takfiri - Perspectives on World History and Current Events. Retrieved 30 Dec 2013.

more tolerant figures like Mohammad Abdu, Jamal al-Din al-Afghani, and Rashid Rida. According to Bernard Haykel, those moderate Salafis of the Abdu category no longer existed. The term Salafis has been hijacked by Salafis of the Ahl al-Hadith/Saudi Salafi variety. [163] Salafis did not acknowledge or follow any of the four schools of thought to which Sunni Muslims adhered. They had their own beliefs and laws.

Demographics of Salafism and Salafi Groups: The majority of the world's Salafis are from Qatar, U.A.E., and Saudi Arabia. 46.87% of Qataris, 44.8% of Emiratis, 5.7% of Bahrainis, 2.17% of Kuwaitis are Salafis. Salafis are the "dominant minority" in Saudi Arabia. There are 4 million Saudi Salafis, 22.9% of Saudi Population, (concentrated in Najd). The Movement is divided into three groups – purists, activists, and jihadis: **Purists:** They work on Education and advisory work and do not oppose rulers and support autocratic regimes of the Middle East.[164]

Activists: They aim to establish a caliphate through evolution, without engaging in violence. Because of being active on social media, they have earned some support among more educated youth.[165]

Salafi jihadists: They encourage and promote violence against those they deem to be enemies of Islam. Sayyid Qutb of Egypt developed an ideology of Salafi Jihadism, and later, his devotees followed it in Egypt. They carried out many terror attacks against government targets. This ideology of violence was later adopted, by international Muslim volunteers, in the Afghan Jihad against the Soviet forces. In the 1990s, extremist jihadis returning to their home countries, after the Afghan Jihad, started fighting their secular governments, to replace them with an Islamic State. Salafi Jihadists allied themselves with the jamaat al-Islamiyah in Algeria and

---

[163] anatomy of Salafi movement- by QUINTAN WIKTOROWICZ, Washington, D.C.
[164] Richard Gauvin, Salafi Ritual Purity: In the Presence of God, p. 41. New York-Routledge, 2013.
[165] George Joffe, Islamist Radicalisation in Europe and the Middle East: Reassessing the Causes of Terrorism, p. 317.- London IB Tauris, 2013.

contributed toward the Algerian Civil War.¹⁶⁶ The most famous jihadist-Salafist attack was the September 11,2001 attacks, against the United States, by al-Qaeda, followers of this ideology. While Salafism had little presence in Europe in the 1980s, by the mid-2000s, Salafist jihadists had a significant presence in Europe, having tried more than 30 terrorist attacks among E.U. countries, since 2001. The Movement, however, had grown in the wake of the Arab Spring and breakdown of state control in Libya and Syria. The most prominent Salafi Jihadi group is al-Qaeda, set up by Osama bin Laden and Abdullah Azzam in Peshawar, Pakistan in 1984, with first funding from Osama himself. In Syria and Iraq, al-Nusra and ISIS were other groups of Salafi Jihadists, who fought to topple the Shia-led governments and engaged in the killing of Shia populace of these countries. The main goal of these groups had been to kill the Shias whom they considered apostates, following the ideology of Saudi / Salafism, which preaches violence against Shia Muslims.¹⁶⁷

Sayyid Qutb: (October 1906 – August 29 1966): Sayyid Qutb, the Egyptian writer, and activist and mentor of Osama bin Laden and the terrorist groups, wrote in his most popular book, "Signposts on the Road" (1964): "This is the most dangerous Jahiliyyah which has ever menaced our faith. For, everything around is Jahiliyyah: the beliefs, manners, morals, culture, art, and laws. He said: "the Muslim rulers are no longer Muslim and advocated their overthrow." He was a leading member of Muslim Brotherhood, and an accomplished writer who wrote 24 books, covering literature, Education, and the political role of Islam. His books in the Education field were part of curricula in schools of Egypt. He disapproved of the life and culture of the U.S., which he considered to be obsessed with materialism, violence, and pleasures.¹⁶⁸

---

166 "Jihadist-Salafism" is introduced by Gilles Keppel, Jihad: The Trail of Political Islam (Harvard: Harvard University Press, 2002)
167 "Jihadist-Salafism" is introduced by Gilles Kepel, Jihad: The Trail of Political Islam (Harvard: Harvard University Press, 2002)
168 James Toth, Sayyid Qutb : The Life and Legacy of a Radical Islamic Intellectual, OUP USA (2013), p. 12.

Views on Qutb: According to writer Mark Weston, Qutb was one of the most important authors of the twentieth century. Qutb is comparable to Karl Marx. Both men had broad interests, a lively writing style, a mistrust of money-controlled democracies, and a belief that a determined elite can seize power and change the world. While Marx dismissed religion as the opiate of the people that took away independent thinking and action from human beings, Qutb spent most of his adult life writing about Islam. His writings were read in homes and mosques throughout the world. His most influential work 'Milestones' was published in 1964 and a few years later translated into Persian by Ayatollah Khamenei, the current leader of Iran, who then began to read the thirty volumes of his 'In the shade of the Quran'. Al Zawahiri, the al-Qaeda leader in his book 'Knights under the Prophet's Banner,' defended the killing of Western civilians and said: "Sayyid Qutb's call to acknowledge God's sole authority was the spark that ignited the Islamic Revolution against the enemies of Islam, at home in Egypt and abroad." After his death, Al-Azhar University of Egypt declared Syed Qutb to be a deviant and put his name on their index of heresy.[169]

Spread of Qutb's ideas: Ideology of Syed Qutb influenced terrorist groups, such as al-Qaeda, ISIS, and the Taliban. Abdullah Azzam, who had been very close to Sayyid Qutb throughout his life, influenced al-Zawahiri with Qutb's character and with the torment, Qutb had endured in prison. Zawahiri admired Qutb in his book "Knights under the Prophet's Banner." Osama bin Laden regularly attended weekly public lectures by Mohammad Qutb, Sayyid Qutb's brother at King Abdelaziz University in Medina, and was deeply influenced by Sayyid Qutb. Qutb's ideas were spread, through his writings, his followers, and particularly through his brother Mohammad Qutb who, after his release from prison in Egypt, migrated to Saudi Arabia and became a professor of Islamic Studies at King Abdul-Aziz University in Medina. He edited, and published his brother's works, and promoted them. Ayman al-Zawahiri who became a member of the Egyptian Islamic Jihad was one of Mohammad Qutb's students and, later, a mentor of Osama bin Laden and a leading member

---

[169] Kepel, Jihad, 1986, p. 58.

of al-Qaeda. Abdullah Azzam was first introduced to Sayyid Qutb, by his uncle, Mahfouz.[170]

Osama bin Laden: (1957-2011) He followed the ideology of Ibn Taymiyyah, Ibn Abdul Wahhab and Sayyid Qutb of Egypt. He belonged to the Athari school of Islamic theology. He believed that the restoration of God's Law will set things right in Muslim countries. Saudi Salafism dictates to its followers that only a Muslim ruler can declare Jihad and that followers must, under all circumstances, obey the ruler unless he commands his subjects to violate the religious commandments. Osama did not agree with this contention of Saudi Salafism. Like Sayyid Qutb, Osama's basic goals were to resist western domination and to combat Muslim Regimes that did not rule, according to Islamic Law. He believed that the Government of the Taliban under Mullah Omar was the only true Islamic state on earth. [171] Bin Laden was born in Saudi Arabia and had a close relationship with the Saudi royal family, but he opposed inviting U.S. forces to defend Saudi Arabia against an attack by Saddam Hussein. The Saudi Kingdom felt threatened, after Saddam's attack on Kuwait. Osama went to see King Fahd and the defense minister Prince Sultan. He told them, not to depend on non-Muslim help, and offered to defend the kingdom with his legion of 100,000 Jihadis. Prince Sultan asked him, how he planned to mount a defense as there were no caves in Kuwait, and how he would defend against chemical weapons of Saddam. He replied, 'with faith in God.' Bin Laden's offer was rejected, and the King invited deployment of U.S. troops in the Saudi kingdom.

Afghan Jihad: In 1979, Osama opposed the Soviet invasion of Afghanistan and answered the call to arms by Afghan freedom fighters. Bin Laden used his own resources to get volunteers from Arab countries such as Egypt, Lebanon, Kuwait, and Turkey to join the Afghans in their battle against the Soviets. The U.S. and Saudi Arabia gave $40 billion worth of financial aid and weapons to Bin Laden's Afghan mujahidin. He met and built

---

[170] The Political Thoughts of Sayyid Qutb, Ch. 3, p. 56. 14 = Qutbism- ideology of islamic fascism- by Dale C. Eikmeier. From Parameters Spring 2007, pp. 85–98.
[171] oct 6,2002- appeared on al-Qaeda website-also on 24 Nov, the Guardian and the Observer.

relations with Gen. Hamid Gul, head of I.S.I. of Pakistan. Although the United States gave the money and weapons, the Pakistan Armed Forces and the I.S.I., conducted the training of militant groups. Osama and Azzam established al-Khidmat, which funneled money, arms, and fighters from around the Arab world into Afghanistan. Through al-Khidmat, bin Laden's inherited family fortune paid for air tickets and accommodation, paid for paperwork with Pakistani authorities, and gave other such services, for the jihadi fighters. Bin Laden set up camps inside Pakistan, near the Afghan border. where he trained the volunteers for Afghan jihad.[172]

Battle of Jaji: Osama personally took part in the Battle of Jaji—a defensive fight against the airborne soviet forces who, backed by their Afghan allies, attacked Osama's camp at Jurji, to cut off their supply line from Pakistan. Participants of this battle were Jalaluddin Haqqani, Abdullah Azzam, Ahmed Khadr, Bin Laden, and his Afghan Arab fighters. 50 Arab fighters and 70 Afghans were killed in this battle, with the camp holding its system of tunnels and caves successfully.[173] Journalist Jamal Khashoggi reported this battle in Saudi Arabia, leaving an impression of Bin Laden as a victorious military leader who then attracted many followers in Saudi Arabia. Bin Laden also took part in the 1988 Gilgit Massacre in which large numbers of Shias of Gilgit were massacred by a group of Sunni tribe members. (detail of this event is available in a relevant section)[174]

Formation of Al-Qaeda: Al-Qaeda was formed on August 11,1988, at a meeting of senior leaders of Islamic Jihad, Abdullah Azzam, and bin-Laden. It was agreed to use bin Laden's money, with Jihadis ability, to take up Jihadi activity elsewhere, after the Soviet withdrawal from Afghanistan. After the Soviets withdrew in 1989, Osama returned to Saudi Arabia in

---

[172] Gardell, Matthias (2003). of the Blood: The Pagan Revival and White Separatism. Durham and London: Duke University Press. p. 325.
[173] Bergen, Peter (May 28, 2002). Holy war, Inc..—inside the secret world of Osama—free press- pp. 56–57
[174] Murphy, Eamon (2013). Routledge. p. 134.- October 3, 2017. Shias in the district of Gilgit were assaulted, killed and raped by an invading Sunni lashkar-armed militia-comprising thousands of jihadis from the North West Frontier Province.

1990 and was welcomed by the people as the 'Hero of the Jihad,' who had defeated a superpower.[175]

F.B.I. Raid in the U.S.: On November 8, 1990, F.B.I. raided home of al-Nusairi, a member of al-Qaeda and discovered evidence of terrorist plots including the bombing of New York buildings. This was the earliest discovery of al-Qaeda plots outside Muslim countries. Nusairi was convicted of world trade center bombing and later admitted to the killing of Rabbi Meir Kahani in New York. Bin Laden continued speaking against the kingdom, and this resulted in his banishment from Saudi Arabia. In 1992, he moved to Sudan, where he invested heavily on various projects. He built a base for Mujahideen operations in Khartoum. In 1995, Islamic Jihad tried to assassinate Hosni Mubarak, the President of Egypt. As a result, Islamic Jihad as well as Al-Qaeda operatives were expelled from Sudan. Saudi officials wanted Bin Laden expelled from Sudan but could not tolerate his presence in Saudi Arabia. Also, Bin Laden no longer felt safe in Sudan, where he had already escaped, at least one assassination try that he believed to have been the work of the Egyptian or Saudi regimes, and paid for by the C.I.A.[176]

Return to Afghanistan: Due to the increasing pressure on Sudan from Saudi Arabia, Egypt, and the United States, bin Laden could leave for a country of his choice. In winding up his businesses in Sudan, Bin Laden lost $20-300 million because of a distress sale of his assets, including his horses. The Sudan Government seized his construction equipment. He contacted his friends in Jalalabad who said they would be honored to welcome a veteran of their long War, against the Soviets. So, he left Sudan aboard a chartered flight on May 18, 1996, with 3 wives, 15 of his 19 children, his closest followers, and his bodyguards. One of his wives, unwilling to live in Afghanistan, asked for and received a divorce, and returned to live in Saudi Arabia, with a son and 2 daughters. Bin Laden's eldest son Abdullah also left Sudan at this time and today runs an

---

[175] The Great War for Civilisation', Robert Fisk, 2005, p 4.
[176] Gallab, Abdullahi A. (2008). the first Islamic republic: development and disintegration in Sudan. Ashgate Publishing, Ltd. p. 127. -Retrieved May 7, 2011.

advertising and marketing business in Jeddah. Khalid Sheikh Mohammad, along with dozens of other bin Laden followers, arrived in Afghanistan on later flights. After the Taliban took Kabul and Jalalabad, Mullah Mohammad Omar invited Bin Laden to move to Kandahar, where he built a new training camp outside the city, in the desert, paid for mosques, irrigation channels, a large dam, and trucks. He already had several other camps to train fighters, bound for Chechnya and Kashmir. He realized he had a lot more freedom in Afghanistan than he had in Sudan. Members of al-Qaeda could come and go without visas or border searches, and they could import vehicles, weapons, and bags of cash with no questions asked. In his mountain quarters, made of mud and tree branches, it was a challenge to keep warm in below zero winter temperatures. Still, his office had a Macintosh computer, a fax machine, and hundreds of books on Islam and on horses, according to Abdul Bari Antwan who visited him in Afghanistan. There was no girls school at his compound, so he himself taught math and science to his two teenage daughters. By 1998, al Qaeda had more than 2000 members, and by 2001, more than 10,000 militants had received training, at Bin Laden camps, according to U.S. estimates. A Pakistani report said that al Qaeda members came from Egypt, Saudi Arabia, Yemen, Algeria, and Jordan. Although Afghanistan was harboring someone who wanted to overthrow the monarchy in Saudi Arabia, the Saudis gave $100 million in aid to Bin Laden, in 1997 and seemed relieved just to have bin Laden out of the way, in desert mountains. Two midlevel Saudi princes were so pleased with bin Laden's training of Chechen and Kashmiri guerrillas, according to a U.S. Intelligence report, that they sent him money despite his anti-Saudi views.[177]

Osama's Declaration of War against the U.S.: On August 23,1996, only 3 months after arrival in Afghanistan, Bin Laden faxed a 10,000-word essay "A declaration of War against the U.S., occupying the Land of the Two Holy Places" to several Arabic newspapers in London. In this declaration, he said that The Saudi Monarchy had given up its right to exist because it had replaced Islamic Law with civil Law; had lowered oil production to suit the American economy; had rejected clerics petitions

---

[177] profile-mullah Omar- BBC News. September 18, 2001. Retrieved May 28, 2010.

and had allowed American Forces to occupy the land of the two holy places.[178]

1998 U.S. Embassy Bombing: Bin Laden and Al-Zawahiri organized an al-Qaeda congress on June 24, 1998. Two simultaneous truck bomb explosions occurred at U.S. embassies in Nairobi, Kenya, and Dar as Salaam, Tanzania, killing over 213 people and wounding 4000 in Nairobi; killing 11 and wounding 85 in Dar as Salaam. Most of the casualties were local citizens but included 12 Americans. Further attacks planned, included—a triple attack on January 3, 2000, on Radisson Hotel in Amman, a tourist resort at Mount Nebo, the sinking of a U.S. destroyer in Yemen and at a target within the U.S. The plan was defeated by arresting the members of Jordanian Terrorist cell and the arrest of Ahmed Ressam, in the U.S. Ressam is currently serving a 37 years sentence in Florence, Colorado.[179]

9/11 Attacks: Osama was accused of the 9/11 attacks. An F.B.I. Investigation in the U.S. said the involvement of Osama and al-Qaeda was irrefutable. The attacks killed about 3000 people.[180]

Death of bin Laden: (April 2011)-President Obama ordered a covert operation to catch or kill Osama who was killed by U.S. Navy SEALs on May 2, 2011.[181]

Muslim Brotherhood: It is an Islamic political Organization, founded in Ismailia, Egypt by Hassan al-Banna, in March 1928. Hassan al-Banna was an Egyptian schoolteacher and Imam. His writings presented a modern ideology based on Islam. He considered Islam to be a comprehensive system of life, with the Qur'an, as the constitution. He appealed to Egyptian

---

[178] Bin Laden's Fatwa-. Pbs.org. August 20, 1998. -Retrieved June 25, 2011.
[179] World Islamic front for jihad against Jews and Christians- al-Quds al-Arabi (in Arabic). Retrieved May 28, 2010.
[180] Watson, Dale L., Executive Assistant Director, Counterintelligence Division, FBI (February 6, 2002). FBI Testimony of 9/11-. Federal Bureau of Investigation – (Representative Press). Retrieved February 11, 2011.
[181] Cooper, Helene (May 1, 2011). Obama announces killing of Osama bin laden- The New York Times. Archived on May 2, 2011. Retrieved May 1, 2011.

pan-Arab patriotism but rejected Arab nationalism and regarded Muslims as members of a single community. The Muslim Brotherhood advocated a gradual moral reform and had no plans to take power by force. After the abolition of the Ottoman Empire, al-Banna warned Muslims to prepare for a struggle against the colonial rule. He encouraged the people of Egypt to give up Western customs. He was assassinated by Egyptian secret police in 1949. His son-in-law Said Ramadan became a major leader of the Muslim Brotherhood in the 1950s.[182]

---

[182] Mura, Andrea (2012). the discourse of al-Bannah- *Journal of Political Ideologies* 17 (1): 61–85.

CHAPTER 4

House of Saud

It is essential to study the Saudi Dynasty which has dominated the middle east region for 300 years, and survived upheavals of its surrounding countries, because of World Wars 1 and 2 which affected all the nations of the world, including the Middle East and Africa. Many kingdoms of the region including Egypt, Libya, India, Russia, and Japan were replaced with nationalist governments, but the Saudi Dynasty withstood the challenges because of its brave policies which were aimed at strengthening the Kingdom, ignoring all other considerations. During the World Wars, the House of Saud sided with whoever served their political interests. They maintained neutrality in the world Wars but sided with the British in fighting the Ottoman Empire because they wanted to wrest control of Arabia from the Ottomans, to establish the Saudi Kingdom and because their Saudi/Salafi religion was at odds with the Ottoman Sunni perspective. Saudi Family consists of descendants of Mohammad bin Saud, the ancestor of the Saudi dynasty and the founder of the First Saudi state (1744–1818) in Arabia. The present ruling faction of the family is primarily led by the descendants of Ibn Saud, the founder of modern Saudi Arabia. The most dominant figure in the family is the King. The family has over 15,000 princes, 2000 of the inner circle possess all the power and wealth. [183]

---

[183] Sir James Norman Dalrymple Anderson. The Kingdom of Saudi Arabia. Stacey International, 1983. Pp. 77.

The House of Saud has gone through three phases: The First Saudi State (1744–1818), when the Kingdom expanded, the second (1824–1891) in which there was infighting; and the Third Saudi State (1902–present), which turned into the present day Saudi Arabia in 1932. The dynasty fought against the Muslim Ottoman Empire, the Muslim Sharif of Mecca, the Muslim Al Rashid family of 'Ha'il and their vassals in Nejd. It also fought its own Shia Muslims, to consolidate the Kingdom, although their Shia populace only asked for more freedom and public facilities and never challenged the empire. The succession to the throne was designed to pass from one son of the first king of modern Saudi Arabia, Ibn Saud, to another. The present King is Salman bin Ibn-Saud, with his son as the crown prince. A royal decree in 2006 stated that a Committee of Saudi Princes should elect future Saudi Kings. Ottoman Empire was divided into nation-states of Iraq, Syria, Kuwait, Jordan, UAE, Egypt, and Oman, after world war 1, as the Ottomans joined the War with the losing side and after the War, the victors imposed punitive measures on the defeated powers, like Germany, Japan, and the Ottomans. Saudi Royals, mainly, King Abdelaziz bin Saud, the founder of the Kingdom of Saudi Arabia, was wise enough to side with whoever suited his political agenda which was always the survival and progress of the country. He sided with the British when he needed their support and later switched to the Americans when they offered him better terms. Ibn Saud even turned against his allies, the Ikhwan, who were instrumental in establishing the Kingdom but opposed his friendship with the British because they insisted on raiding the British Protectorates of Transjordan to expand the territory, thus alienating the British who were a formidable power at the time. He even managed to avoid the calamities of the world wars, by not committing his forces for combats. Ibn Saud only acted against the Ottoman vassals in Arabia, after World War 1, to strengthen his own Kingdom, when it was clear to him the Ottomans could not confront him. He deserves praise for his courage, statesmanship, and perseverance, which provided an excellent example for his successors, some of whom, being incompetent, have put the future of the Kingdom in jeopardy, by not being firm and decisive in dealing with the senior clergy in the country, and by not reviewing the 'Kingdom's policies to conform with modern times, like not softening their religion, to accommodate other faiths and lifestyles.[184]

First Saudi State: (1744–1818): Establishment of the First Saudi State is closely related to the teachings of Imam ibn Abd al-Wahhab which provided a religious sanction for the raiding of neighboring Muslim tribes, in the name of Jihad, to the ruler of Diriyah, Mohammad bin Saud, with whom the Imam sought refuge, after expulsion from his hometown of Uyaynah. In the absence of a religious sanction, raiding fellow Muslims, to expand his domain, would not have been possible. The pact between Imam ibn Abd al-Wahhab and Mohammad bin Saud, the ruler of Diriyah, set up the first Saudi state in 1744, also known as the emirate of Diriyah. They consolidated their pact by Saud's son Abdul-Aziz marrying the daughter of the Imam. Ibn 'Saud's forces first conquered Najd and expanded the Saudi Salafi doctrine to most of present-day Saudi Arabia, eradicating various popular practices, they viewed as akin to idolatries and propagating the theories of Ibn Abd al-Wahhab. After Najd, Saudi forces expanded their control over the eastern coast from Kuwait to Oman, followed by the highlands of Asir in Arabia. Imam Mohammad ibn Abd Al Wahhab wrote letters to people and scholars to join the field of Jihad. After many military campaigns, Mohammad bin Saud died in 1765, leaving the leadership to his son, Abdul-Aziz bin Mohammad. Imam Mohammad ibn Abd Al Wahhab also died in 1792.[185]

Attack on Karbala (1801): Abdul-Aziz bin Mohammad sent a force of 12,000, led by his son Saud, to attack the mosque of Husayn ibn Ali (a.s) in Karbala, Iraq, on 10th of Muharram. They put everything to fire and sword—the elderly, women, and children—everybody was killed. More than 4000 people perished. Rousseau, a Genevan philosopher, writer, and composer, who was there at the time, wrote that the Saudi Salafis loaded 4000 camels with booty, consisting of donations of silver, gold, and jewels to the Imam's shrine, and those brought by Nadir Shah from India, including his personal wealth. They destroyed the 'Imam's shrine,

---

[184] Madawi al-Rasheed -2010, A history of Saudi Arabia.
[185] Saud's campaign for Hijaz and the two holy cities- archived 2010-09-14 at the Wayback machine- Islam Life online magazine.

damaging structures, minarets, and the domes, thinking they were made of gold bricks.[186] According to author Litvak, Meir, Fateh Ali Shah of Iran offered military Help, which was rejected by the Ottomans, and instead, they sent 500 Baluchi families to settle in Karbala and defend it. These defenders, however, escaped when they saw the formidable Saudi army and the Saudi Salafis were left free to loot the city.[187]

Assassination of Abdul-Aziz bin Mohammad: In 1803, Abdul Aziz was stabbed and killed by an Iraqi Shia assassin, in retaliation for his role in the Karbala massacre, when he was leading Asr prayer in Diriyah. In 1803, His son, Saud bin Abdul Aziz Bin Mohammad, sent out forces to bring the region of Hijaz, under his rule. He captured Mecca and Medina, challenging the Ottoman Empire which had ruled the cities since 1517.[188]

End of the First Saudi State (1818): The Ottoman Caliph asked the ruler of Egypt to deal with the House of Saud. His son Ibrahim Pasha led ottoman forces to Hijaz, capturing town after town. 'Saud's successor, his son Abdullah failed to put up a defense against the Ottoman armies which besieged the Saudi capital Diriyah until it surrendered, after several months, in the winter of 1818. Members of Al-Saud and Imam Mohammad Ibn Abd al-Wahhab were shipped to Egypt and the Ottoman capital. They destroyed the Saudi capital, and Abdullah bin Saud was executed, and his severed head thrown in the waters of Bosporus.[189]

Second Saudi state: (Emirate of Nejd - 1824–1891) - The second Saudi State was marred by infighting, among the House of Saud and its last ruler Abdul Rahman bin Faisal was expelled from Najd, after being defeated by Ibn-Rashid at the battle of Malandain in 1891.[190]

---

[186] Rosseau, Description, pp. 74–75
[187] Litvak, Meir (2010). Karbala-Iranica Online.
[188] Vassiliev, Alexei. -History of Saudi Arabia- Retrieved 9 August 2016.
[189] Abdullah ibn Saud's capture and - execution—2010-01-06 at the way back machine., King Abdullah Ibn Saud Information Resource.
[190] Alexei Vassiliev- The History of Saudi Arabia, London, UK: Al Saqi Books, 1998, p.165,177, 185,186.

Third Saudi State (1902-1921): It was set up by Ibn Saud, father of the present King Salman, in 1902. He was the son of the last ruler of the second Saudi state Abdul Rahman bin Faisal. Ibn Saud was 15 when his family sought refuge with Al Murrah, a Bedouin tribe in the southern desert of Arabia. Later they moved to Qatar where they stayed two months. They finally settled in Kuwait where they remained for a decade. In 1901, Ibn Saud asked the Emir of Kuwait for men and supplies for an attack on Riyadh. The Emir agreed to the request, as he had been involved in several wars with the Rashidis of Riyadh. He gave Ibn Saud horses and arms. Ibn Saud left with around 40 men, who included a half-brother Mohammad and several cousins. They set out on a raiding expedition into Nejd, targeting tribes associated with the Rashidis. The raiding proved profitable as their number grew to over 200. They reached Riyadh in Ramadan. At night, Ibn Saud, with his 40 men, climbed the walls of the fort, over the tilted palm trees and took the city, killing the Rashidi Governor ibn Ajlan, on January 15, 1902.[191] In 1906, Ibn Saud defeated Rashidi forces in the battle of Qassim, capturing the al-Qassim region. With Ikhwan forces, Ibn Saud took al-Hasa from the Ottoman garrison which had controlled the area since 1871. People of this region were Shia Muslims who were subjected to severe persecution as opposed to the tolerant Ottoman rule. Ibn Saud captured half of Najd from the Rashidis who asked the Ottomans for Help. Ibn Saud suffered a crushing defeat from the combined forces of the Rashidis and the Ottomans, on June 15, 1904. Ibn Saud reorganized his forces and embarked on guerrilla warfare against the Ottomans, disrupting their supply lines. Abdulaziz Al-Rashid, the Ottoman ruler, was killed by Ibn Saud forces, along with hundreds of his Qassimi and Ottoman allies, in a battle on September 29, 1904, ending the Ottoman presence in Nejd. In 1912, Ibn Saud founded the Ikhwan, a military-religious brotherhood, which assisted him in his later conquests, with the approval of local Salafi Ulama.[192]

---

[191] Madawi Al-Rasheed. A History of Saudi Arabia. Cambridge, England, UK: Cambridge University Press, 2002. Pp. 40.

[192] Mikaberidze, Alexander (2011). conflict and conquest in isl. world ABC-CLIO. p. 807

King of Nejd and Hejaz: The First Saudi-Hashemite War took place in 1918–1919 between Abdul-Aziz (Ibn Saud) and the Kingdom of Hejaz which resulted in the victory of the Saudi forces, but the British prevented the Kingdom's collapse, and a ceasefire remained until 1924. Saudi troops conquered 'Ha'il, incorporated it into the Sultanate of Nejd. In Dec.1925, King Abdulaziz (Ibn Saud) again attacked and defeated the Kingdom of Hejaz, capturing the city of Mecca, ending 700 years of Hashemite rule.[193]

Treaty of Jeddah: This treaty between the British government and Ibn Saud, recognized the independence of the Hejaz and Nejd, with Ibn Saud as the ruler. Ibn Saud forbade the Ikhwan from any further raiding of the British controlled areas of Arabia as he was unwilling to provoke the British. This led to the Ikhwan's Rebellion in 1927.[194]

Kuwait–Najd War: (1922) This War took place because Ibn Saud considered Kuwait to be part of his Kingdom. Thousands of Kuwaitis were killed in this War. After this War, the boundaries of Najd and Kuwait were established.[195]

Battle of Sabilla (1929): This battle took place on March 29,1929, between the rebellious Ikhwan and the army of Ibn Saud. The defiant, but technologically inferior Ikhwan were defeated by the Saudi forces, which used machine-guns and cavalry. In the eyes of Ibn 'Saud's supporters, the battle was necessary for the ability to continue the Saudi conquest of the peninsula. The Ikhwan regarded it as a massacre, a betrayal, and a sign of Saudi capitulation to British colonialism. 500 Ikhwan and 200 Saudis were killed in the battle. The survivors were jailed, but their descendants remained opposed to the Saudi rule, and one such descendant, Juhayman later led the Grand Mosque of Mecca Seizure in 1979.[196]

Declaration of the Kingdom of Saudi Arabia (1932): The Kingdom of Saudi Arabia was proclaimed on September 23, 1932. Ibn 'Saud's eldest

---

[193] Mikaberidze p.799—Dr. Fattouh al-khatrash- hejaz-nejd war- 1924-25-
[194] treaties and agreements—01 March 1948
[195] Michael S. Casey. History of Kuwait—pp. 54–55
[196] battle of sabilla -King Abdul Aziz (Ibn Saud) Information Resource.

son Saud became the heir in 1933. The region of Asir became part of the Saudi Kingdom in 1934.[197]

Oil Discovery: Oil was discovered in Saudi Arabia in 1938 by American geologists working for Standard Oil Company of New York in partnership with Saudi officials. Ibn Saud's concessions to the American oil companies in 1944 much irked the British who had helped Ibn Saud's rise to power.[198]

British Help after world war 1: Jeddah conference of 1927 allowed Ibn Saud to extend his boundaries. The aim of the Darin treaty, for the British, was to save their Persian Gulf protectorates from Saudi raids. The Jeddah treaty in 1927, recognized Ibn Saud's sovereignty over Hejaz and Nejd. By this treaty, Ibn Saud agreed not to attack neighboring British protectorates. The British provided him with surplus munitions of world war 1, and a tribute of 5000 pounds per month.[199] Ibn Saud positioned Saudi Arabia as neutral in World War 2 but favored the allies, without committing his forces.

Meeting with U.S. President Roosevelt: The meeting took place on February 14, 1945, onboard USS Quincy, in the Suez Canal, to formalize future relations.[200]

Railway: Ibn Saud wanted a railway from the Persian Gulf to Jeddah, which was opposed by his advisors, but eventually, ARAMCO built it, costing $70 million. After the road was paved in 1962, the railway lost its traffic.

Personal life of Ibn Saud: following the customs of his people, Abdul Aziz headed a polygamous household making up several wives and concubines.

---

[197] Vassilev -1998, pp. 283–285.
[198] Morton, Michael Quentin (2006).—In the Heart of the Desert: the Story of an Exploration Geologist and the Search for Oil in the Middle East. Green Mountain Press.
[199] The Historical Journal, Vol. 14, No. 3 (Sep., 1971), pp. 627–633.
[200] Rudy Abramson (9 August 1990).-1945 meeting of ibn Saud and FDR- Los Angeles Times. Washington DC. Retrieved 22 July 2013.

According to some sources, he had twenty-two spouses, and about a hundred children, including 45 sons.[201]

Family Relations: bn Saud was very close to his aunt Jawhara bint Faisal, who from childhood motivated him to recover the lost glory of his family. The King visited her daily until she died in 1930. On March 15, 1935, some men tried to kill the King, during Hajj rituals, but he survived the attack unhurt.[202]

Overview of King Abdul-Aziz (Ibn Saud) (1902-1953): The modern Kingdom of Saudi Arabia owes its existence to the military courage and political skill of one man ' Abdulaziz ibn Abdul Rahman ibn Faisal ibn Turki bin Abdullah bin Mohammad Al Saud ', Known as Ibn Saud to westerners and as Abdul Aziz to the Arabs. Unlike his ancestor Mohammad bin Saud, whose raids into Ottoman territory led to the downfall of the first Saudi state in 1818, Ibn Saud understood the importance of restraint. He never threatened the British protectorates on the Persian Gulf, and he waited until 1924 to conquer Mecca when the British themselves had become disgusted with the holy city's King. Sir Percy Cox, 'Britain's Political Resident in the region, once said that he never knew Ibn Saud to make a wrong move. Under the reign of Abdul-Aziz, political considerations superseded religious idealism. His political and military success gave the Saudi Salafi ulama control over religious institutions, and in later years, Saudi Salafi ideas formed the basis of all the rules and laws of the country. Protests from Saudi Salafi ulama were overridden when they conflicted with his political interests. His support from the Saudi Salafi Ulama was so overwhelming that they issued a fatwa saying: "Only the ruler can declare Jihad." As the realm of Saudi Salafism expanded under Ibn Saud into Shiite areas of al-Hasa (conquered in 1913) and Hijaz (captured in 1924–25), Saudi Salafis advocated forced conversion of the Shia to Saudi Salafism, banning Shia practices of mourning, during Ashura, (Husayn ibn Ali (a.s)'s

---

[201] Lacey, Robert (2009-10-15).-inside the kingdom—. Penguin Group US. p.16. -Retrieved 14 November 2013.

[202] Stig Stenslie (2011). power behind the veil- Saudi princesses- Journal of Arabian Studies: Arabia, the Gulf, and the Red Sea. 1 (1): 69–79.- Retrieved 15 April 2012.

martyrdom. Despite the Ulama's objections, Ibn Saud allowed the Shia at hajj. Saudi Salafi warriors traditionally swore loyalty to the monarchs of Al Saud, but there was one major rebellion by the Ikhwan – nomadic tribe members turned Saudi Salafi warriors, who opposed modern innovations and insisted on Jihad against the infidel British by raiding their territories in Jordan and Palestine. Ibn Saud acted against them, defeating them in the battle of Sabilla, described before.

King Saud bin Abdulaziz Al Saud: (Reign: November 9, 1953 –November 2, 1964) Being the eldest son of Ibn Saud, Saud bin Abdul-Aziz became King of Saudi Arabia on November 9, 1953, after his 'father's death. His extravagance, mismanagement of the 'Kingdom's economy, nepotism, ill-health, and ineptitude, caused the bankruptcy of the government, and, eventually, led to his downfall. He alienated all his brothers by giving all the top government jobs to his sons. As soon as he became King, he built a 1300-acre complex of huge pink palaces, at the cost of about $300 million (in 'today's currency). Each palace was provided with big Persian carpets, Chinese vases, and crystal chandeliers and was surrounded by luxurious gardens, palm groves, fountains, and swimming pools (one was scented with Chanel No.5). The complex was looked after by 2500 servants and mechanics, guarded by 1000 soldiers, and surrounded by a high pink wall 7 miles long, with entrance gates, the size of 'Paris's Arc de Triomphe. Altogether, the Nasiriyah Palace used as much water and electricity, as all the rest of Riyadh.[203] By contrast, his brother 'Faisal's palace was modest and tasteful and had no walls. While Saud had a fleet of gold-plated Cadillacs, Faisal had a Chrysler which he drove himself to work every day. The government was really run by 'Saud's sons and their friends, who continued to enrich their cronies with large building contracts, and by the end of 1957, the 'government's debts exceeded a year and a 'half's oil revenues. Banks stopped lending money to the Kingdom, and finally, even Aramco refused to pay any more advances against oil royalties. Money spent on the royal family amounted to half of the national budget by 1956. The government spent only 5% of its income on healthcare. In the whole of Saudi Arabia, there were only 150 hospital beds. Only 6% of

---

[203] Al Rasheed M. (2002) A History of Saudi Arabia Cambridge University Press; pp. 108–9.

the annual budget was earmarked for education. 95% of adults remained illiterate, and only 8% of children went to school. Saudi police arrested five Palestinians, for plotting to blow up the 'King's palace. When questioned, they admitted they were led by an Egyptian military attaché. Rejecting Egyptian government apology, King Saud at once deported hundreds of Egyptians and Palestinians and announced that Egypt would have to buy Saudi oil with US dollars, instead of Egyptian pounds. In 1966, When Saud, with his group of 130 moved from Athens to Nile Hilton in Cairo, taking with him, 3 boxes holding gold, jewelry, and cash worth about $500 million, he was informed by the Egyptian government that he was no longer welcome, and he had to move back to Athens. In response, King Saud hatched his own plot. He sent checks worth $30 million to Syrian Chief of Intelligence Siraj, to blow up President 'Nasser's plane as it approached Damascus. Siraj publicized the plot, in a press conference, on March 5, 1958. As a result, Nasser started calling for the overthrow of the monarchy in Saudi Arabia. Saudi Government employees had not been paid for weeks. When Faisal opened the treasury vaults, he was shocked to find only 317 riyals and $50. Osama bin 'Laden's father lent the government enough money for the payrolls and interest payments. When, Saud stayed 11 months in Europe, staying at clinics and luxury hotels in Paris and Nice, he seemed to be eighty, due to ill-health. Still, 160 wives, children, and servants went with him. They gave $600 tips to waiters, sent limousines to restaurants, to fetch whole roasted sheep to their suites. The hotel bills amounted to about $500,000 per week. In 1965, he bought 23 US planes, to set up his own personal air force, and smuggled them to Portugal. CIA learned about the plot, and the Portuguese confiscated the planes. Because of these activities and policies, Saudi princes and the clergy started consultations as to what to do. Two meetings took place, while Prince Faisal was on a week-long trip to the desert. 65 leading clergymen met at the home of Mohammad ibn Ibrahim, the top clergy, a descendant of Mohammad ibn Abd al-Wahhab. In the other meeting, 100 princes, consisting of about 30 sons of King Abdelaziz, about 15 grandsons, several brothers, and 45 nephews, took part. In the evening, the clerics joined the princes at Sahara Palace. There was a unanimous decision that Saud must go, and Faisal should be the next King. The delegation of the clergy and Princes went to 'Saud's palace and asked him to abdicate, but for 3 days,

Saud refused.[204] Finally, the oldest prince Mohammad barged into 'Saud's palace and told him that if he did not abdicate, his properties would be confiscated, and he will have to live the rest of his life under house arrest. Saud had a discussion with his sons and signed the abdication papers. A month later, Saud's 52 sons swore allegiance to the new King, their uncle Faisal.

Faisal bin Abdelaziz Al Saud (Reign:1964 to 1975): King Faisal was a competent king who carried out many basic reforms within the Kingdom. He inherited the financially bankrupt, backward, and politically isolated Kingdom. As the King, Faisal is credited with rescuing the 'country's finances and implementing a policy of modernization and reform. His main foreign policy aims were Muslim unity, anti-communism, and pro-Palestinian efforts. He carried out the following reforms:

Abolition of slavery (1962): there were 1682 slaves in Saudi Arabia. King Faisal abolished slavery in 1962 at the insistence of US President Kennedy. It cost the government $2000 per slave to free them.[205]

Religious inclusiveness: King Faisal carried out comprehensive reform, acknowledging his 'country's religious and cultural diversity, which included the Shia Muslims whom he gave jobs in the government, and allowed their tribal affinities to Yemen, especially the Ismaili tribes of Najran and Jizan and the Kingdom of the Hijaz, with its capital Mecca. He reduced the Saudi/ Salafi Ulama power and influence, by ensuring that extremists do not rise to powerful religious posts, like the Grand Mufti, a politically recognized senior expert, charged with maintaining the entire system of Islamic law. King Faisal rejected the 'ulama's opposition to aspects of his accelerated modernization attempts. King Faisal did not tolerate Sheikh bin 'Baz's activism and removed him from his position,

---

[204] Vassiliev, Alexei, *The History of Saudi Arabia*, London, UK: Al Saqi Books, 1998, p. 366-7
[205] Nehme, Michel G. (1994). "Saudi Arabia 1950–80: Between Nationalism and Religion". Middle Eastern Studies. 30 (4).

but his teachings had already affected his students, one of whom was Juhayman al-Otaybi who, in 1979, occupied the holy mosque of Mecca.[206]

Steps against coups d'état: There were several coups in the region in the 1950s and 1960s. The Gaddafi's coup in the oil-rich Kingdom of Libya, which resembled the desert kingdom of Saudi Arabia was especially significant. To forestall such a happening, King Faisal built a sophisticated security apparatus in the country, dealing severely with dissent. In 1969, he had hundreds of military officers arrested, on suspicion of hatching a plot by the generals, The action was based on a CIA tip.[207]

Foreign Relations: King Faisal continued close cooperation with the US and refused relations with the socialist countries, saying that Islam was incompatible with communism. In September 1969, he organized a conference in Rabat, Morocco, attended by 25 Muslim countries, which issued a joint statement asking Israel to give up territory conquered in 1967.

1973 oil crisis: During the 1973 Arab-Israel war, King Faisal withdrew Saudi oil from the world market, creating a global crisis. This action was to be the defining act of King Faisal's career and gained him lasting prestige among many Arabs and Muslims worldwide. In 1974 he was named "Time Magazine's Man of the Year." After the War, he increased the aid and subsidies to Egypt, Syria, and the PLO, to recover their losses from the War against Israel. [208]

King 'Faisal's Assassination: On March 25, 1975, King Faisal was shot and killed by his half-brother's son Faisal, when the King bent down to kiss his nephew, following Saudi custom. The first shot hit Faisal's chin, and the second went through his ear. The King was taken to hospital where he died shortly afterward. The 'nation's high religious court sentenced the

---

[206] Mai Yamani (February–March 2008). the two faces of Saudi Arabia-. Survival. 50 (1): 143–156.
[207] Mordechai Abir (1987). "The Consolidation of the Ruling Class and the New Elites in Saudi Arabia". Middle Eastern Studies. 23 (2): 150–171.
[208] Official website of the Saudi Deputy Minister of Defense,, quoting from the official Saudi government journal Umm Al-Qura Issue 2193, 20 October 1967.

assassin to death, and he was beheaded in the public square in Riyadh, on June 18, 1975, at 4:30 pm.[209]

Ideas on Assassination: King Faisal had instituted new and secular reforms that led to the installation of television, which provoked violent protests. In one of these protests, led by Prince Khalid (the 'assassin's brother), the protesters attacked a TV station, and police shot the protesting prince Khalid, to death.[210]

King Khalid bin Abdelaziz Al Saud (Reign: 1975-1982): King Faisal's action of oil embargo during the 1973 Arab-Israel war, caused an increase in oil prices from $3 to $12, resulting in a financial windfall of profits. A lot of development took place in the Kingdom due to phenomenal oil revenues. The number of schools doubled, and King Faisal University was established during Khalid's reign. Despite his friendly message to Imam Khomeini, following the Iranian revolution, King Khalid encouraged Saddam Hussein of Iraq to attack Iran, promising to fund the War. As King Khalid suffered from heart ailment, Crown Prince Fahd oversaw ruling the country. King Khalid died on June 13, 1982 (aged 69) because of a massive heart attack in Taif, Saudi Arabia.[211]

King Fahd bin Abdelaziz Al Saud: (Reign June 13, 1982 – August 1, 2005) - Fahd became King on June 13, 1982, after King 'Khalid's death. Due to his heart condition, like his predecessor, he was also unable to perform his duties as King. Prince Abdullah, therefore, served as de facto ruler, conducting the Kingdom's policies. CIA quoted Fahd as saying: "After God, we can count on the United States." In 1990, When Saddam of Iraq placed his forces on the Saudi-Kuwait border, King Fahd felt threatened and asked the US to help and agreed to host American-led coalition troops in the Kingdom, and later allowed American troops to

---

[209] 1975 King Faisal's assassination- *BBC*. 25 March 1975. Retrieved 17 July 2013.
[210] Ludington, Nick. "Public Execution Expected." Daily News [Bowling Green, Kentucky] 24 March 1975:
[211] Khalid ibn Abdulaziz al-Saud- (6th edition). *The Columbia Encyclopedia*. Columbia University Press. 2013. Retrieved 7 September 2013.August 2012

be based there. This decision brought him considerable criticism and opposition from many Saudi citizens, including Osama bin Laden.

Reform and industrialization: King Fahd was intolerant towards the reformists, and treated them very harshly, including their imprisonment, and firings from their jobs. During his reign, the royal family squandered the country's wealth. He signed the Yamamma Arms Deal, the most significant and most controversial military contract of the century, costing more than $90 billion, initially reserved for hospitals, schools, universities, and roads.[212] On March 1, 1992, King Fahd issued a decree to expand the criteria for succession, which had been only seniority and family consensus, up to that time. The proclamation gave the King of Saudi Arabia, the right to appoint or dismiss his heir, based on suitability.

Wealth: His wealth has been estimated by Forbes, to be $ 25 billion. He owned a palace in Marbella. He had a $ 100 million yacht, which had a ballroom, 2 swimming pools, a theater, and a hospital with an ICU, two operating rooms, and four American Stinger Missiles, onboard. He also owned a $ US 150 million Boeing 747 jet. He preached the strict Sharia of Islam at home but, abroad, he engaged in abominable anti-Islam activities such as drinking and gambling. During his visit to London, he lost many millions in casinos and continued gambling, even during curfew hours in London, by employing blackjack and roulette dealers in his hotel so that he could gamble through the night.[213]

Death: King Fahd died at 07:30 on August 1, 2005, at the age of 84.[214]

King Abdullah bin Abdelaziz Al Saud: (Reign: 2005-2015): Abdullah was named heir by King Fahd, but when Fahd suffered a severe stroke in 1995, Abdullah became the de facto ruler of Saudi Arabia. He was the most dictatorial figure in Saudi Arabia who oppressed his subjects

---

[212] Wood, Paul. Life and Legacy of King Fahd- BBC News, 1 August 2005. Retrieved 10 June 2008.
[213] Marie Colvin, 'The Squandering Sheikhs, Sunday Times, 29 August 1993
[214] Fattah, Hasan M. (28 May 2005).Saudi king hospitalised- The New York Times. Beirut. Retrieved 2 February 2013.

and was extremely intolerant toward journalists, reformers, human rights activists within the kingdom and abroad. On world stage, he instigated the Iran/Iraq war, 2003 Iraq insurgency and civil war, through the Saudi jihadis who crossed the border into Iraq, joining up with the Iraqi Sunnis, forming ISIS which mercilessly massacred the Iraqi Shias, culminating into a dreadful civil war in which hundreds of thousands perished, including US forces and their allied Iraqi government troops. He constantly pressed the US to attack the Shia-led Iran, due to his extreme hatred of the Shia Muslims. He stayed in power for 33 years, as follows:—as Crown Prince (1982-1995)—de facto ruler (1995-2005)-and the King, from 2005 to 2015—during a very crucial period of history, which consisted of the following important events:—1979 Iranian Islamic Revolution—the invasion of Afghanistan by the Soviet Union—1980 Invasion of Iran by Iraq—1990 and 2003 US 'coalition's Invasion of Iraq—Iraqi and Syrian Civil Wars. In most of the said events, King 'Abdullah's policies and influence played a very destabilizing and destructive role. He promoted the Iraq Insurgency in 2003, due to his extreme hatred of the Shia Muslims, after the US coalition attacked Iraq, to remove the brutal regime of Saddam Hussain. He covertly, encouraged and funded, Saudi Jihadis to join up with Iraqi Sunnis, to fight the US and Shia-led Iraqi government forces. These jihadis, in league with the Iraqi Sunnis, eventually turned into ISIS, and posed a formidable threat to 'Iraq's security, resulting in a full-fledged civil war in Iraq, followed by the Syrian Civil War in 2011, causing over a million deaths, including thousands of US security personnel. He supported the Taliban of Afghanistan in their atrocities, financially and politically, as detailed, in various sections of the book. In Saudi Arabia itself, his policies were the most tyrannical of all the Saudi kings, regarding the Shias, the Ahmadis, treatment of women, and a travel ban on critics of the Saudi government. He gave a free hand to Osama bin Laden to operate anywhere, except in the Kingdom itself, in return for $200 million, as reported by Laurent Murawiec, in his book "Princes of Darkness". This resulted in 1998 Al-Qaeda attacks on US embassies in Africa, followed by the 9/11 attacks in the US. Prince Mohammad bin Salman, recently, underscored, over 4 decades of misrule by the Saudi kings, referring to Abdullah, which damaged the reputation of Saudi Arabia, throughout the world, tarnishing the legacy of their illustrious father King Abdulaziz.

Policy on Iran: Saudi 'Arabia's Ambassador to Washington, Adel al-Jubeir said the King often encouraged the US to attack Iran, to demolish its nuclear program.

Policy on Iraq: The Bush administration ignored advice from King Abdullah and Saudi foreign minister, against invading Iraq, as the King feared the strengthening of the majority Shia Muslims of Iraq, after Saddam Hussain. During and after the 2003 US invasion of Iraq, King Abdullah encouraged and funded Saudi Jihadis, to covertly join up, with Iraqi Sunnis across the border to fight the US-allied forces and Iraqi Shias, gradually turning into an Iraqi Insurgency, led by ISIS and other insurgent groups. This activity of the Saudis started in 2003 and continued incessantly, developing into a full-fledged Civil War which continued for over a decade, resulting in thousands of deaths in Iraq, and widespread instability. According to Iraqi Prime Minister Nouri al-Maliki, King Abdullah did not allow his government in Iraq to function.

Criticism of Abdullah as the King: On February 16, 2003, Parade Magazine evaluated King Fahd and Abdullah as the second worst dictators of the world. Abdullah was very repressive and intolerant towards the Shia Muslims and ordered arrests of the Shia during Hajj. In October 2007, during official visit to the UK, protesters accused him of tortures and murders, shouting insults at him.[215]

Death: King Abdullah died at the age of 90 on January 23, 2015.

Wealth: His wealth was estimated at $21 billion by Forbes. His stables in Saudi Arabia had 1000 horses, looked after by his son Prince Mutaib. He also owned a massive palace complex, with several residential compounds in Casablanca, Morocco, equipped with two heliports.[216]

---

[215] Brown, Colin.-shouts of 'murderer, torturer greet king Abdullah - The Independent, 31 October 2007. Retrieved 17 May 2008.

[216] the stables of king abdullah—Janadria Farm. Riyadh. 2013. Retrieved 16 February 2013.

King Salman bin Abdulaziz Al Saud: (Current King since January 24, 2015) - He became King after Abdullah's death on January 23, 2015. During his watch, he ordered an aggressive military campaign against the impoverished Shia Houthis of Yemen, resulting in over 100,000 deaths since the onset of the conflict, as reported by the US-based Armed Conflict Location and Event Data Project (ACLED)" on Fri Nov 1, 2019 saying that 20,000 people had been killed in 2019 only, thousands injured, with widespread destruction of Yemen's infrastructure. Cluster bombs have been used against Yemeni civilians, in violation of the International laws of War.[217] In January 2016, prominent Saudi Shia Cleric Sheikh Nimr was executed in Saudi Arabia.[218]

King 'Salman's Views: In November 2002, charity organizations sponsored by Saudi Arabia such as al-Haramain Foundation, the Saudi High Commission for Relief of Bosnia, and the International Islamic Relief Organization, were accused of terrorism. When confronted, the king said: "Aid was meant to help, and if some misused it for other purposes, the kingdom cannot be held responsible."

General: Salman bin Abdulaziz has married three times. As of 2015, he had 13 children. According to Forbes, his personal wealth was estimated at US$17 billion in 2016.

Prince Mohammad bin Salman: He was appointed heir in June 2017. Prince Mohammad holds a bachelor's degree in law from King Saud University. His reforms have included reducing religious police powers and allowing women to drive and work. On November 4, 2017, billionaire Al-Waleed bin Talal, as well as over 40 other princes and ministers were arrested on money laundering charges. The commander of National Guard, minister of economy, and commander of Saudi naval forces Admiral Abdullah bin Sultan were also fired. Despite the promised

---

[217] father of Ali—father of execution victim speaks out. 12=Zafar Gondal- analysis of court judgement and conviction- 13=al Nimr-Saudi Arabia- Retrieved 20 February 2015.

[218] Saudi led coalition strikes rebels in Yemen-CNN- 27 March 2015. 4= Saudis using cluster bombs—Human Rights Watch. 3 May 2015.

reforms, the repression of activists has risen during King Salman's reign. Mustafa al-Hassan, Abdullah al-Maliki, Essam al-Zamel—all arrested on September 12, 2017. Also significant is the killing of Jamal Ahmad Khashoggi, a renowned journalist, by Saudi agents, in the Saudi embassy in Istanbul. Khashoggi wrote newspaper articles critical of the Saudi government. He had been sharply critical of Saudi Arabia's crown prince, Mohammad bin Salman, and the country's King, Salman of Saudi Arabia. ("Jamal Khashoggi:[219] An unauthorized Turkey source says journalist was murdered in the Saudi consulate." BBC News. October 7, 2018.) [220] CIA report concluded that the crown prince ordered Khashoggi's killing.[221]

A Big Hope for the Future: in October 2017, The Prince admitted that the Saudi state had not been normal, as a reaction to the Islamic revolution of Iran, which Saudi leaders didn't know how to deal with. He and King Salman promised to moderate their religion—rhetoric which has not been acted upon, as of June 2019. On June 6, 2019, the King adamantly said on Saudi television that he had called Muslim countries for a meeting to form a united front against Iran, although Iran was neither attacking nor threatening Saudi Arabia.

Personal life: In 2015, Mohammad bin Salman bought A YACHT for $ 617 million US. In December 2017, a few sources reported that Crown Prince Mohammad bin Salman had bought Leonardo da 'Vinci's Salvatore Mundi painting for $450.3 million. The painting is presently kept at its permanent home in the Louvre 'Museum's extension in Abu Dhabi, UAE. He also bought a $300 million villa in France. Mohammad bin Salman got married in 2008 and has four children.[222]

Challenges to the House of Saud (Inside the Kingdom): Several events affected the 'Kingdom's image and policies, over the years. Among them

---

[219] Turkey has recordings proving Saudi murder—*BBC News*. 12 October 2018.
[220] Hearst, David (21 June 2017). Mohamad bin Salman—prince of chaos *HuffPost*. Retrieved 19 November 2017
[221] Julian E. Barnes and Eric Schmitt, New York Times- Dec. 2, 2018
[222] Mulholland, Rory (16 December 2017—Saudi prince buys world's most expensive home-*The Telegraph*. Retrieved 24 May 2019

is the role of Egyptian refugees, belonging to Muslim Brotherhood whose members preached change-promoting concepts like anti-colonialism and gave a radical twist to the Saudi Salafi values, which the Saudi students had been taught in childhood. Saudi/ Salafism taught unquestioned obedience to the King while with the 'Brotherhood's concept, Jihad became a "practical possibility," not just part of history. However, the Brethren were ordered by the Saudi clergy and government, not to preach or discuss doctrinal matters but they took control of Saudi 'Arabia's intellectual life, by publishing books and taking part in discussions, held by the princes. [223] Later, they assumed leading roles in key governmental ministries, and had an influence on the education curriculum. An Islamic university in Medina was set up, in 1961, to train mostly non-Saudi preachers in Saudi Salafism. The ideas of Brothers eventually spread throughout the Kingdom, and had long-lasting effects, one important effect being the radicalization of Osama bin Laden, and his colleagues.[211]

Non-Saudi/Salafi influence on the Kingdom: Most of the conversion to Saudi Salafism, took place in the institutions, within the Kingdom, like the Islamic University in Medina, for which generous scholarships and monetary benefits were given to ulama of Sufi doctrine of Islam, resulting in their conversion to Saudi Salafism.

World Muslim League: Many of the leading figures in this organization were not Saudi Salafis. It distributed literature and cassettes by foreign Salafis like al-Banna, and Syed Qutb (founder of radical Islam). They staffed the Muslim world league and other Saudi organizations. Saudi Arabia successfully attracted Salafis of al-Azhar to teach in Saudi universities where they radicalized Saudis like Osama bin Laden. Muslim Brotherhood members fleeing the persecution of Arab nationalist regimes in Egypt and Syria, were given refuge in Saudi Arabia and sometimes ended up teaching in Saudi schools and universities. Hassan al-Turabi of Sudan, a prominent political and religious personality of Sudan, spent several years, in exile, in Saudi Arabia. "Blind Sheikh" Omar Abdel-Rahman lived in Saudi Arabia from 1977 to 1980, teaching at a girls college in Riyadh. Al-Qaeda

---

[223] House, Karen Elliott (2012). *On Saudi Arabia: Its People, past, Religion, Fault Lines and Future.* Knopf. p. 156

leader, Ayman al-Zawahiri, was also admitted into Saudi Arabia in the 1980s. Azzam also taught at King Abdelaziz University in Jeddah. His 'fatwa' Defense of the Muslim Lands, the First Obligation after Faith", was supported by the leading Saudi Salafi, Shaykh Abd al-Aziz ibn Baz.[224]

Saudi Arabia backed the Pakistan-based Jamaat e Islami movement, politically and financially, even before the oil embargo of 1973. Non-Saudi Salafis such as Said Ramadan, son-in-law of Hassan al-Banna (the founder of the Muslim Brotherhood), Abul 'A 'la Maududi, founder of Jamaat-e-Islami, and Maulana Hassan Nadvi of India, were leading figures of World Muslim League. In 2013, when the Bangladeshi government acted against Jamaat-e-Islami, the Saudi government reduced the Bangladeshi workers who sent desperately needed remittances from Saudi Arabia. Muslim Brotherhood played an essential role in the choice of organizations and individuals likely to receive Saudi subsidies. Analyst Roy describes the "MBs"[225] and the Saudi Salafis as sharing "common themes of reformist and puritanical preaching, with virulent opposition to both Shiism and Sufi religious practices (the cult of ''saints`).There were, of course, ""significant doctrinal differences"" between Saudi/Salafism and Salafism of the Muslim Brotherhood, the latter preaching unity of Muslims against western imperialism, and emphasized education, healthcare, and a constitutional government, to eliminate backwardness of Muslims, encouraging revolutionary activities. The ISIS, whose roots are in Saudi Salafism, has vowed to overthrow the Saudi Kingdom. In July 2015, Saudi author Turki al-Hamad said in an interview, on Saudi TV: "you see ISIS volunteers ripping their Saudi passports. It is our Saudi youth doing bombings in Iraq and Syria." About 2,500 Saudis had fought alongside ISIS, in Iraq and Syria.[226]

---

[224] Azzam, Abdullah (c. 1993).—defence of Muslim lands—*archive.org*. Retrieved 15 April 2015.
[225] Muslim Brotherhood members
[226] Blair, David (4 October 2014). Qatar and Saudi Arabia have ignited time bomb by funding global spread of radical islam—The Telegraph. Retrieved 12 May 2015.

Occupation of the Kaaba (20 Nov-4 Dec 1979): An important event which shocked the world and affected the Saudi image, was the occupation of the Kaaba, in November 1979. Juhayman al-Otaybi was its leader, who declared his brother-in-law Mohammed Abdullah al-Qahtani, to be the Mahdi (a.s) or the redeemer, who arrives on earth, several years before the Day of Judgment. His followers said Qahtani's name and his father's name were the same as the Prophet's, and the date of the attack was the first day of the year 1400 which matched the tradition of the Mujaddid that appears once in every century. 'AL-Otaybi's grandfather had been a close associate of Ibn Saud, the founder of the Saudi Kingdom, and his other family members were prominent members of the Ikhwan. He was a preacher, a member of the Saudi National Guard, and had been a student of Shaykh Abdel Aziz al-Baz who later became the Grand Mufti of Saudi Arabia.[227]

Rebel Objectives and Grievances: Al-Otaybi advocated, a return to the original ways of Islam, the abolition of television, and the expulsion of non-Muslims from the Holy land of Arabia. He said the Saudi family had corrupted Saudi culture by westernization. Otaybi said he had a vision that Qahtani was the Mahdi (a.s). They aspired to establish a theocracy, in preparation for the imminent apocalypse. They were well-armed and trained former National Guards members who had smuggled weapons, ammunition, gas masks from National Guard armories, to the mosque compound, and hidden in the tiny underground rooms, used as hermitages.[228]

Events: On November 20, 1979, armed men interrupted the Imam of the Grand Mosque, Sheikh Mohammad al-Subayyil, when he was starting Fajr prayers at about 5:00 am. They locked the entrance doors and shot a policeman who was armed with, only a wooden club for disciplining unruly pilgrims. The number of insurgents was about 500 and included several women and children. Luckily, an employee of Bin Laden Company reported the incident before telephone lines were cut by the insurgents, who took up sniper positions in the minarets, from which they commanded the

---

[227] Benjamin, *The Age of Sacred Terror*, (2002) p. 90
[228] 1979 seizure of the Grand Mosque in Mecca—the attack and the siege that inspired Osama bin Laden—Retrieved January 15, 2014.

grounds. No one outside the mosque knew about the number of hostages or the number of militants in the mosque and their preparations. About 100 Saudi Security officers tried to retake the mosque but retreated after heavy casualties. At the request of the Saudi Government, Pakistani and French Commandos arrived to help recapture, the holy compound. Before the rescue operation, the Saudi Government approached the Ulama, led by Abdul Aziz bin Baz, to obtain Religious Sanction for armed intervention, because Islam forbids any violence within the Grand Mosque. Eventually, the ulama issued a fatwa, allowing the deadly force, in retaking the mosque.[229]

Operation and Backlash: The battle lasted for more than 2 weeks resulting in 255 pilgrims, troops and fanatics killed and 560 injured. Shortly after news of the takeover, anti-US demonstrations started in Muslim countries. In Pakistan, on the day after the takeover, the U.S. embassy in Islamabad was burned to the ground by protesters. A week later, in Tripoli, Libya, a mob attacked and burned the U.S. embassy.[230]

Trials and Executions: Al-Qahtani was killed, during the operation. The King secured a fatwa from scholars who found the defendants guilty of following crimes: 1=violating the sanctity of Masjid-e-Haram 2= violating the sanctity of the month of Muharram 3= Killing fellow Muslims and others 4= Disobeying authorities 5= Suspending prayers at Masjid-e-Haram 6= Exploiting innocent, for criminal acts 7= Erring in identifying the Mahdi (a.s). On January 9, 1980, 63 rebels were publicly beheaded in the squares of eight Saudi cities, carefully chosen, to give maximum exposure.[231]

Saudi Policies after the Holy Mosque Seizure: Saudi King Khaled, however, reacted to the upheaval, by not cracking down, on the religious

---

[229] audi opposition group lists insurgent demands- in MERIP Reports, No. 85. (February 1980), pp. 16–17.
[230] Wright, Robin B., 1948. Sacred Rage: The Wrath of Militant Islam. Simon & Schuster, c 2001, p. 149.
[231] Saudis behead zealots—The Victoria Advocate. AP. 10 January 1980. Retrieved 7 August 2012.

establishment. He gave the Ulama and religious conservatives, more power over the next decade. He believed that "the solution to the religious upheaval, was simply, more religion." First, photographs of women in newspapers and television were banned. Cinemas and music shops were shut down. School curriculum was changed to, give many more hours of religious studies, ending classes on subjects like non-Islamic history. Gender segregation was more strictly enforced, and religious police became more assertive.[232]

1979 Qatif Uprising: (November 26 – December 3, 1979): Uprising of Shias of Qatif, was another event, affecting the Saudi image and their policies, towards their Shia subjects. Since the conquer and annexation of Al-Hasa and Qatif, in 1913, the Shia had faced repression by the government. The bulk of Saudi oil reserves are in this region. Also, the main Saudi refinery and export terminal of Ras Tanura is situated near Qatif. The area was left undeveloped. Shiite workers of Aramco were paid less than Sunni workers, leading to increased anti-Western feelings. When US planes landed at King Abdelaziz Air Base, a big demonstration was organized on November 11, 1979, against the US and the royal family.[233]

Shia Community Tensions: With the 1979 Islamic Revolution in Iran, Shiites of Saudi Arabia, were very receptive to Imam Khomeini of Iran who said that Islam and hereditary kingship, are not compatible. Shias of the region, therefore, felt encouraged to try and secure a treatment equal to the Sunnis. Large Shia Marches were held in Dammam and Khobar during Muharram, to commemorate the martyrdom of Husayn ibn Ali (a.s). Security forced carried out a crackdown resulting in 24 deaths, hundreds of injuries, and thousands of arrests. At the time, the Saudi authorities were also busy, dealing with the Seizure of the holy mosque in Mecca.[234]

---

[232] Lacey, Robert (2009). Inside the Kingdom : Kings, Clerics, Modernists, Terrorists, and the Struggle for Saudi Arabia. Viking. pp. 49–52.
[233] Frederic Wehrey- (11 December 2012). Shia Days of Rage - Foreign Affairs. Retrieved 4 January 2013.
[234] Jones, Toby Craig (2006).Shia Uprising of 1979- *International Journal of Middle East Studies*. Cambridge University Press. 38 (2): 213–233 [228]. Retrieved 31 December 2012.

Saudi Government Response: In response to the protest movement, the Saudi government acknowledged the poor conditions in Qatif and increased local spending, to address discontent. The local administration of Qatif was granted an extra 700 million Saudi Riyals, in early December, and later an extra 1 billion in spending, on various local projects, to develop the Qatif region. Other projects included new hospitals, schools, and a Real Estate Development Fund, designed to help locals build new homes for themselves. The first government response was successful, and Shia groups in the Qatif region gave up their protests. However, the main aim of the projects was to appease the protesters rather than signal a structural change in the Saudi government attitudes towards the Shiites in the Kingdom.[235]

1979 Iranian Islamic Revolution (Feb. 1979): Islamic Revolution of Iran also posed a serious challenge to the Sunni governments of the Middle East, particularly the Saudi Kingdom, in that, it called for the overthrow of monarchies and autocratic governments, replacing them with Islamic republics. Sunni Arab neighbors of Iran, including Iraq, Kuwait, Saudi Arabia, Jordan, and other Gulf states were alarmed, as most of them, had large Shia populations. Imam Khomeini, the leader of the Iranian Revolution, tried his level best, during his lifetime, to stress the brotherhood of Shia and Sunni Muslims. The antagonism of the Saudis, due to their Saudi Salafi Religion, which considered the Shia Muslims in general, and Shia Iran in particular, apostates resulted in Shia Genocide all over the world. A devastating Iran/Iraq War of 1980-88, was imposed on Iran, to crush the 1979 Shia-led Islamic revolution, in its infancy. Iraq was encouraged by Saudi Arabia, with the tacit approval of the United States, to attack but the Revolutionary government of Iran could not be toppled, and antagonism towards Iran has continued to this day. Iran/Iraq War, Gulf Wars of 1990 and 2003, followed by Iraq / Syria Civil Wars and the Yemeni War, have all been, parts of a broader policy of a Shia Genocide by Saudi Arabia, due to its extreme hatred of the Shia Muslims, whom they consider to be non-Muslims, deserving extermination.[236]

---

[235] Wilson, Peter W.; Graham, Douglas F. (1994). Saudi Arabia:The Coming Storm., New York: M.E.Sharpe Inc. p. 251
[236] Wright, Robin (1989) In the Name of God. Simon & Schuster. p. 126.. 2= Iran-Iraq War 1980-88 - Efraim Karsh—*osprey Publishing 2002-p.72*

CHAPTER 5

Persecution of the Prophet and Followers

To understand the factors behind terrible persecution of the Prophet (pbuh), at the advent of Islam, in Mecca, for 13 years, and later imposition of dreadful wars on him, after migration to Medina, in-depth study of the historical background of the Quraysh of Mecca, to whom the Banu Hashim and Banu Umayya belonged, is necessary. Historians opine that although most of the Quraysh of Mecca became Muslims at the conquest of Mecca, the staunch opponents of the Prophet, like members of the Banu Umayya clan, had, probably, just accepted defeat in the face of the overwhelming Muslim forces, accompanying the Prophet. This stance of scholars seems credible considering the attitude of Banu Umayya toward Ali (a.s) when he became the 4th caliph and, was adamantly, opposed by members of Banu Umayya community in Medina. Instead of pledging allegiance to him as Caliph, most of them fled to Syria, to take refuge with their clan member Muawiya, the Governor of Syria, who had also refused to accept the Caliph, and later opposed him militarily in the Battles of Camel and Siffin, in which thousands of Muslims were killed, including several senior companions of the Prophet(pbuh).[237]

---

[237] *Armstrong, Karen—2001—Muhammad—a biography of the Prophet- p66.*

The Quraysh of Mecca: Quraysh were a powerful merchant tribe that controlled Mecca and its Kaaba. Quraysh hailed from a common ancestor called Fihr Quraysh, who traced their ancestry to Ismael bin Ibrahim, the Prophet. For several generations, Quraysh were spread about among other tribal groups in Arabia and lived in dismal financial conditions. Qusai bin Kilab, an ancestor, got the trusteeship of the Kaaba from another tribe, and brought his relatives of Quraysh to Mecca and settled them there. They built houses around the Kaaba and some settled in ravines of the surrounding hills and in the countryside near Mecca. Qusai died in 480. Before his death, he transferred all his powers, and handed over keys of the Kaaba and the Assembly Hall in Mecca, to his elder son Abd ud Dar, leaving out his second son Abd Manaf, the ancestor of Banu Hashim. After some time, both brothers began fighting over the father's inheritance. The difference became so serious that they decided to go to war, to settle their dispute. In this tussle, Members of the two groups, swore oaths of allegiance, to stick together and never to abandon each other. They stuck to this oath for generations to come. The dispute, however, was resolved amicably when brothers agreed to split the inheritance. One group was given the custody of the Kaaba, while the other was entrusted with supplying food and water to the pilgrims.[238]

Hashim bin Abd Manaf: He was an ancestor of the Prophet, and Ali bin Abi Talib. Hashim and Abd Shams (stepfather of Umayya, the ancestor of Abu Sufyan, and Muawiya) were conjoined twins, such that, at the time of birth, Hashim's toe was embedded into Abd Shams's ear. Abd Manaf, their father, separated them with his sword. The astrologers and priests of those days forecasted that there will be bloodshed between their descendants. This prophecy, unfortunately, proved to be true, during and after the time of the Prophet Muhammad (pbuh), as several bloody wars took place between Hashim (Banu [239]Hashim) descendants, and Abd Shams (i.e. Banu Umayya descendants). [225]After Abd Manaf died, Hashim

---

[238] Subhani, Jafar. "Chapter 4: Ancestors of The Prophet".—The Message—. P O Box 5425 Karachi, Pakistan: Islamic Seminary Publications. Retrieved 10 September 2017

[239] Maqsood, Ruqaiyyah Waris. –the Prophet's family line no.4—Hashim— Retrieved 3 August 2011.

demanded that Kaaba and Assembly Hall rights be transferred from Abd Dar group to him, with the support of his brothers Abd Shams, Motleb, half-brother Nawfal, Banu Asad, Banu Zuhra, and Banu Teym. The only person who challenged his authority was Umayya, an adopted son, of his brother Abd Shams. Umayya, however, did not have enough support to compete with Hashim who eventually banished Umayya from Mecca, due to his nefarious activities, and Umayya then moved to Syria and spent the rest of his life there.[226] Hashmi's real name was Amr al ula, but he was given the nickname Hashim, which, in Arabic, means, 'The man who feeds the starving", depicting Hashim's character i.e. his benevolence and generosity. Hashim was a man of exceptional talent and personality. He was an extremely generous person. Being an affluent merchant, he fed the starving people of Mecca in famine season. He personally fetched immense stock of flour from Syria by camel-caravans, slaughtering the camels, and crushing the meat and bread to give a broth to his people, at his own expense.[240] Hashim was an able administrator. He set up League of the Virtuous in Mecca. This league acted as the Arbiter of disputes and prevented wars between tribes. After Hashim, his descendants, known as Banu Hashim, were the hereditary custodians and caretakers of the KAABA, and therefore commanded profound respect among the people of Mecca and the Arabs in general. Hashim died, at the age of 33 in the year 497, due to illness contracted on a journey, returning from a business trip to Syria and Palestine. Hashim's tomb is beneath the tomb of Syed Al-Hashim Mosque in Gaza's al-Darraj, named in his honor. The mosque itself was built in the 12th century.[241]

Umayya/ Hashim Enmity: The chiefdom of Bani Hashim was spiritual, while that enjoyed by Bani Umayya was political and financial. They were tradesmen and had enormous wealth. Umayya's enmity and malice against Hashim were unjustified because his own Stepfather Abd Shams was Hashim's supporter because he did not consider Umayya to be a responsible candidate for the custody of Kaaba and its pilgrims. Umayya's banishment

---

[240] 'Lata'if al-ma'arif, Tha'alibi, Edinburgh, 1968, p.42; Ibn Kathir 1.132, from Ibn Ishaq; Ibn Sa'd vol 1 p.77

[241] Hooda, Samreen (September 2006). - Mosque of Sayyed Hashim-Gaza-Palestine: *This Week In Palestine*. Retrieved 17 January 2012

from Mecca by Hashim was the primary cause of his enmity and grudge against Hashim. He fostered this enmity during the rest of his life and passed it on to his descendants, Banu Umayya. This hereditary enmity and desire for vengeance of kinsmen killed in battles (of Prophet Muhammad (pbuh) against the Quraysh of Mecca) played a key role in the brutal and relentless wars waged by Banu Umayya (Abi Sufyan and his descendants) against Banu Hashim (Prophet Muhammad (pbuh), Ali bin Abi Talib, and their descendants). Teachings of Islam and the kind, forgiving personality of the Prophet of Islam, did little to reduce the grudge and animosity of Banu Umayya against Banu Hashim. Islam had ended the discrimination of families and united everybody in a single brotherhood. The Prophet (pbuh) showed clemency towards the Quraysh of Mecca, particularly to the Banu Umayya clan, when he conquered Mecca. On submission and conversion of Abu Sufyan to Islam, the Prophet (pbuh) declared the house of Abu Sufyan as a safe sanctuary for Meccans, and welcomed the participation of all the Meccan tribes, including Banu Umayyad, in his newly founded Islamic State, including his long-time adversary Abu Sufyan who had led an incessant opposition to him in Mecca, and later waged brutal wars against the Muslims, after the Prophet's migration to Medina. After the conquest of Mecca, Abu Sufyan and his clan members could take part in all the Islamic battles, and State politics. Usman (r. a), also of Banu Umayya clan, was a high-ranking adviser, and son-in-law of the Prophet (pbuh). So, the Prophet (pbuh) held no grudge, and showed profound goodwill and brotherhood towards all Meccans, although he himself belonged to the Banu Hashim clan. But, as soon as an opportunity arose, Banu Umayyad revived tribal prejudice and discrimination. The pre-Islamic rivalry of two brothers, Hashim and Umayya, resurfaced in their progeny, spearheaded by Muawiya ibn Abi Sufyan who refused to swear allegiance to the fourth Caliph Ali, on the pretext of failing to deal with rebels who had killed Caliph Usman (r.a), although Ali had asked Muawiya for respite until he had established himself. This caused a huge split in the Muslim Ummah. Caliph Usman (r.a) started appointing inept family members and relatives from Banu Umayya, as Governors of Provinces and to other lucrative posts in the government and ruined the administration of the caliphate. He allowed Marwan ibn Hakam to run the government which caused general outrage and dissatisfaction among the people, culminating into a rebellion in the caliphate, and eventual assassination of Caliph Usman (r.a).

Miracles of Abdul-Muttalib: Historians have recorded the events signifying the spirituality of the Prophet(pbuh)'s grandfather Abdul-Mottalib as follows:

Digging of ZAMZAM Well: Abdul-Mottalib said that while sleeping in the sacred enclosure of the Kaaba, he had a dream, telling him to dig between the idols Isaf and Naila, to find the Zamzam Well which tribe of Jurham had filled in, during Prophet Ismail bin Ibrahim's time, before leaving Mecca. [242] The Quraysh tried to stop Abdul Mottalib from digging in that spot, considered sacred by them. He, therefore, asked his only son al-Harith to stand guard, against intruders. After three days of digging, Abdul-Mottalib found the well. Some Quraysh elders disputed his claim to sole rights over water, but eventually allowed him to keep it. Thereafter, he supplied pilgrims with Zamzam Water, which soon eclipsed all the other wells in Mecca because it was considered sacred.[243]

Sacrificing of Abdullah: During the digging of the well, Quraysh harassed Abdul Mottalib so much that he swore to sacrifice one son for Allah if God gave him ten sons. Later, when nine more sons were born to him, he told his sons he must fulfil his vow. He drew lots and the divination arrow fell on his most beloved son Abdullah (father of the future prophet of Islam). The Quraysh protested his intention of sacrificing Abdullah and demanded that he sacrifice something else. Abdul Muttalib agreed to consult an astrologer who suggested to draw lots between Abdullah and ten camels. If Abdullah was chosen, ten more camels to be added, and keep doing this until the Lord accepted the camels in Abdullah's place. When the number reached 100, the lot fell on the camels. Abdul

---

[242] Muhammad ibn Saad. *Kitab al-Tabaqat al-Kabir.* Translated by Haq, S. M. (1967). *Ibn Sa'ad's Kitab al-Tabaqat al-Kabir Volume I Parts I & II.* Delhi: Kitab Bhavan.

[243] Zam Zam—Ibn Ishaq/Guillaume P.62-65

Mottalib confirmed this by doing the test three times. Then 100 camels were sacrificed, sparing Abdullah's life.[244]

Year of the Elephant (570 CE): This was another miracle of Abdul Muttalib that happened in 570, just before the birth of the Prophet (pbuh). In 570, Abraha, the ruler of Yemen, built a great Church at Sana'a known as al-Qullays, to compete with the Kaaba. The Arabs, however, could not be diverted to this church. Abraha sent a messenger to Mecca saying that his church was better as it had no idols. According to the historian Ibn-Ishaq, a man from Quraysh, annoyed by Abraha's pronouncement, slipped into the church at night and defecated in it. Angered by the incident, Abraha, launched an expedition of forty thousand men against the Ka'bah at Mecca, with the intent to demolish it, led by a white elephant named Mahmud, along with many other elephants. Several Arab tribes tried to fight him on the way but were defeated. When news of the advance of Abraha reached Mecca, Arab tribes prepared to fight Abraha who sent a message that he meant no harm to the people, and only wanted to destroy the Kaaba.[231] Near Mecca, Abraha sent for Abdul Mottalib to talk. After the meeting, Abdul Muttalib was heard murmuring: "owner of the house will defend it and will not dishonor the caretakers." 'Surah al-Fil' of the Quran, describes the event saying: Ababeel appeared with small rocks in their beaks, and bombarded the forces of Abraha, smashing them like eaten straw."[245]

History and Current Persecution of Banu Hashim: Shias (the followers of Ali) are a minority among Muslims, only 10-15% of the entire 1.6 billion population of Muslims in the world. It is proven from history, that Shias are a peaceful, submissive community, but resist tyranny and injustice of the rulers, following their Imam (Leader and role model) Husayn (a.s) who refused to submit to an aggressive Umayyad Caliph Yazid who sent 12000 men army to subdue the Imam and his 72 family members and friends. The standoff resulted in a massacre of almost all his family members, and

---

[244] Muhammad ibn Ishaq. *Sirat Rasul Allah.* Translated by Guillaume, A. (1955). *The Life of Muhammad.* Oxford University Press
[245] Qur'an sura 105

companions, including women and children, who were beheaded, along with the Imam himself.[246]

This chapter details the persecution of Shia Imams (descendants of the Prophet, through his daughter Fatima and cousin Ali) and their followers in history. Also in modern times, worldwide persecution of Shia Muslims is being spearheaded by Saudi Arabia, the self-proclaimed leader of Sunni Islam, and its allied countries, since the Iranian Revolution of 1979, with the unfortunate and reckless support of the United States and the West, even when the persecution of Shias, a minority among Muslims, is a blatant infringement of Human Rights and disregard of the sanctity of human life. The terrorist groups of extremist Saudi Salafi ideology had been killing the Shia Muslims and other non-Salafis, in Iraq, Syria, Yemen, Pakistan, Afghanistan, Indonesia and the African countries, for decades, since 2003. The Shia Persecution included, imposing Iran/ Iraq War of 1980-88 on Iranian Shias, followed by Iraqi and Syrian Civil Wars and the Yemen War, targeting, mainly the Shia populace of these countries, by means of the Jihadi groups, ISIS, al-Qaeda, Taliban, Boko Haram, al-Shabaab, (Lashkar-e-Jhangvi), and (Lashkar-e-Tayyiba)[247] of Pakistan—all supported and funded by Saudi Arabia and its allied Gulf countries. Scholars consider these Jihadi activities, as a broader policy of Shia Genocide, throughout the World, especially in Muslim majority countries.

Persecution of Ali (a.s). Ibn Abi Talib - the 1ˢᵗ Imam: There was a controversy among the companions of the Prophet (pbuh), about who should succeed him, after his passing, although the Prophet (pbuh) had nominated Ali (a.s) to be the Leader of the Muslim community, at Ghadir Khumm, which is a place located between Mecca and Medina. This took place, when on return from farewell Pilgrimage, Ayah 5.67 of the Quran known as the 'verse of announcement', was revealed to the prophet, directing him to make an important announcement to the pilgrims. The prophet gathered all the pilgrims and gave a long sermon. This sermon

---

[246] Madelung, Wilfred—Husayn bin Ali—*Encyclopedia Iranica*. Retrieved 2 November 2015.
[247] Lashkar-e-Jhangvi and Lashkar-e-Taiba groups of Pakistan

included a declaration of Muhammad (pbuh), holding Ali's hand up, saying: "to whomsoever I am Mawla, Ali is their Mawla." After the sermon, Muhammad (pbuh) instructed everyone to pledge allegiance to Ali. All Sunni sources admit that the prophet (pbuh) uttered these words but stress that it did not mean Ali (a.s) will be the ruler, after the prophet (pbuh). He meant that Ali (a.s). should be accorded due respect, due to his kinship with the prophet (pbuh) and exalted position among the Muslims. This contention, however, seems to be just an excuse because the ruler and the religious head were not two persons in Islam, but one person, who is both a religious leader, as well as the ruler, like the Prophet (pbuh) himself. The gathering, the Prophet addressed, consisted of thousands of Muslims, around 10,000, according to some accounts. It means that there were lots of witnesses of this event at Ghadir Khumm. Detail of this event, and other related incidents are described in Chapter 1. The way the companions of the Prophet (pbuh) dealt with Ali (a.s), on the question of succession to the Prophet (pbuh), amounts to his persecution and a disregard of the Prophet's declaration of the phrase "to whomsoever I am Mawla, Ali is their Mawla." which clearly indicated Ali (a.s.)'s stature among Muslims. While Banu Hashim were busy in funeral arrangements of the Prophet, Abu Bakr (r.a) was appointed as the Successor to the Prophet (pbuh), without consulting or at least informing Ali (a.s). This caused a serious split among Muslims, from this point onwards. Supporters of Ali (a.s) became the Shia, and the rest of the Muslim Ummah was called the Sunnis. Ali 's reluctant acceptance and support of the rule of Abu Bakr (r.a) and Umar (r.a), was, because he had neither the support of Meccans, nor willingness to fight, to assert his right to the caliphate. Ali (a.s). believed that he could fulfil his Imamate (leadership of the Ummah), without fighting. Among most of the companions of the prophet (pbuh), no one doubted his prestige and ability, as a prominent Muslim leader but he was not considered for the caliphate, most probably, due to his age which was only 32 at that time while Abu Bakr (r.a) was 59 and Umar (r.a) 49 years old. Another important and more plausible factor causing extreme opposition of Ali (a.s) was the killing of many Quraysh leaders by Ali (a.s) in Islam's battles of Badr, Uhud, and others. As an example, Abu Sufyan's son, his wife Hind's father and brother were killed by Ali (a. s). The feelings of vengeance united all the Meccan tribes against Ali (a.s) for the killing of their relatives in Islam's battles, by Ali (a.s), although the killings took place in a fair fight in the battlefield, mostly in individual combats, each combat initiated by Ali's adversary.[248] However, If the events, narrated below and reported by Historians, really took place, after Abu Bakr(r.a) got elected as the first Caliph, they clearly show extreme disrespect and disregard for Ali (a.s), by the companions of the Prophet(pbuh) who did not consider him as their MAULA (the leader), the status declared for Ali (a.s), by the Prophet (pbuh), at Ghadir Khumm, and on other occasions. According to writer Wilfred Madelung, Abu Bakr (r.a) and a few other companions went to Fatima (r.a)' s house to force oath of allegiance from Ali (a.s), and his supporters, gathered there. When Umar (r.a) threatened to set the house on fire, unless they came out, Zubayr came out with his sword drawn. He stumbled and lost his sword, and Umar (r.a) 's men carried him off. Evidence exists that Fatima (r.a)' s house was searched, and Ali (a.s) said that if he had had forty men he would have resisted. Abu Bakr (r.a) isolated the Banu Hashim (who, according to historian Al-Zuhri, refused to swear allegiance) for six months. According to Lesley Hazleton, Umar (r.a) decided to break into Fatima (r.a)' s house and flung himself at the door. Twelver Shia sources relate that Umar (r.a) set fire to Fatima (r.a)' s door before kicking it open, crushing Fatima (r.a) (who was trying to hold the door shut). The blow killed Mohsin, Fatima (r.a)'s unborn son, broke her ribs which later caused her death). Sunnis believe that no such conflict ever occurred. Twelvers believe that Ali (a.s), under orders from Muhammad (pbuh), not to fight Abu Bakr (r.a), and Umar (r.a), was put in chains; when Abu Bakr (r.a)'s election to the caliphate was a fait accompli, Ali (a.s). withheld his allegiance until after Fatima (r.a) 's death because he did not want to displease his wife, and because he did not desire strife in the nascent Muslim community. He buried Fatima (r.a) at night, with none of Abu Bakr (r.a)'s supporters present, and the location of her grave remained uncertain. [249] Ali (a.s) finally pledged allegiance to Abu Bakr (r.a) six months after he became the first Caliph.

---

[248] Ali (a.s) ibn Abi Talib—Encyclopedia Iranica.—archived from the original on April 29, 2011. Retrieved December 16, 2010.
[249] Vaglieri, Veccia. "Fatima". Encyclopedia of Islam. Leiden, The Netherlands: Brill. p. Vol. 2 844–850.

Caliphate of Ali (a.s): (656 to 661) Ali became caliph after the assassination of the third caliph Usman (r.a). All historians agree that he ruled during his brief tenure according to the Quran and the Sunnah of the Prophet(pbuh). He is noted for the rigorous observance of his religious duties, and detachment from worldly possessions. The rebels, who had assassinated Usman r.a, consisted of several groups. These groups were the people of Egypt, Kufa and Basra, the Muhajir (Meccans who had immigrated to Medina during the prophet's time) and the Ansar (the people of Medina). There were three candidates for the caliphate: Ali (a.s), Talha and Zubair. First, the rebels approached Ali (a.s), who declined the offer, preferring to be a counsellor, instead of the Chief. Talha and Zubayr also refused. The rebels warned the people to select a caliph or they will apply drastic measures. Muslims gathered in the 'Mosque of the Prophet' in Medina, on June 18, 656, to appoint the caliph. Initially, 'Ali (a.s refused to accept it, simply because his most vigorous supporters were the rebels. However, when some notable companions of Muhammad (pbuh), insisted Ali agreed. Talha and Zubayr later claimed they supported him reluctantly. However, people pledged their allegiance publicly, in the mosque, and force was not used. While most of Medina's population as well as many of the rebels gave their pledge, some prominent figures or tribes did not do so. The Umayyads, relatives of Usman (r.a,) fled to Syria or remained in their houses, later refusing Ali's legitimacy. Saad ibn Abi Waqas was absent, and Abdullah ibn Umar abstained from offering his allegiance, but both assured 'Ali (a.s) that they would not act against him. Soon after, Ali (a.s). dismissed governors appointed by Usman (r.a,), replacing them with his own men, against the advice of prominent leaders, who had told him to proceed with his governing cautiously. Historian Madelung says Ali (a.s) was convinced of his rights and religious mission and did not shy away from fighting against heavy odds. Muawiya, the governor of Syria, and the relative of Caliph Usman (r.a), belonging to the Banu Umayyad Clan of Mecca, refused to submit to the new Caliph.[250]

First Fitnah: Ayesha (r.a) Talha, Zubayr, Marwan and Muawiya wanted Ali (a.s) to punish the rioters who had killed caliph Usman (r.a). Ali (a.s)

---

[250] Madelung 1997, pp. 141–145, pp. 148 and 149.

needed time to get set, and under the present situation, he did not have enough force to control or punish the rioters who had killed the caliph. Under such circumstances, a serious split took place which led to the first civil war in Muslim history, which created permanent divisions within the Muslim community, about who had the legitimate right to be the caliph. The first Fitnah followed the assassination of Usman (r.a) and continued during the caliphate of Ali (a.s) and was ended by Muawiya (r.a)'s assumption of the caliphate, in 661.[251]

Battle of the Camel (Nov. 656): Ali (a.s) did not want to fight. Talha and Zubayr also did not want to fight, but the Qurra and the Sabaites who had killed caliph Usman were displeased, as they feared they would not be safe if there was an armistice. So, they launched a night attack and started burning the tents. Ali (a.s) was restraining his men but nobody was listening, as everyone thought that the other party had breached the truce. Confusion prevailed throughout the night. Zubayr was killed by a man called Amr ibn Jamroz who had followed him and murdered him while he was praying. Talha also left. On seeing this, Marwan shot Talha with a poisoned arrow, saying that he had disgraced his tribe, by leaving the field. With the two generals, Zubair and Talha, gone, confusion prevailing, and the Qurra, the Sabaites and the Umayyads fought. Marwan and the Qurra caused a lot of trouble. Marwan was arrested but he later asked Imam Hassan (a.s) ibn Ali (a.s) and Husayn ibn Ali (a.s), for help, and was released. Marwan later became an Umayyad Caliph, setting up his own dynasty, after the abdication of Yazid's son Muawiya II who refused to become his father's successor, due to his father's and his grandfather's cruelty and injustice towards the Ahle Bayt.[252]

Battle of Siffin: (657). Muawiya, the governor of Syria, refused to pledge allegiance to Caliph Ali (a.s). When all efforts of a peaceful settlement failed, the Battle of Siffin started. Muawiya (r.a)'s army was on the point of being defeated when Amr ibn al-Aas advised Muawiya (r.a) to make his soldiers raise 'verses of the Quran' on spearheads, to cause confusion

---

[251] Tabatabai 1979—, p. 53 and 54.
[252] Madelung 1997—, pp. 267–269 and 293–307

in Ali's forces. Most of Ali's forces, the Qurra, left the fight.[253] It was decided to settle the dispute by arbitration which was vehemently rejected by the Qurra who left the ranks of Ali. These dissenters (later called the Kharijites) insisted that Muawiya (r.a) was a rebel and did not deserve arbitration and must be fought until he surrenders and repents. They quoted the verse 49.9 of Quran: "If two parties of believers fight, then fight the aggressor until he returns to God's command." The dissenters believed that in agreeing to arbitration, Ali (a.s), had committed the grave sin of rejecting God's judgment and tried to substitute human judgment for God's clear injunction.[254] They considered everyone to be their enemy. They started killing Ali (a.s) 's supporters and other Muslims.

Battle of Nahrawan: The Kharijites proclaimed Ali's caliphate to be invalid. They gathered at Nahrawan and began to agitate against Ali (a.s), and raid his territories. When efforts at reconciliation failed, Ali's forces attacked the Kharijites in their camp, inflicting a heavy defeat on them in 658, killing their leader Ibn Wahb and most of his supporters.[255]

Assassination of Ali: On 27 January 661, Ali (a.s), was assassinated, by a Kharijite Ibn Muljam, during prayers at the Kufa mosque. He ordered his sons to give only one equal hit to ibn-Muljam, as retribution, whether he died from that hit or not.[256]

Hassan (a.s) ibn Ali (a.s), the 2nd Imam: Just like his father, Imam Hassan (a.s) was also abandoned by the people of Kufa, during the critical period of his caliphate, which he assumed, after the assassination of his father by a Kharijite named Ibn-Muljam. As soon as, news of Hassan (a.s)'s choice reached Muawiya, who had been fighting Ali for the caliphate, he condemned the choice, and declared his decision, not to recognize

---

[253] Ali, Ameer. 'A Short History of the Saracens' (13th ed.). London 1961: Macmillan and Company. p. 51.
[254] Levi Della Vida, G. (2012). In P. Bearman, Th. Bianquis, C.E. Bosworth, E. van Donzel, W.P. Heinrichs. Encyclopaedia of Islam (2nd ed.). Brill.
[255] Francesca, Ersilia (2006)-In khawarij. -Damme McAuliffe. Encyclopaedia of the Qur'an. Brill.
[256] Jafri, Syed Hussain Mohammad—2002—origins and development of Shia Islam—oxford university press

him. Letters exchanged between Hassan (a.s) ibn Ali (a.s) and Muawiya (r.a), produced no result. Letters, recorded in historical accounts compiled by Madelung and Jafri, give useful arguments concerning the rights of the caliphate which led to the origin of the Shia (the party of Ali and the Household of Muhammad). Imam Hassan (a.s) urged Muawiya (r.a) to pledge allegiance to him. In response, Muawiya (r.a) told Hasan he would succeed him after his death, if he submitted to him.[257] Muawiya (r.a) assembled an army of 60,000 men at Maskin, on the outskirts of Mosul. As the news of Muawiya's army reached Hassan (a.s) ibn li (a.s), he also prepared an army, and sent his vanguard of 12,000 men, under the command of Ubayd Allah ibn al-Abbas to Maskin. He instructed him to hold back Muawiya until Hassan (a.s) arrived with the main army.[258]

Hassan (a.s)'s Sermon and its Aftermath: While Hassan (a.s)'s vanguard was waiting for his arrival at Maskin, Hassan (a.s) ibn Ali (a.s) himself was facing a serious problem at Sabat near Madain, where he gave a sermon, after morning prayer, in which he declared that he prayed to be the most sincere of God's creation to His creatures and wanted good for the people. The sermon gave the impression to the troops that he was about to give up the battle. They looted his tent and took away even his prayer rug. Hassan (a.s) ibn Ali (a.s) shouted for his horse and rode off, surrounded by his guards, On the way, a Kharijite named al-Jarrah ibn Sinan managed to stab him in the thigh, with a dagger. News of this attack spread and further demoralized the already discouraged army and led to extensive desertion from his troops. When Hassan (a.s)'s army led by Ubayd Allah arrived, Muawiya (r.a)'s forces were already there. Muawiya (r.a) sent a message to Ubayd Allah that Hasan had asked for a truce, and privately offered 1,000,000 dirhams if Ubayd Allah accepted to join him. During the night, Ubayd Allah joined Muawiya's camp. In the morning, when Ubayd Allah did not show up to lead the prayers, the Kufans came to know what had happened. Qays took charge and, in his sermon, severely denounced Ubayd Allah, his father and his brother. Muawiya sent some soldiers, to make them give up but Qays attacked and drove them back. The next day,

---

[257] Madelung—1997—pp. 314–318, p. 320, 322.
[258] Donaldson, Dwight M. (1933). The Shia Religion: A History of Islam in Persia and Iraq. BURLEIGH PRESS. pp. 66–78.

a larger number of soldiers were sent, but they were also defeated. Muawiya then sent a letter to Qays offering bribes but Qays rejected the offers. Both sides abstained from fighting and waited for Hasan's arrival.[259]

Treaty with Muawiya: Muawiya (r.a) who had already started negotiations with Hassan (a.s), now sent high-level envoys, and wrote a letter saying that he was making peace with Hassan (a.s) ibn Ali (a.s), on the basis that Hassan (a.s) ibn Ali (a.s) would succeed him, and would be paid 1,000,000 dirhams from the treasury every year, plus tax of Fasa and Darabjird. Muawiya gave him a blank paper, with his seal at the bottom, inviting Hassan (a.s) ibn Ali (a.s) to write on it whatever he wanted. Madelung's view is, that Hassan (a.s) ibn Ali (a. s) surrendered the reign over the Muslims to Muawiya (r. a) on the basis that he acts, according to the Quran and the Sunnah. Hassan (a.s) ibn Ali (a.s), thus, surrendered his control of Iraq in August 661, after a reign of only seven months.[243]

Abdication of Hassan (a.s): Imam Hasan announced his abdication in favor of Muawiya in the mosque of Kufa and left for Medina. While he was on the way to Medina, Muawiya faced a revolt from the Kharijites who defeated his troops. He sent a message to Hasan to come and help but Hasan declined and said that he gave up the fight although he was justified to fight Muawiya. So he would not fight for or against him. During the nine-year period between Hassan (a.s)'s abdication in AH 41 (661), and his death in AH 50 (670), Hassan (a.s) ibn Ali (a.s) retired in Al-Medina, He was considered the chief of Muhammad' (pbuh)'s household, by Banu Hashim themselves, and the followers of Ali (a.s), who pinned their hopes on his final succession to Muawiya. Occasionally, the Shiites, mostly from Kufa, went to Hassan (a.s) and Husayn ibn Ali (a.s), asking them to claim the caliphate, but they declined saying they had an agreement with Muawiya. Hassan (a.s) ibn Ali (a.s) has been quoted as commenting "If Muawiya (r.a) was the rightful successor he got it. And if I deserved it, I have handed it over to him, and that is the end."[260]

---

[259] Madelung—1997—pp. 314–318, p. 320, 322.
[260] Momen, Moojan (1985). An Introduction to Shi'i Islam. Yale University Press. pp. 14, 26, 27.

Oath of allegiance to Yazid: Despite the promise not to appoint a successor, Muawiya appointed his son Yazid as caliph after him. Upon succession, Yazid asked governors of all provinces to take an oath of allegiance to him. The necessary oath was secured from all parts of the country. The governor of Madinah, Waleed bin Utbah summoned Husayn ibn Ali (a.s) and Abdullah ibn Zubayr, the former answered the summon and went to the governor, When asked to pledge allegiance, Imam Husayn said that the proper way was to do so is in public, and not in private, and exited the governor's mansion. Marwan bin al-Hakam asked the governor to force Husayn's bayah but the governor refused, saying that he did not want to ruin his Day of Resurrection. The next day, Imam Husayn proceeded to Mecca, to put up a resistance to Yazid. Abdullah ibn Zubayr had already left Medina at night, heading for Mecca. In the morning, Waleed sent men after him, a party of eighty riders under the command of a retainer of the Banu Umayya. They pursued Ibn al-Zubayr but could not catch up with him.[261]

Caliph Muawiya's Persecution of the Shia: Muawiya (r.a) is the most unpopular figure, particularly in Shia Islam, for his rebellion against Caliph Ali (a.s) ibn Abi Talib, by refusing to pledge allegiance which resulted in the Battle of Siffin, described above, the bloodiest battle of Islam, in which over 70,000 Muslims, including some very senior companions of the prophet (pbuh), were killed. Ammar ibn Yasir (r.a), an old man of 95, at the time of his death, was one such companion who was martyred, fighting alongside Ali (a.s) ibn Abi Talib. There is a well-known hadith, present in both, the Shia and Sunni books of hadith, about Ammar ibn Yasir, recorded in Sahih Muslim and Sahih Bukhari, narrated by Abu Hurairah and others, in which Muhammad (pbuh) said, addressing Ammar ibn Yasir: "The transgressing party shall kill you".[262] Muawiya's governor of Basra, Mughira in Shu'ba collected 3000 Shias of Rabbi's tribe, on the false

---

[261] The History of Al-Tabari: Vol. XIX (The Caliphate of Yazid bin Muawiya). Al-Tabari, Muhammad ibn Jarir—(English Translation by I. K. A. Howard). State University of New York Press.—alsunnahfoundation.org/ Karbala—(Pg. 7)

[262] Jami at-Tirmidhi—Vol. 1, Book 46, Hadith 3800. Narrated Abu Hurairah: that the Messenger of Allah (ﷺ) said: "Rejoice, 'Ammar, the transgressing party shall kill you."

pretext of fighting the Kharijites, and had them killed. Similarly. another governor Ziyad bin Sumayya had about 100,000 Shias killed, during his rule of Basra.²⁶³

Umayyad Tradition of Cursing Ali (a.s): The Umayyad tradition of cursing Ali (a.s). was performed in state-controlled mosques in Syria for a period of 65 years from c.657 to c.717 CE, an abdominal practice decreed by Muawiya. The cursing finally ended, with the fall of the Umayyad Dynasty. Sistan governor Saad ibn Abi-Waqqas refused to comply with the order of cursing Ali (a.s), giving three reasons: 1) according to Quran 33:33, Ali (a.s) was a member of Ahl-e-Bayt whom God had purified of all sins. 2)According to the prophet (pbuh), Ali (a.s) 's rank, in relation to him, was the same as that of Aaron (Haroon) in relation to Moses. 3) The prophet (pbuh) gave the banner, to Ali (a.s), at the battle of Khyber.²⁶⁴ Omar bin Abdul Aziz (r. a), an Umayyad Caliph, forbade the cursing of Ali (a.s). on the minbar (pulpit), during Friday prayers, replacing it with verse 15 from Surah 59 (al-Hashr) and verse 19 of Surah 90 (al-Nahl) from the Quran. When Caliph Muawiya Ibn Abi Sufyan put al-Mughira Ibn Shu'ba in charge of Kufa, (on September 2- October 30, 661), he summoned him. After praising and glorifying God, he said: "do not refrain from abusing Ali (a.s) and criticizing him; Continue to shame the companions of 'Ali (a.s)²⁶⁵

Muawiya II s/o Yazid: Atrocities of Yazid and his father, Muawiya, are verified beyond any doubt by what Yazid's successor, his son Muawiya II said, after Yazid's death. He gathered the people of Damascus and said: "My grandfather Muawiya, stripped the command from one who deserved it the most, with your help, as you are fully aware. My father Yazid, and grandfather Muawiya killed the progeny of the Messenger of Allah. My

---

263 Al-Waqidi—1423—p. 352-353
264 Sahih Muslim, English version, v4, chapter MCCV, Tradition #6968, # 6970.
265 Reza Shah Kazmi—2007—justice and remembrance—introducing spirituality of imam ali—I.B. Tauris. pp. 62, 63. Retrieved 2013-07-08

father permitted drinking alcohol and he fought in the sanctuary of Mecca and destroyed the Kaaba.[266]

Husayn-ibn- Ali (a.s)—The 3rd Imam: After receiving letters from the people of Kufa, Husayn ibn Ali (a.s), the grandson of Muhammad (pbuh), proceeded to Kufa. On the way, he received the report of Muslim ibn Aqeel's death, at the hands of Yazid's men and that the Kufans had changed their loyalties, pledging allegiance to Yazid. Ubaid Allah ibn Ziyad, governor of Basra, warned the citizens to avoid the insurgency, and sent a message to Husayn (a.s), on the instruction of Yazid, saying, "you can neither go to Kufa nor to Mecca, but you could go elsewhere."

Battle of Karbala: The battle resulted from Yazid's succession to the caliphate after his father Muawiya's death in 680 who nominated Yazid as his successor despite his agreement with Imam Hasan not to nominate his successor. After taking over as Caliph, Yazid asked his governor in Medina to secure bayah from all the leading companions of the Prophet, including Abdullah bin Zubair, Abdullah in Umar, and Husayn bin Ali, all of whom declined. Imam Husayn proceeded to Mecca to gather support there. During his stay there, he received letters of support from Kufa. [267]To assess the situation, he sent his cousin Muslim bin Aqeel to Kufa who wrote back that the situation was favorable, and he could come to Kufa. In the meantime, the new governor Obaidullah bin Ziyad executed Muslim bin Aqeel and his host Hani bin Urwa, without much resistance from the people of Kufa.[268] Also, Yazd sent an army to Mecca, with instructions to kill Husayn bin Ali wherever they found him during the Hajj. Imam Husayn, therefore left Mecca just one day before Hajj, to prevent violation of the sanctity of the Kaaba, contenting only with an Umrah. When senior companions of the Prophet came to know about his plan, they implored him to leave women and children in Mecca, but the Imam refused their

---

[266] Khulafaa al-Rasool, by Khalid Muhammad Khalid, p.531. 2= Sawaiq al-Muhriqah, by Ibn Hajar AL Haytham end of Ch. 11, pp 336

[267] Cornell, Vincent J. (December 2006—voices if Islam—Greenwood Publishing Group. Retrieved 15 August 2016

[268] The Tragedy of Karbala, pg. 23

pleas.[269] Imam Husayn was at 2 days journey from Kufa, when his caravan was stopped by 1000 men of Yazid's army. Imam addressed his adversaries: "If you are not the people who wrote to me to come to Kufa, then i will return to medina." Their leader Hurr refused to allow the Imam to return unless he pledged allegiance to Yazid. Ubaydullah ibn Ziyad, the governor of Kufa, appointed Umar ibn Sa'ad as the commander of his army. Ibn Ziyad also ordered Umar ibn Sa'ad to start the battle on the sixth day of Muharram.[270] Umar ibn Sa'ad moved towards the battlefield with an army and arrived at Karbala on Muharram 3, 61 AH (October 3, 680 AD). Ibn Ziyad ordered the commander to prevent Husayn and his followers to get water, and 5000 men blocked access to the river. This blockade continued until the end of the battle. [271]Husayn asked ibn Saad to wait until the next morning so that he and his men could spend the night praying. At night, Husayn gathered his men ad told them they were free to leave the camp during the darkness to escape certain death but many did not leave.[272] Husayn had 32 horsemen and 40 infantrymen, to confront 12,000 soldiers of Yazid.[273] Affected by Imam Husayn's speech, Hurr, the opposition commander defected to Husayn's ranks. Before the battle, it was agreed between the warring factions, not to use arrows and lances in the battle due to a small band of Husayn's men but the agreement was breached by ibn Ziyad, and they started showering arrows. After Husayn's other companions were killed, his family members asked his permission to fight. Ali al-Akbar ibn Husayn, the middle son of Husayn ibn Ali, was the first one of the Hashemites who received permission from his father. Casualties of Banu Hashim included sons of Ali ibn Abi Talib, sons of Hasan ibn Ali, a son of Husayn ibn Ali, a son of Abdullah ibn Ja'far ibn Abi-Talib and Zaynab bint Ali, sons of Aqeel ibn Abi Talib, as well as a son of Muslim ibn Aqeel. Altogether, there were seventy-two Hashemites killed in all (including Husayn ibn Ali).

---

[269] Maqtal al-Husayn—Journey to Iraq—p. 130.
[270] al Qazwini, Radiyaddin ibn Nabi. *Tazallum al Zahra*. p. 101
[271] Maqtal al-Husayn–the watering place-p. 162
[272] Tabari, Al. *Tarikh*. 06. p. 337
[273] Lohouf, Tradition No. 140

Abbas bin Ali's Martyrdom: Abbas, the imam's brother, went to the river to fetch water for Ahl-Bayt who were very thirsty, particularly Bibi Sakina, Imam's daughter. Ibn Saad confronted him, to stop him from accessing water. They cut his right arm, and he shifted the water bottle to the other arm, which was also cut, forcing him to grab the water skin with his teeth which was also pierced by an arrow, spilling all the water. At this, he charged the enemies and fought bravely, killing many soldiers. An arrow hit his eye, blinding him, and someone hit him with a spear on the head and he fell off the horse.[274]

Martyrdom of Husayn: When a soldier wanted to kill Husayn, his underage nephew Abdullah bin Hasan ran out of the tents and defended his uncle with his arms which were cut, and the boy died at the Imam's feet.[275] Shimr bin Thiljoshan attacked the Imam who asked him to let him offer Asr prayers. Shimr agreed but when the Imam went down in Sajda, Shimr beheaded the Imam.[276]

Aftermath of Karbala: All the valuables were looted, and the tents were set on fire by the Umayyad army. Imam's family members were captured, and Imam's head, and the dead bodies were sent to Ibn Ziyad in Kufa. Women, children, and Imam's ill son Ali were despatched to Yazid in Damascus.[277]

Caliph Abdullah ibn Zubayr (Reign as Caliph: 683-692): Yazid took over the caliphate, after his father's death. Abdullah ibn Zubayr refused to pledge allegiance to him, and launched an insurgency against Yazid, in 683. After Husayn (a.s) ibn Ali' s martyrdom at Karbala, ibn-Zubayr gathered the people of Mecca and said: "The people of Kufa promised Husayn ibn Ali (a.s) to support him for his caliphate. But when Ibn Ziyad, Yazid's governor came to Kufa, they rallied around him and abandoned Husayn ibn Ali (a.s), who was pious, observed the fast, read the Quran and deserved the caliphate in all respects". The people were impressed

---

[274] Calmard, J. (13 July 2011). Abbas bin Ali—*Encyclopedia Iranica*.
[275] Lohouf, Tradition No.184, 185
[276] Lohouf, Tradition No. 192 and 193
[277] Lohouf, Tradition No. 222, 223

and nominated ibn-Zubayr for the caliphate. Eventually Ibn Zubayr strengthened his control of Iraq, Southern Arabia, parts of Syria, and parts of Egypt. Ibn Zubayr received support from the populace who were dissatisfied with the Umayyad rule.[278]

Sack of Medina by Yazid: (26 August 683): People of Medina expelled the Umayyad Governor, Uthman ibn Mohammad, as well as his aide, Marwan ibn Hakam, along with their Umayyad supporters. Yazid sent an army of 10,000 fighters from Syria, against the forces of Abdullah ibn Zubayr, the ruler of Mecca and Medina, and the people of Medina. After winning the battle, Yazid's forces looted the city, for three consecutive days, massacring many of its inhabitants, including women and children. Many senior companions of the Prophet (pbuh), were also killed in this battle, called the battle of Harrah.[279]

First Siege of Mecca: After taking Medina, Yazid's forces, led by Muslim ibn Uqba, known by Historians as 'heathen incarnate' (the butcher) for his sack of Medina, and atrocities committed there, marched to Mecca. On the way, ibn Uqba died, the leadership going to Husayn ibn Numayr who besieged Mecca. A wooden structure was erected by Ibn-Zubayr around the Kaaba and covered with mattresses, to protect it. The wooden structure caught fire and burned down, and the sacred black stone (Hajr-e-Aswad) was damaged and broken into 3 fragments. The siege continued for a month. When news of Yazid's death, reached the besiegers, the Umayyad commander, left for Syria.[280] Ibn Zubair proceeded to obtain his own legitimacy from Banu Hashim clan in Mecca by pressuring them. They were led by Muhammad ibn Hanafiyyah who was imprisoned by bn Zubair, to force their pledge of allegiance.[281]

Second Siege of Mecca: In 692, Abd al-Malik ibn Marwan, after strengthening his position in Syria, sent his capable but brutal General Hajjaj ibn Yusuf, with 12,000 men, to confront Abd Allah ibn al-Zubayr,

---

[278] Abd Allah ibn -Zubayr". Encyclopedia Britannica. Inc. 2010. p. 17
[279] Ahmed 2010, pp. 65–66.
[280] Gibb 1960, p. 55.
[281] Anthony 2016, pp. 12–13, 21

in Mecca. Hajjaj was able to coerce 10,000 men of ibn-Zubayr, along with his two sons, to switch sides, who then went over to Hajjaj. As a result, ibn-Zubayr was left, with only a few loyal followers, including his youngest son, and they were all killed in the fighting, around the Kaaba.[282]

Sulayman b. Surad al-Khuzai (684): People of Kufa blamed themselves for not supporting Husayn ibn Ali (a.s) in the Battle of Karbala and wished to make up for their failure. They volunteered to avenge the massacre of Karbala and were known as the Penitents. They were first led by Suleiman ibn Khuzai and later by Al-Mukhtar Saqafi. They were able to kill most of the perpetrators of the Karbala massacre, during their battles with the Umayyads. Both Shia and Sunni Historians consider Sulayman to be a devout, virtuous, and renowned person who prayed a lot. He was a strong Tribal leader who commanded respect and loyalty in his tribe that obeyed him. He fought many battles beside Ali (a.s). He led the Penitents Uprising in 684. Sulayman was martyred in The Battle of 'Ayn al-Warda which was fought in early January 685 between the Umayyad army of 20,000 and the 4000 Penitents or Tawwabin Volunteers, most of whom were martyred in this battle, including Sulayman who was 93 at the time. The survivors, led by ibn Shaddad, later joined al-Mukhtar and formed the backbone of his movement.[283]

Al-Mukhtar (622-687): In 680 AD, Obaidullah bin Ziyad, the governor of Kufa, arrested al-Mukhtar, imprisoning him in al-Tamura, a dreadful prison. Al-Mukhtar was released by Obaidullah bin Ziyad, on order of Yazid bin Muawiya, who was persuaded by Abdullah bin Umar, Mukhtar's sister Safiyyah's husband. He supported Abdullah bin al-Zubayr and defended the Kaaba against the Syrian Army, sent by Yazid under the command of Husain ibn Neumayr. After four years' stay in Mecca, Mukhtar decided to go back to Kufa, which was, then, under Abdullah bin Zubair. In Kufa, he was imprisoned again, by Obaidullah bin Ziyad, the governor. After Yazid's death, the people of Kufa took advantage of the situation and started supporting Abdullah bin Zubair. Mukhtar sent a message, from the prison to Rifaah bin Shaddad and his companions.

---

[282] Gibb 1960, p. 55
[283] Daftary—1992—p. 51

Rifaah headed the Tawwabin (penitents) army, after Sulayman bin Surad. Mukhtar was freed from prison again through Abdullah bin Umar bin al Khattab's intercession.[284]

Mukhtar uprising (66 AH, 685 AD): In 685, Mohammad bin al-Hanafiyah, son of Ali (a.s) wrote to Mukhtar, announcing his support to Mukhtar. Ibn al-Hanafiyah's support encouraged people to join Mukhtar. Mukhtar's Army of 3000 volunteers fought two battles with Umayyad forces, winning both. Mukhtar reinforced his troops with another 7,000 under Ibrahim al-Ashtar, who executed Harmala bin Kahil (killer of Husayn ibn Ali (a.s) 's baby, Ali Asghar; Sanan bin Anas (who had taken part in Husayn ibn Ali (a.s) 's killing) ; Umar ibn Saad, leader of Umayyad army in the Karbala massacre; Shimr bin Zil Jawshan, who had beheaded Husayn ibn Ali (a.s). Shimr had fled but was caught in a village and executed.[285]

Battle of al-Khazir: In August 686 CE (66 Hijri), Ibrahim al-Ashtar met the Army of Obaidullah bin Ziyad, in a violent battle. Kufan Army attacked the Umayyad headquarters and killed senior leaders such as Obaidullah bin Ziyad and al-Husain bin Neumayr. Ibrahim al- Ashtar's army of 13,000 defeated Obaidullah's Army of 40,000, losing only 1000 soldier.[286]

Shia Persecution by Caliph Ibn-Zubayr: Ibn Zubayr, initially pretended to support Ahl Bayt but turned against the Shias after he became the Caliph of Hejaz and Iraq, although he had gained support of Meccans, and nomination to Caliphate, after his touching rhetoric, expressing his deep sorrow for the events of Karbala, and the treachery of Kufans. Al-Mukhtar had helped him defend Mecca against the Umayyad forces in 683 CE. But in fact, Ibn- Zubair disliked the Alawites, the followers of Ali (a.s), as the later events proved. In Mecca, he assembled the Shias, near a mountain

---

[284] al-Abdul Jader-2010—p. 6.
[285] Donner-2010—p. 185
[286] Hawting, Gerald R. (2002)-p.52

and kept them there against their will. He destroyed their houses. Mukhtar rescued them from the siege with 5000 fighters and rebuilt their homes.[287]

Defense of Medina: When the Umayyad Caliph Abd al-Malik sent a big army to occupy al-Medina, Mukhtar sent three thousand fighters to save the Prophet's City. Ibn Zubayr, the Caliph, sent another army of two thousand warriors to defend Medina against the Umayyad army, but his real aim was to attack Mukhtar's Army. When Mukhtar's soldiers were busy fighting the Umayyads, ibn Zubair's army took advantage of the situation and attacked Mukhtar's soldiers. They killed many soldiers, and the rest escaped to the desert where they died of hunger and thirst.[288]

Mukhtar's Last Stand (67 AH 686CE): Ibn Zubayr appointed his brother Mu'sab bin al-Zubair, as the ruler of Basra. Mu'sab formed a large army and headed for Kufa. He took Mukhtar by surprise. Ibrahim al-Ashtar was in Mosul. Mukhtar faced Ibn-Zubair with his small Army. Ibn-Zubair's Army launched a strong attack and forced Mukhtar's Army to come back to Kufa. Mus'ab's Army followed Mukhtar to Kufa. They then proceeded to besiege his palace. The siege went on for four months. Mukhtar tried to raise the siege but failed due to the formidable forces of ibn-Zubayr. Finally, he came out with only 17 men, and fought bravely, and was killed.[289] Mu'sab ibn Zubayr cheated the people, who remained in the palace, promising not to harm if they came out, but all the seven thousand of them were put to death when they opened the gates.[290] Mu'sab ordered his soldiers to arrest Mukhtar's wife Umrah, who was taken to the desert and beheaded. In 691, Hajjaj attacked Mus'ab's weakened Army in Kufa, by bribing many of his soldiers to switch sides and kill their leader.[291]

Ali ibn Husayn (a.s): the 4th Imam (4 January 659-20 October 713): Ali ibn Husayn (a.s), also called Imam Sajjad, and Zayn al-Abidin, was ill during the battle of Karbala and on his aunt Zainab's plea to the Umayyad

---

[287] Dixon, Abd al-Ameer A. (1971).-p.56-58.
[288] Dixon, Abd al-Ameer A. (1971)-p.56-58
[289] Sachedina-(1981) p.10
[290] Kennedy 2016—p. 83.
[291] Wellhausen, Julius (1975)-p.139

commander, he was spared and was taken to Yazid in Damascus. He was later allowed to return to Medina. Whenever food was brought to him, he wept excessively. A servant once said to him: Is it not time for you to end the sorrow? He answered: "Jacob the prophet (pbuh) had twelve sons, and Allah made one of them disappear although he was alive, whereas I witnessed all of my family members being massacred."[292]

Imamah of Ali ibn Husayn (a.s): Mohammad ibn al-Hanafiyah (r. a), was the 3rd son of Ali ibn Abi Talib (a. s), from his wife Khawla bint Ja'far whom he married after the death of Fatima (r.a). She was brought to Medina, as a slave from Yamama, with other women of her tribe. Her tribesmen approached Ali (a.s) and asked him to save her from slavery. Hanafiyah was her son. He was a pious, brave man whom many considered as their Imam. Other Shia sects said Zayn al-Abedin (a.s) had the right to inherit the Imamah because his father Husayn ibn Ali (a.s) had designated him as the next Imam. Mohammad ibn al-Hanafiyah said he was worthier because he was the son of Ali. Zayn al-Abidin (a.s) replied to his uncle, Fear God and make no such claim. After the death of Caliph ibn Zubayr, the governor of Medina, Zayn al-Abidin (a.s) and Mohammad ibn Hanafiyah agreed to go to Mecca, to determine who was the true successor. They both prayed for a sign. When ibn Hanafiyah prayed, no sign came. When Zayn al-Abidin (a.s) prayed, the Blackstone agitated, and nearly fell off. It showed that Zayn al-Abidin (a.s) was the successor, an answer, to which Mohammad ibn Hanafiyah consented. [293]After this settlement, Zayn al-Abedin (a.s) returned to a quiet life in Medina.[294]

Social status and Caliph's Malice: Ali ibn al-Husayn (a.s) was respected by the Medina scholars who considered him as an eminent personality.

---

[292] Sharif al- Qurashi 2000—p. 163—*His eyes turned white from constant weeping, his head turned grey out of sorrow, and his back became bent in gloom,* though his son was alive in this world. But I watched while my father, my bro.ther, my uncle, and seventeen members of my family were slaughtered all around me. How should my sorrow come to an end?

[293] Donaldson, Dwight M. (1933). *The Shi'ite Religion: A History of Islam in Persia and Iraq.* BURLEIGH PRESS. pp. 101–111.

[294] Madelung Wilford—ali b.Hosayn b. ali bin Abi Taleb—*ENCYCLOPÆDIA IRANICA.* Retrieved August 1, 2011.

The lawyer, Saeed ibn al-Musayyib and the jurist al-Zuhri—though attached to the court of the Umayyads—were among his admirers. Al-Zuhri gave him the honorific title Zayn al-Abidin (a.s)—the ornament of worshippers—and narrated many Hadiths from him. His exalted position is evidenced by an ode composed by a famous Arab poet Farazdaq, who was present, during Hajj rituals when Caliph Hisham and the Imam were both trying to touch the black stone. People showed utmost respect to the Imam and gave way while the Caliph struggled, trying to reach the black stone. The Caliph was offended and asked who that man was, to whom so much respect was being accorded. Answering the Caliph's question Farazdaq composed an ode, which says: "This is he, whose ability the valley of Makkah recognizes and whom, the sanctuary and the area outside the sanctuary (al-hill) recognize. He is the son of the best of all Allah's servants. This is the pure, pious man, the pure eminent man. He is a generous man who never utters "no" except in Tasha Hud. If there were not be the word 'La' (No) in Tasha Hud, he would not say 'No.' Love to him is deen (faith), hostility to him is kufr (infidelity), and nearness to him is protection and refuge. This is Ali b. al Hussein, the son of Fatima. Whoever knows God, knows his Wali (religious leader). Religion is from the house of this man."[295]

Death: Zayn al-Abidin (a.s) was poisoned by Umayyad ruler of Medina, Al-Walid, by order of Caliph Hisham ibn Abd al-Malik although he was not involved in any political activity at that time. The fact that the previous caliphs such as Yazid ibn Muawiya, Abd al-Malik ibn Marwan and Marwan ibn Hakam had left him alone as they perceived him to be harmless.[296] After his death, at 54, many people discovered their livelihoods had come from the Imam. He used to go out with a sack of food, knock at doors of the needy, and distribute food to whoever answered.[297]

---

[295] 7= Al-Farazdaq—Encyclopedia Britannica 8=Al-Farazdaq—Imam Reza network
[296] WOFIS (2001). *A Brief History of the Fourteen Infallibles* (3rd ed.). Tehran: World Organization for Islamic Services.
[297] Donaldson, Dwight M. (1933). *The Shi'ite Religion: A History of Islam in Persia and Iraq.* BURLEIGH PRESS. pp. 101–111.

Mohammad Al-Baqir (a.s), the 5ᵗʰ Imam: al-Baqir (a.s) was born in Medina around 56 AHS (676 AD) when Muawiya (r.a) was trying to ensure that his son Yazid inherits the Caliphate. When Husayn ibn Ali (a.s), was killed in Karbala, al-Baqir was 3 years old. He witnessed the power struggle among the Umayyads, Abd Allah ibn Zubayr and several Shiite parties, including his brother Zaid bin Ali's uprising, and other relatives. Most people accepted al-Baqir as the fifth Imam, but a minority followed his brother Zaid who sought support of the people to stand against the Umayyads. He asked for Imam Baqir's advice who told him not to trust the people of Kufa who had betrayed their ancestors. Zaid dd not listen to the advice and led a fruitless coup in Kufa. According to historian Al-Shahrastani, a dispute developed between Zaid and the Imam. Zaid announced that position of an Imam depended on his appearing publicly to assert his rights. Imam Baqir replied that according to your reasoning, your father was not the Imam because he did not assert his claims.[298]

Views of Imam Baqir (a.s): Someone asked the Imam how he could visualize God. Imam replied: Imagine a thing which is limitless, and the mind cannot contain. Talk about Allah's creations and not about Allah himself for that increases perplexity." He also said: "Rasul is someone who sees and hears the angel, but Imam and a Nabi only hear. The Imam was often asked to explain teachings about the Imamate, which is also explained in his book Mahathir ul-Baqir (a summary of which is translated into English by Canon Sell's 'Ithna 'Asharíyya or The Twelve Shia Imams." He said: "I advise you regarding five things: If you are wronged, do not commit wrong in response, and if you are cheated, do not react by cheating. If you are accused of lying, don't be angry. If you are criticized, think of what is said. He also said: "How beautiful it is when goodness succeeds badness; and how unappealing it is when evil succeeds goodness. Being religious equals being extremely loving and being extremely loving equals being religious". [299]Imam was asked about collective knowledge of the Quran, its apparent and hidden meanings, he answered that no one

---

[298] Tabatabai, Muhammad Husayn (1975). *Shiite Islam*. Translated and Edited by Seyyed Hossein Nasr. State University of New York Press. pp. 68, 179.

[299] Lalani, Arzina R. (March 9, 2001). *Early Shi'i Thought: The Teachings of Imam Muhammad Al-Baqir*. I. B. Tauris. pp. 37–38.

can claim that knowledge except the Prophet himself, Ali bin Ani Talib and the Imams of the Ahl al-Bayt.[300]

Death: Imam Al-Baqir (a.s) was poisoned by Ibrahim ibn Walid ibn Abdallah, the nephew of the Caliph Hisham. He was buried next to his father, the fourth Imam. His grave was destroyed in 1806, and later in 1926 by the Saudis.[301]

Ja'far ibn Mohammad Al-Sadiq (a.s): the 6th Imam (702–765): He was an outstanding personality, in the formulation of Shia doctrine. The traditions recorded from Al-Sadiq (a.s) are said to be more numerous than all Hadiths recorded from all other Shia Imams combined. As the founder of Jafari Jurisprudence, Al-Sadiq (a.s) also elaborated on the doctrines of an Imam's infallibility and Taqiyya. During his time, the region was embroiled, in many conflicts. He was requested by rebels for support which he declined. He was poisoned at the orders of the Caliph al-Mansur.[302]

Imamate: Al-Sadiq assumed Imamate when he was about 35 years old, and held it for 28 years, longer than any other Imam. Before his Imamate, many Shia preferred Zaid's revolutionary politics, as opposed to his father's stance and his grandfather, Zainul Abidin's attitude of quietism. Zaid had asserted that an Imam should assert his rights publicly. Imam elaborated the doctrine of Imamate by saying: "Imamate is not self-assertion or human choice but is a divinely inspired designation and unique knowledge of each imam by the previous Imam, passed down from the prophet Muhammad (pbuh), through immediate descendants of Ali (a.s)." Despite being designated as the Imam, Al-Sadiq (a.s) did not lay claim to the Caliphate.[303]

---

[300] Al-Kulayni, Abu Ja'far Muhammad ibn Yaqoob (2015). *Kitab al-Kafi*. South Huntington, NY: The Islamic Seminary Inc.
[301] Donaldson, Dwight M. (1933). *The Shi'ite Religion: A History of Islam in Persia and Iraq*. BURLEIGH PRESS. pp. 112–119.
[302] Haywood, John A.—Ja'far ibn Mohammad *Encyclopedia Britannica*. Retrieved 2015.
[303] Armstrong, Karen (2002). *Islam, A Short History*. Modern Library; Rev Upd Su edition. pp. 56–57, 66.

Under Umayyad rulers: Al-Sadiq's Imamate extended over the latter half of the Umayyad Caliphate, which was marked by many revolts (mostly by the Shia movements), and eventually the violent overthrow of the Umayyad Caliphate by the Abbasids, descendants of Muhammad (pbuh) 's uncle, Abbas. Al-Sadiq (a.s) maintained his predecessors' policy of quietism and played no part in the numerous rebellions. He stayed out of the uprising of Zaydis, who gathered around al-Sadiq's uncle, Zayd, who had the support of some groups in Medina and Kufa. Al-Sadiq (a.s) also did not support the rebellion led by his cousin, Mohammad al- Nafs al-Zakiyya. Al-Sadiq (a.s) played no part in the Abbasid revolution. His response to Khorasan leader of the uprising, against Umayyads, became famous. Al-Sadiq (a.s) burnt Abu Muslim's letter, saying to the messenger: "tell your master what you saw and that he is not my man and it is not my time to act. Although I am the designated Imam, I will not lay claim to the Caliphate." There were over 4000 students in Imam Sadiq's classes, including some prominent figures such as Abu Hanifa and Malik bin Anas, founders of two primary Sunni schools of law, and Wasil ibn Ata, of the Mu'tazila school.[304]

Abbasi Caliphate was based on their descent from Muhammad (pbuh) 's uncle, Abbas ibn Abd al-Muttalib. They were suspicious of al-Sadiq because Shias had always believed that leadership of the Ummah was a position ordained by divine order, and which was given to each Imam by the previous Imam. Besides, Al-Sadiq (a.s) had a large following, both among scholars, and among those who believed him to be the Imam. During the rule of Al-Mansur, Al-Sadiq (a.s) was summoned to Baghdad along with some other prominent men from Medina, to keep an eye on the Imam but eventually satisfied the Caliph that he need not fear the Imam. The Imam was therefore allowed to remain in Medina. After the defeat and death of his cousin Mohammad al-Nafs al-Zakiyya in 762, however, Al-Sadiq (a.s) decided to go to Baghdad, to comply with the Caliph's summons. Also, the Imam's house was burned on the Caliph's orders, but no harm came to Al-Sadiq (a.s).[305]

---

[304] Jafri, Syed Husain Mohammad (2002). *The Origins and Early Development of Shi'a Islam; Chapter 10.* Oxford University Press.
[305] Gleaves, Robert.—Ja'far al-Sadiq—Life—*Encyclopedia Iranica.* Retrieved 2015.

Death of Imam Al-Sadiq (a.s): He was arrested several times by Umayyad and Abbasid caliphs Hisham, Saffah, and Mansur. According to some sources, he was poisoned at the behest of Mansur in 148/765, at the age of 64. He was buried in Medina, and his tomb was a place of pilgrimage until 1926. When Saudi Salafis conquered Medina for the second time in 1925, they razed many monuments to the ground, including al-Sadiq's, except for Muhammad (pbuh) 's which miraculously escaped. To end the Imamate, the Caliph instructed the governor of Medina to behead whoever was nominated as the successor. The governor found four names, instead of one, in Imam's testament; the Caliph himself, the governor, his eldest son al-Fattah, and the youngest son Musa al-Kazim.[306]

Views and Teachings: Shia jurisprudence became known as Jafari Jurisprudence after Ja'far al-Sadiq, whose legal dicta were the most essential sources of Shia jurisprudence. Like Sunni law, Jafari jurisprudence is based on the Qur'an and the Hadiths, narrated by Shia sources, and based on the consensus. Unlike the Sunnis, Shias preferred reasoning. Imam rejected opinion and analogical reasoning, arguing: "God's law cannot be predicted and is occasional. The servant's job is to obey and not to reason. He also said: "whoever says God ordered the evil or created good and evil, has lied about God who does not order his creatures to do something, without providing for them a means of not doing it. A moderate view between compulsion and choice is the right course to follow as God decreed somethings absolutely and left some others to individual choice. He said the blessings of the Lord are, in the moderate view."[307]

Musa Al-Kazim (a.s)—the 7th Imam: He was Imam, during reigns of Mansur, Al-Hadi, Al-Mahdi, and Harun al-Rashid of Abbasid Caliphate. Al al-Reza (a.s), the eighth Imam, and Fatima Masoumeh (r.a) were among his children. Musa Al-Kazim (a.s) was born during the conflict between the Abbasid and Umayyad Caliphates, He was four when the first Abbasi caliph al-Saffah was enthroned. His mother, Hamida, was a former slave.

---

[306] Jafri, Syed Husain Mohammad (2002). *The Origins and Early Development of Shi'a Islam; Chapter 10.* Oxford University Press.

[307] Donaldson, Dwight M. (1933). *The Shi'ite Religion: A History of Islam in Persia and Iraq.* BURLEIGH PRESS. pp. 115,130–141.

Al-Kazim was brought up in a large family, with nine sisters and six brothers. His oldest brother Ismail whom some Shia considered the Imam, died before his father, Imam Sadiq.[308] According to some sources, Al-Kazim (a.s) was religious-minded as a child. Mohammad Baqir Majlisi relates an incident where Imam Abu Hanifa called on Ja'far Al-Sadiq (a.s) to ask his advice. While there, he met Al-Kazim (a.s), who was then five years old. Hanifa asked Al-Kazim (a.s): "does disobedience issue from God or the servant? Al-Kazim answered, if it issues from God, the servant will not be punished for something he did not do. If it issues from God and the servant, God will not punish, being the stronger partner. If it issued from the servant only and not from God, then it is God's discretion to punish or not, and it is God whose help, we all seek." Hanifa was satisfied and left without seeing the Imam, saying that the answer had been right enough for him. In another incident, Abu Hanifa complained to al-Sadiq, saying: "I have seen your son, Musa praying when people were passing in front of him. He neither prevented them, nor he interrupted his prayers. Imam asked his son to explain. Al-Kazim (a.s) replied: "To whom I pray is nearer to me than the people passing. God says: "I am closer to every human than his jugular vein. "Quran: 50;16.[309]

Imamate: Musa Al-Kazim (a.s) was said to be a gentle and tolerant man. Therefore he was called Al-Kazim (a. s) due to his generosity and forgiveness toward the people. If someone was unfriendly or rude to him, he sent him a pure of money-narrated by historian Ibn Khallikan. In another incident, a man cursed al-Kazim and his grandfather Ali (a. s). Imam's followers wanted to kill him, but the Imam prevented them. He went to the man's farm outside Medina, and sat beside him, treating him kindly. He asked the man how much he paid to sow his land. He replied that it cost 100 dinars. Imam then asked him how much he expected to gain from his crop. The man answered 200 dinars. Imam gave him 300 and left. When he reached the Mosque of the Prophet, he saw the man already sitting there. When the man saw the Imam, he called out: "God knows whom to

---

[308] Sharif al-Qureshi 2000—p. 69, 198,128.
[309] Meaning "people walking before me does not prevent me from facing God, as God is not at Qibla or in Kaaba as people might imagine, but He is with me". 7= Qur'an 50-16.

give his prophetic mission to". The man recounted the events of the day to the followers who were amazed at the change in man's attitude. Imam asked his followers which course was better, his or theirs, and added I' have put right something wrong.' Al-Kazim (a.s) never accepted Harun's government, because he believed al- Rashid looked to destroy Islam, by erasing the truth and justice. Caliph Harun al-Rashid is quoted as saying in his court that al-Kazim was better suited to inherit the Caliphate from Muhammad (pbuh) than al-Rashid. His son Mamun asked him why he glorified the Imam. The Caliph said: "I am Imam by force whereas Musa is really Imam of the people. However, I will not hand over the Caliphate to him as I like to be in power. Even if you attempt to take the Caliphate from me, I will take it back from you even if I had to gouge your eyes. Musa is the inheritor of the knowledge of Prophets. If you want sound knowledge, you will find it with him. "When Mamun became the Caliph after al-Rashid's death, he insisted on giving the Caliphate to his son. Ali al-Reza (a.s), the eighth Imam.[310]

Story of Bishr al-Hafi: al-Hafi led a Bacchic Life. Once during the noise, music, alcoholic drink, and frivolity, Musa Al-Kazim (a.s) happened to pass by his house in Baghdad. Al-Kazim (a.s) saw a servant coming out. He asked her: "Is the owner of the house, a slave or a free man? The servant said: he is free. Imam responded: you are right. if he were a slave, he would have feared his Lord." When she returned to the house, al-Hafi asked what had delayed her. The servant repeated to al-Hafi what the Imam had said. He was so shocked by the words that he ran barefooted in search of the Imam. When he found the Imam, he fell on the ground and began to weep, saying I am a slave, I am a slave. From then on, he was called 'Bishr al-Hafi-the bare-footed one.[311]

Story of a monk: A final incident concerned Al-Abbas (born Hilal al-Shami), who said to Musa Al-Kazim (a.s) that people admire those who eat simple food, wear coarse clothes, and show reverence. Imam gave him an example of Joseph, who was a prophet but wore silken clothes, adorned

---

[310] See Al- Murtaza, Amali, vol. 1, pp. 105-106, and Bihar al-Anwar, vol. 4, p. 1049
[311] Donaldson, Dwight M. (1933). *The Shi'ite Religion: A History of Islam in Persia and Iraq.* BURLEIGH PRESS. pp. 152–160.

with ornaments, and sat on Pharaoh's throne. People did not care about what he wore but needed his justice. An Imam is needed to be just, truthful and fair, in everything he says or does. Then he recited Aya 7:32 of the Quran: "all beautiful things obtained from plants; animals are allowed. Also wearing clothes and lawfully earned foods are for the enjoyment of believers"[312]

Imprisonment and Death: The Historian Al-Fakhri states the reason for his imprisonment, saying that "there were people who carried false reports to the Caliph, particularly, the Imam's relatives who were jealous of the Imam. There were so many reports that he first imprisoned the Imam and then sent orders to put him to death. They then brought several reputable men to Karkh, to act as coroners, and to testify in public that he had died a natural death. He was buried in the cemetery of Quraysh, on the south side of Baghdad. A town called Kazimiyah (the town of the Imam Kazim (a.s) grew around the graveyard. A reputable Islamic school was instituted there. The school is still a source of scholarship for many students.[313]

Ali al-Reza (a.s)—the 8th Imam: (December 765 – 23 August 818)
Imam Reza (a. s) succeeded his father Musa Al-Kazim (a.s). In those days, there were many Shia revolts. The Caliph Al-Mamun thought of solving this problem, by appointing Al-Reza (a.s) as his successor, through whom he could conduct his governance without worrying about Shia uprisings. Al-Mamun first offered al-Reza (a.s) the Caliphate itself. Al-Reza (a.s), politely declined and said: "if Caliphate belongs to you, it is not right to give it to me as God has granted it to you. If it does not belong to you, then you don't have the right to give me something that is not yours. Mamun finally offered him being the Crown Prince. When Imam al-Reza (a.s) declined that position as well, al-Mamun threatened him to say "Your ancestor Ali (a.s) was chosen by the second Caliph to be in a six-member council, to elect the third Caliph, and ordered to kill any one of the six who didn't comply. If you do not accept the position of Crown Prince in my government, I will follow through on the same threat". al-Reza (a.s)

---

[312] Sharif al-Qurashi—2000—p.81,125,129,134,393.
[313] Donaldson, Dwight M. (1933). *The Shi'ite Religion: A History of Islam in Persia and Iraq.* BURLEIGH PRESS. pp. 152-160

finally agreed on the condition that he will be the crown prince in name and will have no part in governing.³¹⁴

Admonishment to his brother: When al-Reza (a.s) was summoned to Khurasan and reluctantly accepted the role of successor to the Caliph, Al-Mamun summoned the Imam's brother, Zayd, who had revolted and brought about a riot in Medina. Al-Mamun kept him free, as an honor to Ali al-Reza (a.s) and overlooked his punishment. One day, however, Ali al-Reza (a.s) heard Zayd praising himself in front of the people. Imam said to Zayd: "Sons of Ali (a.s). Ibn Abi Talib and Fatima (r.a) are worthy if they obey God's commands and shun sins and blunders. You think you are like Musa Al-Kazim (a.s), Ali (a.s), Husayn ibn Ali (a.s) and other Imams? Remember that if a member of the Ahl al-Bayt performs a good deed, he gets twice the reward. Because not only he performed virtuous deeds like others but also that he has kept the honor of Muhammad (pbuh). If he practices something bad and commits a sin, he has performed two sins. One is that he performed a terrible act, like the rest of the people, and the other one is that he has dishonored Muhammad (pbuh).³¹⁵

Death of Imam Reza: Al-Mamun thought he would solve the problems of Shia revolts, by naming al-Reza (a.s) as his successor. After finally being able to persuade al-Reza to accept this position, al-Mamun realized his mistake, for Shia began to gain even more popularity. Moreover, Arabs in Baghdad were furious when they heard that al-Mamun had changed the flag to green, in honor of the Imam. They feared the Caliphate will be taken from them and began plotting to depose Mamun and swore allegiance to Ibrahim ibn al-Mahdi, Mamun's uncle. When Mamun heard this, the Imam recommended to him to solve the problem by dismissing him from his position, but he did not listen and decided to return to Baghdad. On the way, his Vizier was assassinated. When they reached Tus, he had the Imam poisoned, according to Shia accounts. Mamun had the Imam buried next to his father, Harun al-Rashid, in Tus, the present- day

---

³¹⁴ Esposito, John L. (27 December 1999).-History of Islam—Oxford University Press.
³¹⁵ al-Saduq, al-Shaykh-2006—Uyun Akhbar Al-Reza—vol.2 Ansariyan Publications. p. 520.

Mashhad in Iran. He expressed extreme sorrow at Imam's death and stayed at the burial site for three days.[316]

Miracles of Imam Ali al-Reza: Abu Salt Harvie reported that the Imam was passing Din-Surkh, near Nishapur, when it was time for noon prayers. When no water was found for ablution, Imam dug some earth and water gushed out. This place is now called "Qadam Gah." People visit this place to drink from the spring, as a blessing, and as a cure from sickness and skin diseases. Footprints of the Imam are preserved here on a black stone.

Zaamin e Ahoo: The Imam came across a hunter in a jungle who was about to kill a deer. The deer was trying to escape. She saw the Imam (a.s) and requested the Imam to be her guarantor as she wanted to feed her baby. The Imam (a.s) asked the hunter to let her leave and told the hunter she will come back. The Imam waited with the hunter until the deer returned, with her young ones. The hunter was surprised, on seeing this unbelievable event and he set the deer free as a mark of respect for the Imam. (Akhbar al-Reza)

Imam e Zaamin: Imam Ali Reza (a.s) ended the ban on visiting the grave of Imam Husayn (a.s) in Karbala. Al-Mamun, the Caliph, allowed on one condition for anyone who wished to go, to get the permission of the Imam, who gave a guarantee to everyone. This historical event propagated his name as Imam e Zaamin, among the people. By order of the Caliph, coins had Imam's name inscribed on them. It became a custom of that time for people to keep those coins with Imam's name as a Tabarrok (blessing). Some wrapped the coin in cloth and tied it around their arms for safety when traveling. This cultural practice of Imam Zaamin still exists among the Muslims of South Asia, especially India and Pakistan. The reason is obvious. Persia ruled India (present-day Pakistan, India, and Bangladesh) for a long time. The people there, adopted many linguistic, religious, and

---

[316] Donaldson, Dwight M. (1933). *The Shi'ite Religion: A History of Islam in Persia and Iraq*—BURLEIGH PRESS. pp. 161–170.

cultural aspects of Persian traditions, an important one being the Imam Zaamin.[317]

Imam's Knowledge of all Languages: (Human, Birds, and animals): Suleman b. Ja'far said, "I was with Imam al-Reza (a.s) in the garden when suddenly, a sparrow came to Imam and began to chirp. The Imam said: "do you know what she is saying. She says a snake wants to eat my chicks. Imam gave a stick and told Suleman to kill the snake. Sulaiman said, I went to that house and killed the snake." Aba Salt Hirawi reported that Imam al-Reza (a.s) used to speak with people of different languages, in their own languages. One day, he said to the Imam (a.s): "O son of the Apostle of Allah! I am astonished at your knowledge of languages. Imam replied: I am Allah's authority over his creatures. He doesn't assign a person over his creatures unless he knows their language. Ismail Sindi came from India to see the Imam. He went to the Imam and greeted him. The Imam answered him in Sindhi. In the end, he asked the Imam, to ask God to inspire the Arabic language to him, The Imam rubbed his hand on Ismail's lips, and he was able to speak Arabic. In Basra, One of Imam's opponents named Amr bin Haddad wanted the Imam to prove his ability in different languages. The Imam asked Amr to bring in people speaking different languages. Several people were brought to the Imam, and he talked to all of them in their own languages, although the Imam never had any teacher to learn so many languages.[318]

Mohammad al-Jawad (a.s)—the 9th Imam: Al-Jawad (a.s) became Imam, at the age of 7 or 8. He acted like an adult and was very knowledgeable. Shias say he was like Jesus who assumed his prophetic mission in childhood.[319] After al-Reza (a.s) 's death, Al-Mamun summoned al-Jawad (a.s) to Baghdad to marry his daughter, Ummul Fadhl. This provoked strong objections from the Abbasids. According to Ya'qubi, al-Mamun

---

[317] Madelung—(1 August 2011).—Al-Reza—the eighth Imam—*Iranicaonline.org*. Retrieved 18 June 2014
[318] Nicholson, R.A.; Austin, R.W.J. (2012). Maruf al-Karkhi—. *Encyclopaedia of Islam* (2nd Edi.).
[319] Donaldson, Dwight M. (1933) The Shia religion—a history of Islam in Persia and Iraq—. AMS Press. pp. 190–197.

gave al-Jawad (a.s) a hundred thousand dirhams, saying: "surely, I would like to be a grandfather in the lineage of the Prophet. It is reported that al-Mamun's first meeting with al-Jawad (a.s) was coincidental. According to this account, al-Mamun was hunting when he happened upon a group of boys, including al-Jawad (a.s), who were playing. When al-Mamun's riders approached, the boys ran away, except al-Jawad (a.s). This prompted al-Mamun to stop his carriage and ask, "Boy, what kept you from running away with the others?" Al-Jawad (a.s) said:" the road was wide enough for you to pass, and I was not guilty of a crime, and you are not the sort of person who would harm an innocent person." After a while, the Caliph's hunting bird brought him a small fish. The Caliph hid the fish, returned and asked al-Jawad: "what is in my hand? "Al-Jawad (a.s) replied: "the creator made a small fish that was brought to the caliph, to test the progeny of the Prophet. "AL-Mamun was pleased with this answer and asked the child about his lineage. Afterward, the Caliph called a large gathering, during which al-Jawad (a.s) was asked many questions. Ibn Akhtam, the chief justice wanted to test al-Jawad. He asked about a person who hunts in Ihram (the pilgrimage garb). Al-Jawad, in response, asked if the game was inside or outside of the sanctified area; if the hunter was ignorant or aware of his sin; whether he was a minor or an adult; if it was his first sin or a repeated one; and whether he was sorry or not. The exchange of questions and answers evidently impressed the audience. The historian Kulaini recounted another episode in which the superintendent of the Shrine gave al-Jawad (a.s) a test that "lasted for several days, in which he answered thirty thousand questions to their great amazement!" [320] One year after his marriage to the Caliph's daughter, al-Jawad came back to Medina with umme Al Fazal, his wife, and devoted his life to teaching. Al-Jawad (a.s) also married Samaneh, who bore him a son and a successor, Ali al-Hadi who became the tenth Shiite Imam. After al-Mamun's death in 833, his successor, Al-Mu'tasim became the new Caliph.

---

[320] Tabatabai Muhammad Husayn (1981). *A Shi'ite Anthology*. Translated with Explanatory Notes by William Chittick Under the Direction of and with an Introduction by Hossein Nasr—State University of New York Press. pp. 49–50 & 138–139

Death: Al-Mu'tasim did not like Al-Jawad (a.s) and in 835, called him to Baghdad. AL-Jawad (a.s) left his son Ali-al-Hadi with his mother Samaneh in Medina, and his wife Ome Al Fazal accompanied him to Baghdad. They lived there for a year, and AL-Jawad (a.s) was poisoned by his wife, at the Caliph's instigation, and he died at the age of 25 years, the shortest lifespan among all the twelve Shia Imams.[321]

Ali al-Hadi (a.s)—the 10th Imam: Ali Al-Hadi (a.s) assumed the official role of Imamate at the age of 7 or 8, after his father's death in 830.[322] When Al-Moutawakel became Caliph, he summoned the Imam to Samarra. There, the Caliph and his successors maltreated him and, according to Shiite accounts, he was eventually, poisoned through the intrigue of Al-Mu'tazz, the Abbasid caliph, in 868, at the age of 38, and was buried in Samarra.

Summoning to Sammera: The governor of Medina, Abdullah ibn Mohammad, wrote to the Caliph, saying that the people gave him lots of money he could use to revolt. Al-Hadi sent a letter to Moutawakel defending himself against the accusations and complained about the governor. Convinced of the harmless nature of al-Hadi (a.s), Moutawakel wrote back that he had removed the governor from his post but asked al-Hadi (a.s) to please come to Sammera (a military camp) near Baghdad. The Caliph also instructed his Guard Commander to investigate charges against the Imam and bring the Imam with him. Yahya, the guard commander, searched the Imam's house and found nothing more than copies of the Quran and other religious books. Yahya states: "While I took him away, I offered him my services and showed him very high respect. One day, during the journey, when the sky was clear and the sun just rising, I saw the Imam put on a cloak, got on the horse, knotting its tail. Soon afterward, it started raining. Imam turned to me and said, "I did not have any special knowledge of the rain. I was brought up in a desert, and I know the winds preceding a rain. On our arrival in Baghdad, we first visited the governor who pulled me aside and said, "You have influence with the

---

[321] Sharif al-Qurashi 2005—pp. 210–212
[322] Madelung, Wilferd.—ali . al-Hadi—. *Encyclopedia of Iranica*. Retrieved September 14, 2015.

Caliph who might want to kill this man who is the family of the Prophet. So, if you encourage the Caliph to harm the Imam, the Prophet himself will be your enemy. I praised the Imam in front of Moutawakel, who then sent him gifts and treated him with respect. At Samarra, however, the Caliph did not see him at once or receive him, though he assigned a house for his residence. Even though Moutawakel had no reason to be suspicious of al-Hadi (a.s), he insisted that he stay in Samarra, under house arrest. It is said that Moutawakel once gave the order for his assassination. He sent for the Imam and ordered his guards to stand ready to strike him when he gave the order. The Imam, however, left the court unharmed. When he passed the guards, they threw down the swords and fell at the Imam's feet, saluting him. The Caliph asked why they disobeyed. They said they saw a man, with a drawn Sword by the Imam. He warned us we would all be slain if we tried to harm the Imam.[323]

Argument With ibn as-Sikkit: Once, al-Moutawakel organized a conference in his palace, with theologians and jurists. Ibn Sikkit asked the Imam why God had sent Moses with a rod and a white hand, sent Jesus with the healing power, and sent Muhammad (pbuh) with the Qur'an and the Sword? al-Hadi (a.s) replied, "In the times of Moses, people believed in magic. So, Moses was sent to defeat their magic to prove his authority. Jesus was sent with healing power when medicine was an important issue. And Allah sent Muhammad (pbuh) with the Quran and Sword in a time when the powerful things among people were Sword and poetry. Therefore, Muhammad (pbuh) came to them with the Quran to overwhelm their poetry, defeated their Sword, and proved his authority over them."[324]

Disrespect of the Imam and Caliph's Death: It is said that Moutawakel was envious of the Imam because Imam's position was exalted among the public. He wanted to belittle the Imam. His Vizier counseled him and recommended to refrain from opposition to the Imam. However, he ignored the advice and was keen to humiliate the Imam, Moutawakel

---

[323] 4=Donaldson, Dwight M. (1933). *The Shi'ite Religion: A History of Islam in Persia and Iraq*—. BURLEIGH PRESS. pp. 210–216.

[324] Donaldson, Dwight M. (1933). *The Shi'ite Religion: A History of Islam in Persia and Iraq*. BURLEIGH PRESS. pp. 210–216.

ordered that the Imam travel on foot, along with officials, while he himself remained mounted on the horse. The commander narrated that he noticed the Imam had almost suffered a heat stroke, was breathing heavily and sweating profusely. So, he approached the Imam, and tried to calm him down by saying "Your cousin (Moutawakel) did not intend to hurt you particularly." The Imam looked at Zuraqa and recited Qur'an: 11.65: "enjoy for three days. It is a promise." Zuraqa related the event to his friend, a Shia teacher who became alarmed at what the Imam had said and said Al-Moutawakel shall die or be killed after three days. I immediately went to the Caliph's palace and took all the money he owed me and deposited it with one of my friends. Within three days of that event, the Caliph was assassinated. One of the assassins was his son, al-Muntasir.[305]

Character: It is said that al-Hadi (a.s) showed extreme generosity, though, he, at times, had no money. A man came to the Imam saying he was in debt and needed Imam's help. The Imam gave him a note saying that he was in debt to the nomad and asked him to meet the Imam where he had a meeting, and to insist that the Imam pay back the recorded debt. The officials at the meeting reported the Imam's debt to Al-Moutawakel, who then, sent the Imam 30,000 dirhams, which he gave to the nomad.[325] In Twelver Shiism, he is described as endowed with the knowledge of the languages of the Persians, Slavs, Indians, and Nabataeans. Also, he could forecast unexpected storms and other events. He descended into a lion's cage, to prove that lions do not harm true descendants of Ali (a.s). Imam Reza performed a similar miracle during his time.[304]

Death. According to Tabatabai, al-Hadi (a.s) was poisoned at the behest of Caliph Al-Mu'tazz.[306]

Hassan al-Askari (a.s)—the 11th Imam: He was born in Medina during a period when his father Al-Hadi (a.s), the tenth Imam, was suspected of being involved in a conspiracy against Caliph al-Moutawakel. Al-Hadi (a.s) was taken to Samarra, along with his family, and they were kept there under house arrest. Al-Askari (a.s) spent most of his time, reading the Qur'an and the Sharia. According to Donaldson, al-Askari (a.s) must

---

[325] Qureshi—2007 pp. 386–388, 390,391,116

also have studied languages, because, in later years, he could speak many languages. It is said that even as a child, al-Askari (a.s) was religious minded. While playing, a passerby asked him if he would like a toy that he might play with. "No!" said al-Askari (a.s), "From the saying of God, "Did you then think that We had created you in vain." (Qur'an 23.115)[326]

His wife: Various legends relate to al-Askari (a.s) 's wife, Narjis Khatun (the mother of the twelfth Imam, Mohammad al-Mahdi (a.s). It is said that al-Askari (a.s) 's father, al-Hadi (a.s) the 10th Imam, wrote a letter in the 'script of Rom ', and gave it to his friend Bashar bin Suleiman, and asked him to go to a ferry terminal in Baghdad where boats from Syria unloaded, and female slaves sold. Imam instructed him to look for a shipowner Amr bin Yazid who had a slave girl who spoke the language of Rûm. Whenever a buyer approached her, she would say "Cursed be the man who unveils my eyebrow!" Her owner would then say in protest, "What option do I have? I am compelled to sell you?" "You will then hear the slave girl answer", said the Imam, "Let me choose my purchaser, that my heart may accept". When Bashar gave the letter, she read it and started crying. She said to her master, Amr ibn Yazid, "Sell me to the writer of this letter. If you decline, I shall kill myself". Price was agreed on 220 dinars the Imam had sent. When asked by Bashar, she described a dream she had, after which she escaped from her father's palace. The story is recorded in Donaldson's book. [327]

Imamate: Under the rule of the Abbasid Caliphs: Shia believed that Hassan al-Askari (a.s), became Imam at the age of 22. During the seven years of his Imamate, Hassan Al-Askari (a.s) lived, without any social contact, with his followers, due to restrictions imposed on him by the Abbasid Caliph who came to know from Shia sources that the eleventh Imam would have a son who was the promised Mahdi (a.s). Due to these fears, the Abbasis decided to end the Imamate and forced Imam Askari to live under strict house arrest all his life. He criticized the rulers for

---

[326] Donaldson, Dwight M. (1933). *The Shi'ite Religion: A History of Islam in Persia and Iraq*. BURLEIGH PRESS. pp. 217–222.

[327] Corbin, Henry (2001). *The History of Islamic Philosophy*. Translated by Liadain Sherrard with the assistance of Philip Sherrard. London and New York: Kegan Paul International. pp. 69–70

misappropriating the wealth of the nation and subjecting the people, under their rule, to injustice and tyranny. After the death of al-Askari (a.s)'s father, the Caliph Al-Mu'tazz summoned him to Baghdad where he was kept in prison. Most of Imam's prison time was during the reign of the succeeding Caliph, Al-Mu'tamid, who is known by Shia sources, as the main oppressor of the Imam. The Imam's death has been attributed to poisons administered by al-Mu'tamid.[328]

Divisions: Many Shia believed that the Imamate stopped with the seventh Imam, Musa Al-Kazim. Al-Askari (a.s)'s brother, Jafar, claimed to be the next Imam, after Askari (a.s)'s death. but he gave up his claim of Imamate soon afterward.[310]

Death: Hassan al-Askari (a.s) died in his house, at the age of 28, on 4 January 874, in Samarra. He was buried with his father.

The Promised Mahdi (a.s)—the 12th Imam: When Caliph Al-Mu'tamid heard about Imam al-Askari's illness, he sent physicians to inspect the Imam. After death, his female slaves were examined by the midwives, for pregnancy. On the day of Imam's death, his 4-5-year-old son Mohammad al-Mahdi (a.s) disappeared, known as the Minor Occultation, destined to reappear at end times, along with Jesus Christ (a.s) to fill the world with justice, peace, and to set up Islam as the global religion. Shias believe that the birth of al-Askari (a.s)'s son was hidden due to the threats of the time. It is said that when al-Askari (a.s)'s uncle (his father Imam al-Hadi (a.s)'s brother Ja'far) was about to say the prayer at his nephew's funeral, there appeared "a fair child, with curly hair, and shining teeth", who seized Jaffar's cloak and insisted on offering funeral prayers himself. A few days later, some Iranian pilgrims from Qum, unaware of al-Askari (a.s)'s death came. Jafar presented himself as the next Imam. Pilgrims said they would accept if he would tell them their names and how much money each one carried. While Ja'far was protesting, a servant of al-Mahdi (a.s) appeared,

---

[328] Al-Qureshi, Baqir Shareef—life of Imam Hadi—study and analysis—Abdullah al-Shahin. Qum: Ansariyan Publications. p. 82. Retrieved 25 September 2014.. .5= Koleini, Mohammad (1362). *Osule Kafi*. 1. Tehran: Islamie. pp. 509 & 285.

saying that his master had sent him to inform them of their names and how much money they had. It is believed that the Imam has been withdrawn from the eyes of men and that his life has been miraculously prolonged, just like the Prophet Khizr, who is alive and met with Prophet Moses, described in the Quran;18:65–82.[309]

The Mahdi: According to the Quran's interpretations, the Earth has always had a divinely appointed leader for every nation. Imam Jafar Sadiq said that there will always be a leader from the Ahl al-Bayt, according to his interpretation of the 7th verse of Surat Ar-Ra'd. "For every people, there is a guide." Quran (13:7) Also, another ayah of the Quran says: "We wrote in the book of Psalms, after the Torah that the righteous servants shall inherit the earth."—Quran (21:105).

Doctrine about Prolonged Life: Belief in a long life is justified by research in Scriptures and historical accounts, such as: "And We certainly sent Noah to his people, and he remained among them a thousand years minus fifty years, and the flood seized them while they were wrongdoers." Quran 29;14. Another example is about the People of the Cave who lived for 309 years, asleep in the cave. "And they remained in their cave for three hundred years and exceeded by nine." Quran18;25. Also, there is the longevity of Khizr whom Prophet Moses met during his journey.[329] The twelfth Imam, went into Occultation around 873-874, and will appear before the day of Judgement, to restore justice and equity on the Earth, alongside Jesus to fill the world with truth.[330] The Mahdi was born in Samarra in 868 and until 872, he lived under his father's care and tutelage. He was hidden from the public view, and only a few of the elite among the Shi'a were able to meet him.[331] He went into Occultation (ghaybat), and after that, he appeared only to his deputies (na'ib) and even then only in exceptional circumstances.[313] Mahdi chose Uthman ibn Sa'id ' Umari, one of the companions of his father and grandfather, as his first deputy through

---

[329] Kitab al-Ghayba, al-Shaykh al-Tusi, p 155
[330] Sachedina, Abdelaziz (1978). "A Treatise on the Occultation of the Twelfth Imam". p 109–124
[331] Tabatabai, Sayyid Muhammad Hossein (1975)-Shia Islam (PDF) (First ed.). State University of New York Press. pp. 210–211 (185–186 in the Ebook)

whom Mahdi answered his followers' questions. After Uthman, his son Mohammad was deputed, ad after Mohammad Abu'l Qasim Husayn Nawbakhti was appointed. The next appointee was Ali ibn Muhammad Simmari who died in 939, after which Imam's major Occultation began, and would continue until the day God grants permission to the Imam to manifest himself.[313] The Mahdi will appear in Mecca between the corner of the Kaaba and the station of Abraham.[332]

Shia Persecution by al-Mansur (Abbasid Caliph)—139-159 AH: Imam Jafar Sadiq lived during the rule of Abbasid Caliph al-Mansur. Many people approached the Imam to claim the caliphate, but he refused, saying he was content with preaching Islam at Medina. Despite his non-interference with politics, he was distrusted by the Caliph for his huge following. Before his death, Mansour gave a key to his wife and son and asked them to open the house only after his death. After his death, they opened the house and were shocked to see hundreds of dead bodies, stacked in rows, with tags in their ears. They belonged to the progeny of Fatima (r.a) and Ali (a.s). Such was the cruelty of Caliph al-Mansur.[333]

Shia Persecution by the Ottomans: After severe persecution of Shia Imams and their followers, by the Umayyad and Abbasid rulers, described in the earlier sections, the abuse of Shia Muslims, continued through succeeding periods of Sunni Ottoman Empire which mercilessly massacred thousands of Turkish Shias, and deported thousands to other countries of their realm. Sultan Bayezid and Selim were the worst of all the Ottoman Caliphs, described here. Sultan Bayezid (1481-1512) and Sultan Selim (1512-1520): ordered execution of Shia, captured during travel to Iran, and deported thousands to Greece and other regions of their caliphate. The real reason, according to historian Riza Yildirim, was that they were considered infidel. [334] Bayezid II's son Selim did not think his father had taken

---

[332] Momen, Moojan (1985). *An introduction to Shia Islam: the history and doctrines of Twelvers*- G. Ronald. pp. 75, 166–168.
[333] Masa'ibush Shia, vol. 5 p. 125-127 quoting at-Tabari Tarikh Al Umam wal Muluk.
[334] Rıza Yıldırım: *Turkomans between two empires: the origins of the Qizilbāsh identity in Anatolia (1447–1514)*, Bilkent University, 2008, p. 306, 318, 319

sufficiently hard measures against the Shia Qizilbāsh. He killed three of his brothers and deposed his father who was sympathetic towards the Shias. One of the first things Selim did, as sultan, was to get the Ottoman Mufti ibn Kemal (d. 1533), to issue a new fatwa against the Shia Qizilbāsh, to justify and legitimize their killing. He led an army of 200,000 men to attack the Safavid Empire. On the way, he Sought out and massacred some 40,000 Qizilbāsh, during his campaign. The Ottoman Empire waged war against the Safavid dynasty in 1514, which ended with an Ottoman victory. After Selim's reign, the later sultans continued the same harsh treatment towards Shia Qizilbāsh in Anatolia and Shia persecution continued until the end of the Ottoman caliphate. Along with Shia, Bektashi Sufi Order was also disbanded in 1826, by Caliph Mahmud. 4000-8000 Bektashi were killed in a battle and remaining beheaded, following a fatwa allowing extermination and prohibition of the Bektashi Sufi Order.[335]

Turkish Shia Persecution: Due to Ottoman persecution, Alevis sought refuge in the mountains to avoid attracting attention. Therefore, most Alevis live in the mountains of Turkish province Tunceli. Even in present day Turkey, Alevis hide their religion and pray at night, to avoid questions like why they do not pray in mosques or fast during Ramadan. Alevis demand to be accepted as they are instead of being redefined and questioned continuously.[336]

A Bastion for the Shias: Noticing the plight of Shia Muslims in the region and the world, and persecution of Shias, the Safavid King Ismael reunified Iran and Azerbaijan as an independent state, the Shia Bastion, in 1501 and established Twelver Shia as the official religion. Both nations still have large Shia majorities, and the Shia percentage of Azerbaijan's population is second only to that of Iran.[337]

---

[335] Sahabettin Tekindağ: *Yeni Kaynak ve Vesikaların Işığı Altında Yavuz Sultan Selim'in İran Seferi, Tarih Dergisi, Mart 1967, sayı: 22, s. 56 i Saim Savaş: XVI.*
[336] Saim Savaş: XVI. *Asırda Anadolu'da Alevîlik,* Vadi Yayınları, 2002, p. 86–118.
[337] *Andrew J. Newman, Safavid Iran: Rebirth of a Persian Empire, IB Tauris (March 30, 2006).*

Shia Persecution by Regions: There has been widespread persecution of Shia Muslims all over the world ever since the demise of the Prophet(pbuh) in 632. As the reader probably noticed that Shia Imams were exemplary individuals with profound knowledge of the Quran and the Sunnah of the Prophet. They were extremely kind, pious, generous, non-violent, and benevolent personalities of their times, and did not revolt against the rulers despite large followings and immense financial resources due to the payment of Khums by their followers. Of course, they always objected to the injustice and tyranny of the rulers. After the 12th Imam Mahdi (a.s) went into occultation, the Shia Muslims launched no insurrections against the governments and patiently tolerated all kinds of persecutions, by the majority Sunni Muslims, until 1979 when Imam Khomeini led a revolution against the Shah of Iran who had terrorized his people by his cruel policies and anti-Islam legislation. Following the Iranian revolution, Shia persecution has intensified in various parts of the world, spearheaded by the Saudi/Salafis who consider Shias as apostates, who deserve to be killed. In the following sections, Shia persecution in different parts of the world will be discussed.

Kashmir (India): Shias in India have been persecuted by Sunni Rulers and Mughal Emperors. Shias of Kashmir have been persecuted for centuries by Sunni Invaders, resulting in the killing of many Shias, plunder, looting and murder, known as Taarajs (Shia massacres) which took place between 15th to 19th centuries in 1548,1585,1635,1686,1719 1741,1762,1801,1830 and 1872, when Shias were subjected to tyranny. Large numbers were killed, and their properties plundered. During Mughal Emperor Aurangzeb's reign, Shias of North Karnataka were forced to leave their cities. Of course, in present-day India, Shias are free to practice their faith. However, Shias in Kashmir are still not allowed to conduct Ashura rituals, which is against the Indian constitution, which guarantees freedom of religion.[338]

---

[338] Shias of Kashmir- Socio Political dilemma-Kashmir Observer- Retrieved 2010-07-01.

China: Zaidi Shias fled from Umayyad repression and came to China in the eighth century. In Xinjiang, foreign slaves were Ismaili Shias called Ghalchi. They used to be traded by other Turkic Muslims.[339]

Bahrain: The population's majority are Shia Muslims, being 70-75% of the population. The ruling Al-Khalifa Family, who are Sunni Muslims, arrived in Bahrain from Qatar at the end of the eighteenth century. Shiites alleged that Al Khalifa did not gain legitimacy in Bahrain and set up a system of "political apartheid based on racial, sectarian, and tribal discrimination. They are denied rights of assembly, speech, and Worship. There are currently hundreds of Shias under detention in Bahrain. Security Forces consist of Sunnis from Syria, Pakistan, and Baluchistan who get Bahraini citizenship easily, much to the displeasure of the Shiite population.[340]

Egypt: There are 2-3 million Shias in Egypt. They are persecuted by the authorities due to their religion. A December 2012 report by UNHCR showed that Shia are not allowed to observe Muharram rituals in Egypt. Police forcibly removed Shia worshippers from Cairo's Al-Hussein mosque, accusing them of performing barbaric rituals at Ashura.[341]

Indonesia: It is a Muslim majority country where most Muslims are Sunni Muslims. In December 2011 a Shia boarding school was attacked and burnt.[342] Amnesty International recorded many incidents of intimidation and violence against the Shia who were forced to return to their village in East Java. Amnesty urged the government to protect the minority Shia in Indonesia.[324]

Malaysia: The constitution of Malaysia guarantees freedom of religion and Malaysia is a secular state. 61% of Malaysians are Muslims, following

---

[339] Marshall Broomhall (1910). Islam in China: A Neglected Problem. Morgan & Scott, Limited. pp. 20..
[340] Nakash, Yitzhak (2006).- Reaching for Power—Shia in Arab World—(PDF). Princeton University Press. p.24.
[341] Col. (ret.) Dr. Jacques Neriah (September 23, 2012).—Egypt's shia Minority- JCPA.
[342] Amnesty Int. urges Shia minority protection. January 14, 2012.

the Shafii school. Shia Islam is banned in Malaysia. The ISA (Internal Security Act) was used on several occasions to target Shia in Malaysia. Ten Shias were arrested in 1997 under the ISA and another six suffered the same fate in October 2000. In December 2010, 200 Shia were arrested by the Selangor Islamic Religious Department, for celebrating Ashura under the Selangor state sharia criminal enactment law. Four years later, 114 Shia were arrested by the Perak Islamic Religious Affairs Department, with assistance from the Malaysian police.[343]

Pakistan: Saudis had funded Jamaat-i-Islami Educational networks since the 1960s. The party was active in the Saudi-founded Muslim World League. And "segments of the party "followed Saudi Salafism", as their religion. According to a 2008 US diplomatic cable released by WikiLeaks, in one part of Pakistan (the Multan, Bahawalpur, and Dera Ghazi Khan Divisions of southern Punjab),government and non-governmental sources claimed that financial support estimated at nearly $100 million annually was making its way to Deobandi and Ahle-Hadith clerics in the region from "Islamic charitable" organizations in Saudi Arabia and the United Arab Emirates, ostensibly with the direct support of those governments.[344] The Deobandi and Ahle-Hadith madrasa network indoctrinated students into jihadi philosophy and ultimately sent them to terrorist training camps in the Federally Administered Tribal Areas (FATA). With Saudi and the Gulf countries funding, religious schools (madrasas) rapidly expanded during the 1980s in Pakistan, usually Deobandi in doctrine, which is allied with the Saudi Salafi doctrine of Saudi Arabia. Critics (Dilip Hiro) complained of intolerance in teachings, as reflected in the chant, at the morning student assembly at radical madrasas, saying: "When people deny our faith, ask them to convert and if they don't, destroy them utterly. Sufi Mohammad, a former member of Jamaat-e-Islami (JI) fought in the Afghan jihad and later founded Tehreek-e-Nifaz-e-Shariat-e-Mohammedi (Movement for the Enforcement of Islamic Law) in 1992. Described as "an ardent believer in the Saudi Salafi school of thought," he has remained

---

[343] 16 arrested for spreading Shia teachings—says minister Bernama—. themalaysianinsider.com. Archived on 2013-11-10.

[344] Roul, Animesh (June 26, 2015).—growing ISIS influence in Pakistan fuels violence—Terrorism Monitor. 13 (13). Retrieved 30 June 2015

associated with Saudi-sponsored groups, from the Afghan theater of 1980-88". The group bombed the statues of Buddhas in Bamiyan, in Afghanistan. His organization has also forced the closure of some development organizations, accusing them of spreading immorality by employing female staff.[345]

Shia Killings in Pakistan: From 2012 to 2015, 1900 Shias were killed in bombings and gun attacks. Shias make up 5-20% of the Muslim population in Pakistan. 8000 Hazara Shias were killed in Quetta by Lashkar-e-Jhangvi and Sipah-e-Sahaba, Pakistan which were Sunni militant organizations affiliated with Al-Qaeda and the Taliban. Shia doctors, businessmen and other professionals have been targeted in Karachi by Sunni Muslim militants regularly. In the northern areas of Pakistan, such as Parachinar and Gilgit, Baltistan, Muslim militants have continuously been attacking and killing Shias.[346]

Saudi Arabia: In modern-day Saudi Arabia, the Saudi Salafi rulers limit Shia political participation to a few notable people who get certain privileges for their ties to the government, and in turn, are expected to control their community. Saudi Shias make up 15% of the 28 million Saudis (estimate 2012). The majority of Saudi Shias live in the oases of al-Hasa and Qatif in the oil-rich areas of the Eastern Province, but are mostly hand to mouth.[347] There have been no Shia cabinet ministers, mayors, or Police officials. None of the 300 Shia girls' schools have a Shia principal. In Dammam, a quarter of whose residents are Shia, Ashura is banned, and there is no Shia call to prayer. According to Journalists, the Shiite grievances are not merely doctrinal issues but stem from socioeconomic deprivation, because of religious repression and political marginalization

---

[345] Rampant killings of Shia by extremists in Pakistan—Human Rights Watch. 30 June 2014. Retrieved 16 November 2014.

[346] Barelvi against Deobandi/Wahhabi terrorism in Pakistan—by AU Khan. Retrieved 12 December 2013. 7= Produced by Charlotte Buchen.—Sufism under attack in Pakistan—(video). The New York Times. Retrieved 21 May 2012.

[347] Nasr (2006)-Saudi Arabia's Shias press for rights—. p. 84, 236, 237—retrieved 19 July 2012

bordering on apartheid." In January 2016, Shiite cleric Sheikh Nimr called for pro-democracy demonstrations, resulting in his execution, along with 47 other Saudi citizens, by the Criminal Court on terrorism charges.[348] In May 2017, in response to protests, the Saudi military besieged the Shia town of Al-Awamiyah, and indiscriminately shelled the neighborhoods with airstrikes, mortar, and artillery fire, along with snipers, shooting residents. Dozens of Shia civilians were killed, including three-year-old and two-year-old children. The Saudi government claimed it was fighting the terrorists. On July 26, 2017, Saudi authorities began refusing to give emergency services to the wounded civilians. Saudi Arabia has also not given humanitarian help to trapped citizens of Awamiyah. President of the Quran Council and two cousins of executed al-Nimr were also killed by Saudi security forces, in Qatif in 2017.[349]

---

[348] Saudi execution of Shia cleric sparks outrage—.the Guardian 2 January 2016.
[349] Saudi forces kill head of Qur'an Council in Qatif and kill Sheikh Nimr's cousins in Qatif. Press TV report.

CHAPTER 6

Spread of Saudi Salafism

Spread of Saudi Salafism gradually turned into Global Terrorism, because the very teachings of Saudi Salafism breed intolerance and violence against non-Saudi Salafis that includes Muslims who do not agree with them. This includes the Shia Muslims, the Sufi Muslims, as well as Christians, Jews, other faiths, and lifestyles, considering them apostates who deserve to be killed. Wherever the ideology of Saudi Salafism reached, it resulted in discord and strife among communities, which were peaceful and where people of different faiths tolerated and respected each other. Members of terrorist groups believed that they were engaged in a holy war against the infidels; if killed, paradise was guaranteed for them. This Jihadi fervor motivated all the armed groups that had been involved in a Shia Genocide in Iraq, Syria, Afghanistan, Pakistan, East Africa, Indonesia, Russia and Nigeria since 2003, when the terrorist groups were propped up by Saudi Arabia, initially to fight the Shia in Iraq. As of 2019, the Saudi-backed terrorist groups have been defeated in Iraq and Syria due to relentless efforts of the Iranian forces, Russia, and the Hezbollah of Lebanon but sporadic incidents of terror by ISIS still exist in Iraq, Syria, and other places, as of June 2019. However, there is still violence in Pakistan, and Afghanistan where the Saudi-backed Taliban are a menace to the governments. Also, Boko Haram is still active in Nigeria where atrocities are being committed by the group. All the Sunni militant groups such as al Qaeda, ISIS, al Nusra, Taliban, al Shabab, Boko Haram, Let,

LeJ of Pakistan, and the Jamaat Islami of Indonesia, followed the doctrine of Takfir of Saudi Salafi Islam, by which killing of non-Saudi Salafis is sanctioned. All these groups have been receiving overt and covert support from charities or individuals in Saudi Arabia, Qatar, UAE, or Kuwait, with the tacit approval of their governments, to spread Saudi Salafi Islam, by coercion. More than $75 billion was spent to propagate Saudi Salafi Islam in the world, during the period 1982 to 2005. Ideology was spread through mosques religious schools and Islamic centres, which were set up in Muslim and non-Muslim countries. The institutions consisted of about 1500 mosques, 210 Islamic centers, and 2000 schools. Saudis also distributed 138 million copies of the Qur'an (the central religious text of Islam) worldwide. [350] In the 1980s, the Saudi embassies had attaches who oversaw construction in their countries. The Saudi Arabian government-funded Muslim World League, and several relief organizations to preach Saudi/ Salafi doctrine, and other allied foreign ideologies such as Salafism of Muslim Brotherhood and Jamaat -e-Islami of Pakistan and Indonesia, which opposed Shia and Sufi Muslim practices. Followers of Saudi Salafism and Salafism of the Muslim Brotherhood fought together in the Afghan Jihad of the 1980s, against the Soviet Union. After the withdrawal of Soviet forces from Afghanistan, the Jihadi fighters went on to fight Jihad against Muslim governments and civilians in their own and other countries.[351]

Tools of Propagation: Even if the introduction of the Saudi/Salafi brand of Islam, was not ill-motivated, the narrow view about the other faiths and encouragement of violence against those who did not agree, gave rise to terrorism. This section deals with how the ideology was spread and what effect it had in various countries. Spread of Saudi /Salafi doctrine,

---

[350] late king [Fahd] spent 'north of $75 billion' in his efforts to spread Wahhabi Islam. According to Ottaway, the king boasted on his personal Web site that he established 200 Islamic colleges, 210 Islamic centers, 1500 mosques, and 2000 schools for Muslim children in non-Islamic nations. The late king also launched a publishing center in Medina that by 2000 had distributed 138 million copies of the Koran worldwide.

[351] Armstrong, Karen-27 Nov.2014—Wahhabism to ISIS.

throughout the world, has been done in the following, very practical and effective ways:

Religious Funding: From 1975 to 2005, the Saudi Arabia government spent £49 billion on free copies of the Quran and religious texts, distributing them to all the mosques and Islamic cultural centers throughout the world, from Africa to Indonesia, including European cities.[352]

Hajj: The most significant and most sacred annual assembly of Muslims on earth, takes place in Mecca. Since 1979, over 5 million Muslims have been coming for pilgrimage, each year. Saudi control of Hajj, granting or denying the Hajj visa, is an essential influence over Muslims who must perform Hajj at least once during the entire lifetime.[353]

Education: Saudis granted attractive paid scholarships in Saudi Universities and institutes, to train scholars in Islam but analysts, like David Commins, say they propagated Saudi Salafi, rather than Salafi doctrine. Most scholars were probably lured by highly attractive financial incentives, to join the Saudi institutes. [354]The Islamic University of Medina was set up as an alternative to Al-Azhar of Cairo when the latter was under Gamal Nasser's control in 1961. Some famous figures of Islam attended the Islamic University of Medina. For example, the later Grand Mufti of Egypt Allama Tantawi spent 4 years there and became a staunch supporter of the Saudi/ Salafi Islam.[355] Following the October 2002 Bali Bombing,

---

[352] the involvement of Salafism/Saudi Salafism in the support and supply of arms to rebel groups around the world"—(PDF). European Parliament - DIRECTORATE-GENERAL FOR EXTERNAL POLICIES OF THE UNION. June 2013.

[353] Keppel- Jihad-2002—p.75. 2=Lacey, Robert (2009). *Inside the Kingdom-: Kings, Clerics, Modernists, Terrorists, and the Struggle for Saudi Arabia.* Viking. p. 95.

[354] Murawiec, Laurent (2003, 2005)- Princes of Darkness—Rowman & Littlefield. p. 56. Retrieved 2 April 2015.

[355] Abdel Nasser, Walid (2011) [1994]. "The Attitudes Towards Selected Muslim Countries".—islamic movement in Egypt—Routledge. ... it is important to refer to the position of Sheikh 'Abdul-Halim Mahmud (d.1978) Sheikh of al-'Azhar ... towards Saudi Arabia. Sheikh Mahmud had an ideological affinity with the Saudi interpretation of Islam. Due to his links with Saudi Arabia, he moved

an Indonesian commentator (Jusuf Wanandi) worried about the danger of "extremist influences of Saudi Salafism from Saudi Arabia" in the educational system of Indonesia.

Muslim World League: World Muslim League has been a crucial tool, to propagate the Saudi Salafi doctrine of Islam. It was set up in 1962. It played a pioneering role in supporting Islamic associations, mosques, and investment plans. The organization funded the construction of mosques, financial reliefs for Muslims, affected by natural disasters and the distribution of copies of the Qur'an. The League says that they reject all acts of violence and promote dialogue with the people of other cultures, within their understanding of Sharia, but they have been the subject of several ongoing counterterrorism investigations in the U.S., related to Hamas, al Qaeda, and other terrorist groups. The League founded the International Islamic Relief Organization in 1978. It opened branch offices around the globe. It developed a closer association between Saudi Salafism and Salafism; with Muslim Brotherhood of Egypt and Syria; Ahle-Hadith and the Jamaat-Islami of Pakistan, to combat Sufism and "innovative" popular religious practices in their regions and to reject the West, and Western ways which were so harmful to Muslim values.[356] In October 2001, Newsweek writer Evan Thomas reported that Osama bin Laden had used the two interrelated charities-the International Islamic Relief Organization and Muslim World League, to finance his operations. The organizations were omitted, from the list of groups sanctioned by the U.S., to avoid embarrassing the Saudi government.[357] In 2008, MWL invited Yusuf al-Qaradawi to speak at their conference in Mecca in June 2008. During his speech, he said: "I would never sit with Jews on one platform and never hold dialogue with those who do us harm or support Israel."

Scholarships: The Funding available to those who support Saudi Salafi views, gave incentive to scholars around the world, to benefit from Saudi Funding." An example is a salary for "a Muslim scholar spending a

---

closer to al-Ikhwan al-Muslimeen. This position contrasted with the position of al-'Azhar in the 1960s

[356] archive.adl.org/ terrorism/Muslim world league
[357] Intelligence: Gearing Up for A Shadow Struggle. Thomas, Evan.—Newsweek.

six-month sabbatical" at a Saudi Arabian university, which is more than 10 years salary for a teacher of Azhar University in Egypt.[358]

Hajj Visa and Critics of Saudi Salafism: A powerful tool available to the Saudi government is the power to grant or deny, a visa for Hajj. [359]Also, Books by critics of Saudi Salafism have been made scarce by Saudis who have "successfully prevented the republication" or otherwise "buried" copies of their work, according to author Abou El Fadl. Examples of such authors are, early Salafi Scholar Rashid Rida; a Yemeni jurist, Mohammad al-Amir al-Husseini al-San'ani; and Imam Mohammad Ibn Abd al-Wahhab's own brother and critic, Sulayman Ibn Abd al-Wahhab.[360]

Migrant Workers: More than five million foreign workers from Muslim majority countries worked in Saudi Arabia and the Gulf states, in the 1980s. They returned to their countries, with lots of savings, and following the strict Saudi practices learned in Saudi Arabia such as gender segregation, head to toe abayas for women, and men growing long uncut beards.[341]

Revenge of the Migrants' Employer? Bangladesh government declared the Jamaat-e-Islami, a terrorist organization for its role in the Liberation War. Saudi Arabia disapproved of the imminent hangings of the members

---

[358] Abou El Fadl, Khaled (2005). The Great Theft: Wresting Islam from the Extremists. Harper San Francisco. p. 74.
[359] Kepel- Jihad-2002—p.75, 72
[360] Lacey, Robert (2009). *Inside the Kingdom: Kings, Clerics, Modernists, Terrorists, and the Struggle for Saudi Arabia.* Viking. p. 95. In 1984 the presses of Medina's massive $130 million King Fahd Holy Koran Printing Complex rolled into action. That year and every year thereafter, a free Koran was presented to each of the two million or so pilgrims who came to Mecca to perform their hajj, evidence of Wahhabi generosity that was borne back to every corner of the Muslim community. 'No limit', announced a royal directive, 'should be put on expenditures for the propagation of Islam.' The government allocated more than $27 billion over the years to this missionary fund, while Fahd devoted millions more from his personal fortune to improve the structures of the two holy sites in Mecca and Medina. Vast white marble halls and decorative arches were raised by the Bin Laden company at the king's personal expense to provide covered worshiping space for several hundred thousand more pilgrims.

of the party. As a result, the number of workers in Saudi Arabia was cut to only 14,500 people since 2009.[361]

Spread of Saudi Salafism and Resultant Terrorism (by Country): As said before, the spread of Saudi Salafism, resulted in intolerance of other faiths, and lifestyles, giving rise to violence and killing, wherever the ideology was introduced. It transformed peaceful societies into sectarian groups that started fighting each other. This occurred in almost all countries where Saudi money was invested in building mosques, cultural centers, schools, and universities. Due to massive investments, the governments, politicians, and the military could not fathom the motives and consequences of such investments. Even the most learned scholars could not believe that the Custodians of the two Holy Mosques of Mecca and Medina, would mean any ill-will against the Muslim Ummah, but malice and inimical activity of investors was intentional, due to their extreme hatred for non-Saudi Salafis, including Muslims of other sects, Jews, and Christians. This section describes the terrorist incidents that took place in various countries after Saudi Salafism was introduced there.

Tajikistan and Uzbekistan: The leadership of the Islamic Movement of Uzbekistan (IMU), had been influenced by the Saudi Salafi and Deobandi traditions. In 1995, the IMU head, Jumma Namangan, traveled to Saudi Arabia, to undergo "religious and intelligence training from Saudi intelligence." The government of Tajikistan and Uzbekistan accused IMU

---

[361] «Revenge of the migrants› employer?». *March 26th, 2013 economist.com. Retrieved 8 April 2014. Since 2009 Bangladesh has been sending to Saudi Arabia an average of only 14,500 people ... Bangladesh appears somehow to have fallen out of favour as a source of labour with the Saudis. ... Saudi Arabia silently disapproves of the imminent hangings of the leadership of the Jamaat-e-Islami, the religious party that serves as a standard-bearer for its strand of Islam in Bangladesh. ... The current prime minister, Sheikh Hasina, ... has brought back an explicitly secular constitution under which religious politics has no space. It will not have escaped the Saudis' notice that Bangladesh's foreign minister likened the Jamaat, a close ally of theirs, to a terrorist organisation in a briefing with diplomats in Dhaka on March 7th. ... As long as relations are what they are with the Saudis, Bangladesh must keep scrambling to find alternative venues for its migrant labourers. ... as far as Saudi retribution is concerned.*

of training suicide bombers who bombed a police station in Khujand on September 3, 2010, killing two police officers and injuring 25. IMU also launched attacks in Tashkent and Bukhara in March and April 2004, killing 10 police officers, four civilians, and 33 militants. U.S. and Israeli embassies in Tashkent were also attacked, on July 30, 2004, killing two Uzbek security guards. IMU had been funded by the Taliban and al-Qaeda, which are both funded by organizations in Saudi Arabia and the Gulf countries, as shown under these groups in the relevant sections of the book.[362]

Finland: A proposal to construct a large mosque, in Helsinki to "unite all Finnish Muslims" had met with resistance because it is to be built by Bahrain and Saudi Arabia, followers of Saudi Salafism. In Brussels, Saudi-trained preachers taught courses on Islam and supported German Saudi / Salafi Muslims through the mosques. Their preaching was aimed at propagating the radical ideology of Saudi Salafism, which supports terrorism.[363]

Britain: Extremist ideas were spread by Islamic study centers linked to British universities and backed by multi-million-pound donations from Saudi Arabia and its Muslim organizations. A new report, published by Ben Leach, on 13April 13 2008 in the Telegraph, claimed eight universities in England had received £233.5 million from Saudi and other Arab sources, since 1995. Prof Glees said the universities were propagating anti-western views held by fundamentalists, causing security threats. In June 2017, after the London Bridge Attack, Jeremy Corbyn said that serious conversations are needed with Saudi Arabia and other Gulf states which have funded the extremist ideology. in July 2017, a report by Henry Jackson Society said that the Saudi-sponsored mosques were spreading the Saudi Salafi ideology of terrorism and that the number of these mosques had increased from, 68 in 1997, to 110 in 2014.[364]

---

[362] Rashid, Ahmed (14 January 2002). They are only sleeping—militant Islamists are not going away—Retrieved 6 February 2016.
[363] Thomas-Johnson, Amandla (2 May 2017). Bahrain backed mosque sparks row in Finland—*Middle East Eye*. Retrieved 23 June 2017.
[364] Extremism fears over donations-13 April 2008.

Europe: Islamic terrorist attacks included: 1985 El Descanso bombing, killing 18 people in Madrid; 1995 Paris Metro bombings killing 8 people; 11March 11 2004- bombings of trains in Madrid, where 191 people were killed; July 7 2005- London bombings, of public transport, which killed 52 commuters; Hebdo shooting in Paris killed 12, in reaction to cartoons of Muhammad (PBUH); A series of attacks on November 13 2015, claimed by ISIS, which killed 129 people in restaurants, at the Bataclan theatre and the Stade de France;[365] March 22 2016—ISIS terrorists bombed the Zaventem Airport and a metro station in Brussels Belgium, killing 32 people; Most of the deaths by terrorism in Europe from 2001 to 2014 were caused by Islamic terrorism, perpetrated by terrorists of Saudi/Salafi ideology.[366]

Russia: Since 2000, Russia had also experienced many suicide bombings that killed hundreds of people in various parts of Russia, including Moscow. Caucasus Emirate and its affiliates, allied with Salafist Jihadism, aligned with Saudi Salafism of Saudi Arabia, carried out many attacks in Russia. The Emirate sought to advance the cause of Allah, on the earth, by waging War against the Russian government.[367]

Balkan States: Saudi Salafism began to spread among the Muslims of the Balkans, after the Yugoslav Wars. Sources in governments of Bosnia, Kosovo, and Albania had confirmed that Saudi Salafism was being preached through the Saudi-funded mosques in these countries, particularly in remote villages. In the Muslim majority state of Albania, 200 mosques had been built, and King Fahd donated one million copies of the Quran in the Albanian language. The preachers taught the Saudi Salafi doctrine of Islam. The teaching emphasized Saudi Salafism, as the only true doctrine which considers tolerance as being a sign of weakness. It preached hatred

---

[365] Dearden, Lizzie (15 November 2015).—Paris Attack—ISIS warns : this is just the beginning after killing at least 127 people in French capital—The Independent. Retrieved 17 November 2015

[366] Shane, Scott (2016-08-25). Saudis and Extremism—both the arsonists and firefighters—The New York Times. Retrieved 2017-06-22

[367] Darion Rhodes—Salafist /Takfiri Jihadism—ideology of Caucasus Emirate— International Institute for Counter-terrorism, March 2014.

of the Western culture as the cardinal part of the true religion. In Sarajevo, Bosnia, Saudi Arabia financed the King Fahd Mosque, which was a $28 million complex that included a sports and cultural center. According to an intelligence report, "the mosque was well financed and was the most radical mosque in the whole of Bosnia-Herzegovina. All those guys who took part in terrorist activity in Bosnia-Herzegovina were part of that mosque"[368]

Bosnia and Herzegovina: During the Bosnian War, there were several strict Muslim special units. The Bosnian mujahideen unit was made up of foreign fighters and radical Bosnians.[369]

Kosovo: There is a Muslim population in Kosovo who followed 'liberal' and 'moderate' Islam of Hanafi school. Saudi Salafism, which is the religion of Saudi Arabia, had gained a foothold in Kosovo, through Saudi diplomacy. Saudi Arabia paid for new mosques, and Saudi-educated imams arrived in 1999. During the U.N. administration, Saudi Arabian organizations, set up a cultural foothold in Kosovo, and 98 Saudi Salafi schools were set up. Hundreds of Kosovo Albanians joined the Jihad in the Middle East.[370] The Saudi Joint Committee for Collection of Donations for Kosovo and Chechnya, sent $45 million to Kosovo, according to the Embassy of Saudi Arabia in the U.S., to build mosques and schools. 240 mosques had been built since the 1999 war, and Saudis sent 388 teachers to preach Saudi/Salafism. The Kosovo police arrested about 40 suspected Islamist militants on August 11, 2014. By April 2015, 232 Muslims of Kosovo had joined ISIS to fight in Syria.[371]

The Republic of Macedonia, and Croatia: On April 12, 2012, five Macedonians were killed by Albanian Islamic fundamentalists (of Saudi

---

[368] The Balkans—a hub of worldwide terrorist network?
[369] FBI—attack on US Embassy in Bosnia in 2011—Fbi.gov. Retrieved 2012-04-29. 3=Bosnian Imam on trial for ISIS recruitment. middle east updates.
[370] Mincheva & Gurr 2013—, p. 34,35.5=Norman, Laurence (11 August 2014). Kosovo arrests 40 Islamic militants—WSJ.
[371] Yosef Budinski (4 May 2011) Bin Laden—Crown Publishing Group. pp. 398–403.-3=Lyubov Grigorova Mincheva; Ted Robert Gurr (3 January 2013).—crime-terror alliance—. Routledge. pp. 34

Salafi Ideology) near the capitol. Croatian military captured Talat Fouad Qassim, a vital member of the al-Gama al-Islamiyah terrorist organization of Egypt when he attempted to enter Bosnia. Qassim was soon transferred to Egypt with the active help of Croatia. Because of that, a decision was made by them to commit a terrorist attack, called the 1995 Rijeka bombing. The attack took place on October 20, 1995 in Rijeka, Croatia. The next day, representatives of the al-Gama al-Islamiyah terrorist organization from Egypt, claimed responsibility for the attack.[372]

Iraq: Saudi-sponsored jihadis of al-Qaeda, ISIS, and others had been directly involved in the Iraqi Civil War, since 2003, wreaking havoc on civilian and government targets, causing widespread instability in that country. The U.N. accused ISIS of systematic and widespread violence, including holding some 3,500 women and children as slaves. On July 10, 2015, ISIS militants forced victims to lie down in central Mosul in front of a large crowd. A bulldozer was driven over them. On June 4: Two young males and a 60-year-old man, were thrown from a building in Ninawa, for homosexual acts. On 1-2 August: I.S.I.S militants killed 19 women in Mosul, for refusing to have sex with fighters. On 21June: Women were offered as sex slaves, to the top three winners of a Quran memorization competition in Mosul. On 23June: I.S. group video showed men placed in a car and hit by a rocket-propelled grenade; men drowned in a cage; men decapitated with explosives. On 12-15 July: Four imams in Mosul, were accused, by self-appointed ISIS court, of conducting forbidden tarawihs, during Ramadan prayers. They were shot in the head.[373]

East Africa (Somalia): Al-Shabaab is a militant jihadist terrorist group based in East Africa. It was allied with al-Qaeda and participated in the Somali Civil War and was being used by Egypt to destabilize Ethiopia and to attract converts from Christian Kenya. Al-Shabaab terrorists attacked.

---

[372] Macedonia—5 albanians charged with Terrorism—Adnkronos.com—Retrieved 2014-07-12.. 2= Euronews—5 killed in Macedonia.
[373] Altran, Scott-2006—the Moral Logic and growth of suicide terrorism—(PDF). The Washington Quarterly. 29 (2): 131. Archived on June 23, 2015. 2=Report on terrorist incidents—2006.

Garissa University College, using light arms and suicide vests, killing more than 145 Kenyans, most of whom were students.[374]

Sudan: According to Al Jazeera, as of 2012, more than 60% of Sudanese were still affiliated with Sufism, but 10% were tied to Saudi Salafi groups, and that number was growing. It is a poor, Muslim-majority country, located close to the Hijaz province of Saudi Arabia and has had close relations with the kingdom. The Sudanese belonged to the Sufi interpretation of Islam, different from Saudi Salafism. Over the years, this changed, with labor migration, to Saudi Arabia and Gulf states. Sudanese workers returned as successful, affluent, high-prestige religious conservatives. Hassan al-Turabi and his National Islamic Front (funded and strengthened by the Saudis) grew in influence in the 1980s. and in 1989 were brought to power in a coup d'état staged by Omar al-Bashir.[356]

Kenya: Kenya faced an ongoing terrorist threat from the Somalia-based terrorist group al-Shabaab, against which the Kenya Defense Forces engaged in military operations in Somalia, since 2011, as part of the African Union Forces in Somalia (AMISOM). Kenya continued to face serious terrorism challenges, within its own borders in 2015. Most notably, the April al-Shabaab attack on Garissa University College killed at least 147, mostly students, and there were other fatal attacks, particularly in Mandera, Garissa, and Lamu counties, near the border with Somalia. However, there were no major terrorist incidents in Kenya's two largest cities, Nairobi, and Mombasa. Reports of violations of human rights, by Kenya's police and military forces, during counterterrorism operations continued, including allegations of extra-judicial killings, disappearances, and torture.[356]

Algeria: The Armed Islamic Group in Algeria, between 1992 and 1998, was one of the most violent Islamic terrorist groups, which had imposed the Saudi/Salafi religion on the Sufi mystical brotherhoods which were dismantled, their lands confiscated and redistributed by the ruling National Liberation Front (FLN) government in retaliation, for their lack of support

---

[374] BUREAU OF COUNTERTERRORISM AND COUNTERING VIOLENT EXTREMISM, US State Department—Report on terrorism in East Africa

to the FLN, during the fight against the French. The government hired Muslim Brotherhood refugees of Egypt as schoolteachers who propagated Arab Nationalism among the students. When the Algerian government tried to open its political system in 1989, the new Islamic Salvation Front (FIS), supported by the Saudis and other Gulf monarchies, resisted. When FIS was banned, the Algerian Muslims, aided by Jihadis returning from Afghanistan, and supported by the Saudis, rose against the government, resulting in the Algerian Civil War. The Civil War ended in the defeat of the Islamists, with about 200,000 deaths. As of 2010, Non-violent Salafism had been spread in Algeria, telling people: how to dress—how they deal with the state.—how they do business—how to protest a government plan to make women remove their headscarves, for passport photographs—pressuring shopkeepers to stop selling tobacco and alcohol—refusing to stand for the national anthem—to show their rejection of modern political systems, as practiced in Saudi Arabia.[375]

Lebanon: ISIS carried out many terror attacks in 2015 and 2016, in Lebanon, targeting mainly Shia Muslims, killing hundreds. The worst attacks were: On October 31, 2015, a Russian airliner was bombed over Sinai killing 224 people; On November 12, 2015: two ISIS suicide bombers in, Burj-el- Barajneh, near Beirut, killed 37-43 Shia Muslims.[376]

Nigeria, Chad, Niger, and Cameroon: Boko Haram, a very violent jihadi group, allied with ISIS, is based in northeastern Nigeria, also active in Chad, Niger, and northern Cameroon. **The Izala Society-** a Saudi Salafi missionary group, set up in 1978, by the World Muslim League of Saudi Arabia. It fights what it sees as the (innovation), practiced by the Sufi brotherhoods, specifically the Qadri and Tijani Sufi orders. Global

---

[375] John Pike (June 27, 2008).—Armed Islamic Group in Algeria (GIA)—Globalsecurity.org. Retrieved April 25, 2010. 2=Kepel, Gilles, Jihad, (2003) Rose Troup Buchanan (18 November 2015). Boko Haram overtakes ISIS as the deadliest terrorist organisation—The Independent. Retrieved 18 November 2015

[376] 44 killed in Daesh bombing in Beirut—Press TV. Retrieved 13 November 2015. 17=Naylor, Hugh (12 November 2015).—ISIS says it carried out Beirut attacks—The Washington Post. Retrieved 15 November 2015.

Terrorism Index 2015 considers Boko Haram as the deadliest terrorist group in the world. Boko Haram kidnapped 276 schoolchildren from Chibok in April 2014.[377]

Yemen: There have been attacks on civilian targets and tourists, and there was a cargo-plane bomb plot in 2010. In October 2002, suicide bombers rammed an explosive-laden boat into a French oil tanker, killing a sailor, spilling 90,000 barrels of oil into the Gulf of Aden. A Saudi born prime suspect of the USS Cole bombing, paid $40,000 to fund the French tanker attack. In Nov 2002, Hunt Oil Company helicopter was attacked shortly after taking off, A missile and machine gun bullets were fired at the helicopter injuring two American citizens. In December 2002, a suspected Islamic militant killed three U.S. workers and wounded one, in a hospital in Jibla. Jews in Yemen fled their homes due to threats from Muslim extremists. The Jewish community sent a complaint to President Ali Abdullah Saleh and temporarily moved to a hotel near Sana'a.[378]

Bangladesh: Saudi Arabia financed about 14000 radical mosques and madrasas, since the late 1970s, in Bangladesh. About 1.4 million students received Islamic education in these madrasas, without any state supervision. Individuals radicalized in Saudi Salafi-funded mosques comprised Hefazat-e-Islam organization, which was implicated in a January 2014 incident when its members staged violent protests, demanding the implementation of Islamic law in Bangladesh. Attacks by Islamic extremists in Bangladesh had been targeting secularist and atheist writers and bloggers in Bangladesh. They also attacked foreigners, Hindus, Buddhists, Christians, and Shia Muslims. The main proponents of these attacks were the ISIS and Ansarullah of

---

[377] Rose Troup Buchanan (18 November 2015). Boko Haram overtakes ISIS as the deadliest terrorist organisation—The Independent. Retrieved 18 November 2015
[378] 3 Hospital staff killed in Yemen—Domini.org. Retrieved April 4, 2010. 5= Yemeni Jews under pressure from Muslim extremists—World Jewish Congress. 23 Jan 2007. Retrieved 28 September 2016.

Bangladesh. As of July 2, 2016, a total of 48 people, including 20 foreign nationals, were killed in such attacks.[379]

India: From 2011 to 2013, 25000 Saudi preachers came to India, with $250 million, to build mosques and Islamic universities. There was concern about the increasing Saudi- Salafi influence, in the North West and in the East of India. According to Wikileaks, in 2015, 140 Muslim preachers were on Saudi consulate payroll in New Delhi. Kashmir had been the site of the Indo-Pakistan Wars of 1947, 1965, the 1999 Kargil War, about 2 million Muslims are affiliated with Saudi Salafi mosques. The Saudi-funded Jamiat Ahle-e-Hadith built 700 mosques and 150 schools in Kashmir and claimed that 16 percent of Kashmir's population were members. Police in Jammu and Kashmir believed that this was the result of a $35 billion Saudi plan for South Asia, to build mosques and schools.[380]

2001 Indian Parliament Attack: It was an attack, by members of Lashkar-e-Taiba (Let) and Jaish-e-Mohammad (Jem) which killed 14 persons, including 6 Indian police officers, 5 attackers, 2 parliament guards, and a gardener. This heinous attack on the symbol of Indian democracy resulted in a serious standoff between India and Pakistan. Due to the emergency created by the Parliament attack, Pakistan Army personnel, deployed on helping U.S. forces, capture Osama bin Laden, on his exit from Tora Bora, during intense U.S. bombardment of Osama's hideout, were withdrawn for redeployment on the India/Pakistan border. This facilitated the escape of Osama into Pakistan. Was this just a coincidence or a pre-planned operation by al-Qaeda, in collaboration with Lashkar-e Taiba, to divert Pakistan Army attention, enabling Osama to escape?[381]

---

[379] Ansarullah Bangla Team banned—Dhaka tribune.com. May 25, 2015. Archived from the original on May 27, 2015.

[380] Asit Jolly, "the Wahhabi Invasion"—India Today, December 23, 2011—How Saudi Arabia exports Radical Islam—. 8 April 2015.

[381] Govt blames LeT for parliament attack—. Rediff.com (14 December 2001). Retrieved 8 September 2011. 2= Adrian Levy; Catherine Scott-Clark (23 May 2017).—The Exile—the flight of Osama bin Laden—Bloomsbury Publishing—pp. 77–78.

The 2008 Mumbai attacks: The attacks took place in November 2008, when 10 members of Lashkar-e-Taiba, an Islamic terrorist organization, based in Pakistan, carried out a series of 12 coordinated shootings and bombings, lasting four days across Mumbai, from 26November to 29th, killing 164, and injuring 308.Attackers were members of Lashkar-e-Taiba. The Government of India said that the attackers came from Pakistan, and their controllers were in Pakistan. On 7January, 2009, Pakistan confirmed the sole surviving perpetrator of the attacks, was a Pakistani citizen.[382]

Terrorism in Pakistan: Attacks committed by terrorist groups affiliated with Saudi-sponsored ISIS, Al-Qaeda, Sipah-e-Sahaba, Lashkar-e-Jhangvi, Lashkar-e-Tayyiba, East Turkestan Islamic Movement (ETIM), the Islamic Movement of Uzbekistan (IMU), the Haqqani network, Taliban, and Jundullah killed thousands in Pakistan. These groups followed the extremist and violent ideology of the Saudi/Salafi religion of Saudi Arabia. They have all been funded by the charities and individual donors in the Gulf States, including Saudi Arabia, with the support and backing of their governments. In 2000 the deaths were 45, rising to 63,1787 by May 2018, consisting of 22,260 civilians, 6955 security personnel, and 33,963 terrorists-a staggering figure, depicting a dire situation, which the Pakistan government needed to address, eventually, to save Pakistan from destruction. The economic costs of terrorism from 2000–2010 totaled $68 billion, according to the government of Pakistan. Terrorism in Pakistan originated from Pakistan's involvement in the Afghan War. The state of Pakistan and its ISI, in alliance with the CIA, and Funding from the Kingdom of Saudi Arabia, encouraged the "mujahideen" (the holy warriors) to fight against the infidel Soviet forces in Afghanistan. The defeat of a superpower, the Soviet Union, by the mujahideen emboldened and radicalized them. Many of these mujahideen, on return to their home countries, started fighting their governments, to replace them with an Islamic State, giving rise to terrorism. Terrorists in Pakistan have had a similar agenda, to replace the democratic setup of the country, with an Islamic State, like Saudi Arabia. They followed the extremist and violent

---

[382] Schmitt, Eric; Somini Sengupta, Jane Perlez (3 December 2008).—US and India—militants in Pakistan—The New York Times. Retrieved 3 December 2008.

ideology of the Saudi/Salafi religion of Saudi Arabia. They have all been funded by the charities and individual donors in the Gulf States, including Saudi Arabia, with the support and backing of their governments. The Taliban have been fighting the government of Pakistan, while the other groups have been targeting the Barelvis and the Shia Muslims, whom they consider non-Muslims, who deserve to be killed, as preached by the Saudi/Salafi religion of Saudi Arabia, creating a serious law and order situation in Pakistan. These terrorists considered their actions, as Jihad or The Holy War, against the infidels, a powerful motivation for terrorism. Jihadi groups had been waging similar Jihad all over the world, since the 1979 Islamic Revolution of Iran, initially to counter the effects of the Iranian revolution, which appealed, even to the Sunni Muslims, worldwide. However, the terrorism spread to all the Muslim majority countries, like Iraq, Syria, Afghanistan, Pakistan, Philippines, Indonesia, Nigeria, and Yemen, following the spread of Saudi/Salafi religion, which sanctioned the killing of those who did not agree with its interpretation of Islam. As stated before, this religion was spread throughout the world at a phenomenal cost of $ 75 billion in the 1980s. According to the present King Salman, Saudi Arabia made this investment to help the Muslims, particularly in impoverished Muslim nations. Despite good intentions of the Saudis, intolerance of other faiths by Saudi/Salafism resulted in violence against followers of other faiths because the very teachings of this religion promote terrorism, as detailed in the previous chapter. Therefore, the Saudis cannot absolve themselves of the responsibility for the killings which had taken place, because they had been funding the terrorist groups which had been committing these atrocities, as detailed in chapters 6 and 7. If the Saudis are serious about doing good to the Muslims, they have to reform their religion, and put a complete stop to the Funding, by individuals, charities, and Arab governments, and particularly the Saudi princes.[383]

A Synopsis of Terrorism in Pakistan: As described above, Pakistan has been facing relentless anti-Shia crusade for decades, notably after General Zia led a coup, on 5July, 1977, and toppled the democratically elected government of Zulfiqar Ali Bhutto. In League with Maulana Maududi

---

[383] moderndiplomacy.eu/India- destabilizing -Pakistan

of Jamaat-e-Islami, Zia committed himself to setting up an Islamic state and enforcing Sharia Law of Sunni Islam, as practiced in Saudi Arabia. His actions of state-sponsored Islamization increased sectarian divisions in Pakistan, between Sunni and Shia, and between Deobandis and Barelvis. Pakistan's first major Shia/Sunni riots erupted in 1983 in Karachi, during the Shia holiday of Muharram, leaving at least sixty people dead. Further Muharram disturbances followed over the next three years, spreading to Lahore and Baluchistan regions, killing hundreds more. In July 1986, Sunnis, and Shias, many of them equipped with locally made automatic weapons, clashed in Parachinar where over 200 died. Violence against the Shia Muslims has continued ever since.[384]

Shia Massacre in Gilgit: The first major anti-Shia riots in Gilgit broke out in May 1988, during the reign of General Zia, over the sighting of the moon, which ushers the end of the holy month of Ramadan. When Shias in Gilgit were celebrating Eid al-Fitr, a group of extremist Sunnis, still fasting, attacked them. After a brief calm of about four days, the Pakistani military regime used militants, along with local Sunnis, to 'teach a lesson' to the Shias, which resulted in the hundreds of Shias and Sunnis being killed. The Pakistan Army brought Osama bin Laden, along with his Afghan Arab fighters, and thousands of Sunnis from Pakistani tribal area, who invaded Gilgit along the Karakoram Highway. They killed hundreds. The exact number of casualties is not known but, according to sources, about 700 Shias were killed.[385]

Pakistan—A Failed State: The 'Fund for Peace 'characterizes a failed state as having a central government unable to raise taxes, give the needed public services, ensure security for its people, and does not have complete control over all its territories. Pakistan conformed to this definition of a failed state. As of June, 2019 when Imran Khan is the Prime Minister, the

---

[384] Gunman kills 13 at Karachi airport—9 June 2014—BBC News. 5=Pakistan launches offensive near afghan border—15 June 2014.
[385] Humza, Izhar. conflict in Gilgit- (PDF). United States Institute of Peace. Retrieved July 5, 2017. In 1988, a rumor alleging a Sunni massacre at the hands of Shias resulted in an attack by thousands of armed tribesmen from the south, the killing of nearly four hundred Shias.

security situation in Pakistan, is not much better, considering the recent violence in Quetta against the Shia, and unsafe road travel from Karachi to the Iran border. The terrorist groups are still active in Pakistan, and they still receive funding from Saudi Arabia and UAE. How can the Pakistan government stop Saudi funding of terrorists when the government itself receives Saudi funding to run its operations? President Obama declared Pakistan 'a Failed State, 'during his tenure of U.S. Presidency. Obama is a knowledgeable scholar, an accomplished writer, and an eminent political leader, whose remarks cannot be dismissed, without careful consideration. Many other scholars have expressed similar views about Pakistan, such as the British writer Anatol Lieven. The main problem facing Pakistan has been terrorism which has menaced Pakistan since 2001 when Pakistan allied with the U.S. for the War on terror. All the armed groups, committing terror, were supposed to be banned, but they intensified their activities since 2001. As mentioned above, these groups have been the Taliban, Lashkar-e-Jhangvi, Lashkar-e-Taiba, ISIS, al-Qaeda, and their associated groups, which have been targeting the Pakistani Security Forces and the civilians, including women and children. These terrorist groups still pose a serious security challenge in Pakistan. Indonesia had a similar problem, created by their Jamaat-e-Islami, which was banned, its Funding blocked, and members killed or imprisoned. In this way, Indonesia successfully got rid of terrorism, with the help of its security forces. Pakistan's security forces can do a lot better due to their military prowess and expertise.[386]

Pakistan's Existence at Stake: Contrary to the general belief, among the Pakistani public, Politicians, and the Army that India is the Enemy of Pakistan, the real enemies of Pakistan have been, and still are the terrorists, and their funders who are intent on destabilizing and demolishing Pakistan. As indicated earlier, 63,134 Pakistanis have been killed by terrorists since 2000, including 22,239 civilians, and 6940 personnel of Security forces. It seems that We have been in a perpetual state of War, for decades, with an enemy who has not been on the battlefield, in open warfare, but operated

---

[386] terrorism in Pakistan-Murphy, Eamon (2013). Routledge. p. 134.- October 3, 2017. Shias in the district of Gilgit were assaulted, killed and raped by an invading Sunni lashkar-armed militia-comprising thousands of jihadis from the North West Frontier Province

stealthily, and therefore could not be defeated. Our War in the past and today has not been with India, but with the terrorists. The individuals, Charities, and organizations in the Arab countries, described in detail, in Chapter 7, who have been funding the terrorists such as the Taliban, Lashkar-e-Jhangvi, Lashkar-e-Taiba, ISIS, and Al-Qaeda, for decades, have been, and are the real enemies of Pakistan, and should be treated as such. The Sunni Arab countries wanted to replace the tolerant religions of Barelvis and Shias with their intolerant ideology of Saudi Orthodox Islam by force. Their ultimatum to the victims of terrorism was 'convert or die,' giving no other choice. The Quran preaches "No Coercion in religion "(Quran 2;256), as described in Chapter1 on Islam. The Prophet of Islam (pbuh) did not force people to convert to Islam. Therefore, the ideology of coercion, propagated by the Saudi/Salafism, is against the teachings of the Quran and the Prophet (pbuh) and should be rejected. Shia Muslims comprise 15-20% of the total population of Pakistan, amounting to about 30 million, according to the PEW survey of 2012. They are Pakistanis and deserve a life of peace and security, which the Pakistan government is supposed to provide. If the Pakistanis do not wake up to these facts, the existence of Pakistan is in danger.

Funding of Terrorism in Pakistan: Terrorist Groups need funds to operate. They need money to obtain explosives, weapons, and to pay high salaries to their members. The average salary of a jihadi in Syria was at least $1000-1500 per month. Islamic Terrorists are mercenaries who work for money as well as for misguided religious gratification, which promises a high reward in the afterlife. The Funding of terrorist groups must be stopped, to stem terrorist operations, As detailed in Chapter 7 on terrorist groups, the most prominent funders of Terrorist Groups have been the donors in Saudi Arabia, Qatar, UAE, and Kuwait who through intermediaries in Pakistan, gave millions of dollars to Lashkar-e-Jhangvi (LeJ), Lashkar-e-Taiba (Let), the Taliban, ISIS, and their associated groups. They have been funding these groups, from their very start, in 2003. The more active and violent a group is, in killing the Shia Muslims and government personnel, the more money they receive as a reward. They motivate the group members by saying that they are engaged in a Jihad against Infidels who are those who do not agree with their interpretation of

Islam, namely the Shia Muslims, Barelvis, and non-Muslims. The donors and their supporting governments in the middle east are the real enemies of Pakistan. Any individual or organization giving funds or material to a terrorist group such as LeJ, Let, Taliban, ISIS, and their associated groups, must be declared as the "Enemies of Pakistan," and must qualify for capital punishment, like the terrorists themselves. Islamic and Political parties which support the armed ambushes at the India/Pakistan borders and inside India are, in fact, acting against the interests of Pakistan, and should not be sanctioned by the government. The Pakistan Government needs to beware of deception, employed by the Arab billionaires, to propagate their ideology, through enticement with enormous amounts of money to the religious and political parties, apparently for humanitarian purposes, but really for terrorist purposes. Their ulterior motive has usually been the Funding of the Jihadi groups through these organizations. (Please. See Saudi Funding through Maulana Ludhianvi by a Saudi named Mecci, under LeJ Funding in the book, chapter 7)[387]

What to Do? The Government of Pakistan needs to restrain Islamic parties such as JUI(F), and Jamaat-e-Islami, from supporting terrorist groups like the Taliban, LeJ, Let, ISIS, Al-Qaeda, and others, and must ensure that no Imam or Preacher, talks against the other Muslim sects or non-Muslims. Long jail terms and punitive measures must be implemented against violators. Pakistan must not permit its armed forces to act as mercenaries for the Arab countries. Even stationing Pakistan army personnel in Arab countries for whatever aims, contradict the policy of neutrality. The long-held policy of neutrality in regional conflicts must be maintained, to avoid being drawn in the regional Shia/Sunni conflicts. The government must regard its citizens equally regardless of their religious affiliations. It does not matter whether the citizens are Shia, Ahmadi, Hindu, Christian, Sikhs, or Jews. They must all be safeguarded and protected. Foreign donations to religious and political figures or organizations of the country must not be allowed, for any reason, including the humanitarian grounds, which should be the prerogative of the Pakistan Government and not of an individual or an organization.

---

[387] moderndiplomacy.eu/ India- destabilizing -Pakistan

Indonesia: Saudi Arabia spent millions of dollars in Indonesia, to replace its tolerant Islam, with the extremist brand of Saudi Salafism, since 1980, building more than 150 mosques, an Islamic university, and many Arabic language institutes in Jakarta. It had been supplying more than 100 boarding schools with books and teachers. Also, it had been granting thousands of scholarships for studies in the Arab countries, including Saudi Arabia. Salafi radio stations, T.V. channels and websites in Indonesia (and Southeast Asia) preached Salafi ways of life.[388] Saudis got a foothold in Indonesia in 1988, during President Suharto's reign. The Saudi embassy's Religious Attaché Office gave scholarships for students, to go to Saudi Arabia, and paid for "preachers" to give Friday sermons "across Indonesia." There was an all-expenses-paid Salafist university in Jakarta, which produced tens of thousands of graduates, since its founding in 1980. There were schools for the affluent as well as for the poor, in both Java and more remote islands, funded by the Saudis. The libraries in East Java were filled with books from Saudi Arabia. The Saudi embassy in Jakarta provided one million Arabic religious books, translated into Indonesian, every year. The titles were questions answered by Bin Baz, Saudi Arabia's most venerated Mufti. As of 2003, a Pew Research Center poll found Crown Prince Abdullah, was rated as the most trusted leader. As Saudi Salafism expanded, some Indonesians became alarmed at what had taken place in their country and had called for an Islam, with freedom of opinion and tolerance, that did not reject democracy. A graduate of LIPPIA (the Institute of Islamic and Arabic Studies, (Farid Okbah) helped found the National Anti-Shia Alliance (ANNALS) of Indonesia, which preached anti-Shia rhetoric. A series of attacks on Shia had since occurred in East Java. Although Shias make up only about 1% of the population of the country, Okbah had urged the disbanding of the sect.[389] According to analyst Sidney Jones, the director of the Institute for Policy Analysis of Conflicts in Jakarta, Saudis had created intolerant atmosphere and were behind campaigns, against Shia and Ahmadi Muslims, both of which are

---

[388] Commemoration of 3rd anniversary of bombings—AAP. The Age Newspaper. 10 December 2006. Travel warnings—US Embassy Jakarta—10 May 2005. Archived on 11 November 2006. Retrieved 26 December 2006
[389] Vickers, Adrian (2005).—*A History of Modern Indonesia*. Cambridge University Press. pp. 218–219.

considered heretics by the Saudi Salafis. However, according to a 2003 article in the New York Times, Saudis had also secretly provided funds for "militant Islamic groups." The Saudi foundation Al-Haramain, financed educational institutions, with the approval of the Indonesian Ministry of Religion, and transferred money to Jemaah Islamiyah, a Southeast Asian Islamist organization, that aimed to build Islamic states. The spiritual guide of Jemaah Islamiyah (Abu Bakar Bashir) had then pledged his allegiance to ISIS.[390] The deadliest incident that killed 202 people (including 164 international tourists) was in Bali, in 2002.[391]

Counterterrorism in Indonesia: Terrorism in Indonesia could in part be attributed to the al-Qaeda affiliated Jemaah Islamiyah, an Islamic Terror Group and/or ISIS. After the 2002 Bali Bombings, their leaders, Imam Samudra, Amrozi, Abu Dujana, Azahari Husain and Noordin Top, were captured and killed, dismantling the terrorist cells of Jemaah Islamiyah in Indonesia. Samudra, Amrozi, and Amrozi's brother Ghufran were executed by firing squad on November 9, 2008.[392]

The Philippines: Since January 2000, Islamic militant groups and separatist forces in the Philippines, carried out many bombings. From 2000 to 2007, attacks killed 400 Filipino civilians and injured well over 1500. These figures were more than those, caused by bombings and other attacks, in Indonesia, Morocco, Spain, Turkey, or Britain, during the same period. Abu Sayyaf and the Rajah Suleiman Movement, two groups that had claimed responsibility for most of the attacks were affiliated with al-Qaeda. Their stated goal was to create a 'Super Islamic State' across Southeast Asia, including Malaysia, Thailand, Myanmar, and Indonesia.[393]

---

[390] McDonald, Hamish (30 June 2008).—fighting terror—. Sydney Morning Herald. p. 17. .6=Police to quiz Bali mastermind—*BBC News.* November 25, 2002. Retrieved 25 May 2010.

[391] Bali mastermind Dulmatin killed—Times online—2010-03-09

[392] South Asian terrorist leader under arrest—14 June 2007. 8= Noordin Top Killed by police—Jakarta globe—Archived on 25 September 2009.- Retrieved 2 December 2014.

[393] Philippine court designates Abu Sayyaf a terrorist group—Sun Star. 11 September 2015. Retrieved 12 September 2015.

United States: In the 1980's Saudi Arabia spent about $10 million on mosque construction, according to Yvonne Haddad of Georgetown Centre. Academic chairs for Islamic studies at Harvard had been donated by the Saudis. Also, Islamic Research Institutes, at American University in Washington, Howard University, Duke University, and John Hopkins University were all funded by the Saudis. A study of Saudi Salafi publications, by NGO Freedom House, stated "Muslims should oppose infidels for Allah's sake, and that Shia and other Sunni Muslims are infidels, and that democracy is responsible for all the horrible wars."[394]

9/11 Attacks: Four passenger airliners run by two major U.S. passenger carriers bound for California were hijacked by 19 al Qaeda terrorists, and two of them were crashed into the World Trade Center in New York, and the third into the Pentagon building, headquarter of the Defense Department, in Arlington, Virginia County. As a result, two 110-story towers of the World Trade Centre collapsed, within an hour and 42 minutes of impact. The Pentagon building also collapsed partially, when the third plane hit it. The fourth plane initially was steered toward Washington D.C. but crashed into a field in Stony Creek Township in Pennsylvania, after its passengers tried to overcome the hijackers. In all, about 3,000 people were killed in this atrocity. Hijackers were mostly Saudi nationals.

Orlando Bombing: An al-Qaeda terrorist Omar Mateen shot and murdered 49 people in a Gay club at Pulse, in Orlando, Florida. It was also the deadliest terrorist attack in the United States, since the 9/11 attacks.[395]

Canada: There are one million Muslims, in Canada, out of a population of 35 million. Late King Fahd donated $5 million for Salahuddin Mosque and Islamic Center in Toronto. and a further $1.5 million per year for operations. According to the National Post, one of the founders

---

[394] United States. Federal Bureau of Investigation; Terrorist Research and Analytical Center (U.S.) (2007).terrorism in the US 2002-2005—(PDF) (2 ed.). U.S. Department of Justice, Federal Bureau of Investigation. p. 43.

[395] Ellis, Ralph; Ashley Frantz; Faith Karimi; Eliot C. McLaughlin (June 13, 2016). Orlando shooting—49 killed—shooter pledged allegiance to ISIS—CNN.com. Retrieved August 3, 2016.

of the Centre, Hassan Farhat, left Canada to fight in Iraq with ISIS. The center's imam Aly Hindi is known for his "controversial comments" on homosexuality and Canadian law. The Saudi government donated hundreds of thousands of dollars to private Islamic schools in Canada. Canadian government keeps a close eye on home-grown terrorists, and thwarted many terrorist plots, through its alert security agencies.[396]

Turkey: An international airport was bombed. An ambassador was assassinated. A nightclub massacre took place. These and many other attacks showed how terrorism had hit Turkey hard. Turkey had been pushing for Syrian President Bashar al-Assad's fall, ignoring ISIS. At the beginning of the War in Syria, President Recep Tayyip Erdogan backed the Sunni rebels, who were fighting the Shia ruler of Syria. Turkey had left ISIS alone, and ISIS left Turkey alone, in terms of attacks, though fighters and supplies were routed through the country. ISIS had established many footholds and supporters. The Turkish military intervention in Syria had been the first frontal opposition, between ISIS and the Turkish Army, heating up tensions. The main goal of these ISIS attacks on Turkish civilian targets was to set off hatred and division and to harm the unity and stability in Turkey. On January 12, 2016, an ISIS suicide bomber carried out the 2016 Istanbul Bombing. killing 12 people. Turkish army carried out tanks and artillery strike on ISIS positions in Syria and Iraq, killing 200 fighters. On March 19, a second bombing took place in Istanbul's Beyoğlu district. Turkish authorities arrested around 1.200 people inside Turkey, for suspected links with ISIS. On June 28, 2016, the attack on Istanbul airport killed 48 people. On December 10, 2016, a bombing at the sports stadium killed 46. On January 1 2017, A mass shooting took place at the Reina nightclub in Ortakoy, Istanbul, killing 39. ISIS claimed responsibility for these attacks.[397]

---

[396] Seymour, Andrew (2010-08-26). RCMP say homegrown terror suspects were preparing to build IEDs—Ottawacitizen.com. Retrieved 2011-10-16.

[397] Armed attack on the nightclub in Istanbul—. Habertürk (in Turkish). Retrieved 31 December 2016. 5=Graham, Chris (31 December 2016).—istanbul nightclub attack killed 39—The Telegraph. Retrieved 2 January 2017. Walker, Peter (2 January 2017). 6= ISIS claims responsibility for nightclub attack—The Independent. Retrieved 2 January 2017

Saudi Arabia: Over the years, dating back to 1995, there had been many terrorist attacks in Saudi Arabia, mostly targeting foreign civilians, including Americans and Europeans, affiliated with its oil industry. Saudi Arabia has always funded terrorist groups in other countries, including Syria, Iraq, and other Muslim countries where its aim was to replace the non-Saudi Salafi ideologies of Islam, like the Shia and Sufi Islam, by coercion and violence, propounded by its intolerant Saudi Salafi ideology which considers all non-Saudi Salafis apostates who deserve to be killed. However, no harm ever came to any member of the Royal Family in Saudi Arabia or abroad, and their properties, consisting of thousands of palaces, organizations, and offices, in the kingdom and abroad, also suffered no damage. The family consists of thousands of princes, and they have extraordinary holdings all over the world. This proves Saudi complicity in worldwide terrorism, also verified by Laurent Murawiec, who, in his book "The Princes of Darkness "has an explanation. He was told by an Arab foreign minister that a deal had been made between Osama bin Laden and the royal family who were represented by the chief of intelligence, Prince Turki Al-Faisal, who resigned 12 days before 9/11, after 26 years' service. Osama agreed, in return for $200 million, not to do anything, against the kingdom or its interests. However, he will have complete freedom of action anywhere outside the kingdom. Laurent says his source of information is unimpeachable, as several western intelligence services confirmed it.[398]

2015 Bombings against Shia Muslims: On May 22, 2015, a suicide bomber attacked the Ali (a.s) mosque in the village of al-Qadeeh, in Qatif governorate, during Friday prayers, killing 21, injuring 80 in the blast. ISIS later claimed responsibility for the attack. A Shiite mosque in Dammam was bombed on May 29, 2015, killing four people. The bomber detonated his bomb in the parking lot, after being stopped by security guards. On August 6, the Abha bombing, carried out by a suicide bomber, killed 17 people, at Abha.[399]

---

[398] US embassy cables: Hillary Clinton claimed Saudi Arabia was a critical source of terrorist funding—the Guardian—London. December 5, 2010. 2=Walsh, Declan (December 5, 2010)-Wikileaks cables portray Saudi Arabia as a cash machine for terrorists—the Guardian, London 2001

[399] ISIS claims Shia mosque bombing—BBC News. 2= Saudi Arabia: ISIS suicide bomber attacks Shia mosque—kills 4—The Indian Express. 29 May 2015.

CHAPTER 7

Islamic Terrorism and Terrorist Groups

As elaborated in chapter 6, the ideology of Saudi Salafism sanctions violence against those who disagree with it, declaring them apostates and unbelievers, whose killing is a holy act, according to the founder of Saudi Salafism, Imam ibn Abd al-Wahhab. From 1970's to 2002, Saudi Arabia, follower of Saudi Salafism, invested over $70 billion, earned from skyrocketing oil prices, following the 1973 Oil Crisis, to propagate its ideology to Muslims all over the world, including the US and Europe, along with Muslim majority countries, where it aimed to replace other Islamic doctrines, with their intolerant brand of Islam. The result was that, wherever Saudi Salafism was introduced, it resulted in violence against followers of other faiths, such as the Shia and the Sufi Muslims. Although their religion also considers Jews and Christian as apostates whose killing is religiously sanctioned, Saudis have been smart enough to avoid alienating their long-time Christian allies, the United States and Europe. According to US State Department, Saudi Arabia is the World's most significant source of funds, and promoter of Saudi/Salafi Jihadism, which forms the ideological basis of terrorist groups, such as al-Qaeda, ISIS,

---

Archived on 29 May 2015. 3= suicide bomber kills 15 in mosque—Reuters UK. Retrieved 6 August 2015.

Taliban, Lashkar-e-Jhangvi, Boko Haram, and their associates. Wealthy donors in other Arab countries, especially Qatar, Kuwait, UAE, have also been funding the terrorist groups in Iraq, Syria, Pakistan, Afghanistan, and Africa. Scholars such as Dr. Dore Gold, Patrick Cockburn, and others have been pointing out the root causes of terrorism, for decades. The United States and the European countries, who have been the real powers in the world, have chosen to take no notice of the recommendations, due to their fear of alienating their long-time allies who have been motivating the terrorists by their generous funding.[400] The human rights aspect of terrorism, which has been targeting the Shia Muslims, has been ignored by the world powers of the US and UK, probably because, Shias are not considered human beings. This attitude of persecuting the Shias has been going on for centuries, as described in Chapter 5. It is surprising to note that, in the modern world of the 21st century, when even animals have rights, ensuring their protection against violence, killing of the Shias in the world has not been evoking any reaction from the World Powers, such as the US, the UK, and the European countries, which continuously boast about their regard for human rights. They are quick to pounce on every little happening in Iran, branding them as terrorists when all the terrorists, so far, have been the Sunni extremist Muslims, like the al-Qaeda, the Taliban, and the ISIS. Not even one terrorist incident, so far, has been perpetrated by a Shia Muslim. Sunni Muslims or organizations always claimed responsibility for all attacks. This chapter describes the terrorist groups, their origin, logistical and financial support, motivations of terrorism, tactics, aims, and networks, along with a detail of their activities in different countries, and deception employed by them and their supporters, to make their tracking difficult.[401]

Major Terror Attacks in the World (Sept. 11, 2001, to May 2013): Terrorists, claiming to be Muslims, committed the following devastating acts of terrorism, in various countries:

---

[400] Walsh, Declan (December 5, 2010)-Wikileaks cables portray Saudi Arabia as a cash machine for terrorists—the Guardian, London 2001

[401] Holbrook, Donald (2010). "Using the Qur'an to Justify Terrorist Violence". Perspectives on Terrorism. Terrorism Research Initiative and centre for study of terrorism and political violence-4 (3)

Europe: On Nov.13, 2016—-Paris-France: In a series of related attacks across Paris, ISIS terrorists killed at least 129 people. On Jan. 7, 2015, in Paris -ISIS extremists murdered seven people in Paris in the Charlie Hebdo magazine office. On May 24, 2014, in Brussels -A shooter killed four people at the Jewish Museum of Belgium in Brussels. Mehdi Nemmouche, a French national, with ties to Islamic State, was arrested and charged with the killings. On July 7, 2005, in London—Four coordinated attacks, by suicide bombers, ripped through London subway trains and a bus, killing 52. The killers were later named as British al Qaeda sympathizers Shehzad Tanweer, Hasib Hussain, Mohammed Siddique Khan, and Jermaine Lindsay. On March 11, 2004, al-Qaeda bombings in Madrid, Spain killed 191 commuters in train bombings.

Asia: On Nov. 12, 2015, in Beirut: A double suicide bombing, in a Beirut suburb, killed around 43 people, in an attack by Sunni militants, linked to al Qaeda and other extremist groups. On Dec. 16, 2014, in Pakistan: Taliban shooters stormed a military-run school in Peshawar, Pakistan killing 148 people. On Nov. 26, 2008, Mumbai: A 60-hour siege by ten militants from Lashkar-e-Taiba of Pakistan, killed 166 people, in India's biggest city and financial capital. On Oct. 10, 2015, in Ankara, Turkey: Reuters reported that suicide bombers killed 95. On July 20, 2015-ISIS suicide bombing killed 31 people in Suruc, a town in Turkish Kurdistan. More than 100 people were injured. On Oct. 12, 2002, in Bali, Indonesia, al Qaeda, killed 202 people on the Indonesian holiday island of Bali.

Africa: On Oct. 31, 2015, in Egypt: A Russian-operated jet crashed in Egypt, killing all 224 people on board. Islamic State claimed responsibility for the crash. On June 26, 2015, in Tunisia an ISIS lone shooter stormed a beach resort in Tunisia, killing 37 people. On April 2, 2015, in Kenya, heavily armed al-Shabaab shooters killed 150 of a university campus in Kenya. On March 18, 2015, ISIS killed 21 in Tunis. On Sept. 1, 2004, Beslan, North Ossetia: 330 were killed by ISIS terrorists who also took 1200 people as hostages.

Russia: On Oct. 23, 2002, Forty Chechen fighters seized Moscow's Dubrovka Theater and held 1,000 people hostages. In Russian police operation, 40 terrorists and some 130 hostages were killed. As described earlier, in the US, On Sept.11, 2001, ISIS Terrorists crashed passenger jets, killing about 3000 people. A fourth airplane, destined for Washington DC, crashed in a western Pennsylvania field, as a result of brave passengers' struggle with the hijackers, averting another disaster.[402]

Motivations of Islamic terrorism: Terrorists are motivated by several factors that need to be investigated and studied, to solve this menace. Saudi Jihadis, have had powerful indoctrination imparted to them, through textbooks and teachers of schools they attended, from childhood, in Saudi Arabia. Statistics show that about 45% of foreign fighters in Iraq were Saudis, most of whom came as suicide bombers, who were convinced that God would reward them, in the afterlife, which is, undoubtedly, the strongest motivation for a terrorist act. Some terrorists treated it as a regular job, like a soldier, which pays well, as the jihadis' earned $1000-1500 per month in Iraq and Syria. Some, like Osama bin Laden, were upset about the US and European involvement in Muslim countries. These and other motivating factors will be discussed in the following section.[403]

Ideology: First and the foremost, and the strongest motivator of terrorism, for the misguided Muslims, is the ideology. Saudi Salafi religion of Saudi Arabia includes a doctrine of takfir, which declares all those who do not agree with it, including the Muslims of Sufi and Shia faiths, Jews, and Christians, as apostates who deserve to be killed. This doctrine was the main proponent of worldwide terrorism since 2003, according to researchers and historians. Saudi Salafi interpretation of Islam encourages intolerance, in fact, hatred, towards non-Saudi Salafis, and legitimizes, not only violence against them but their extermination. In India, the Deobandi movement follows Saudi Salafism's extremism. This ideology was spread (among other ways) through textbooks in Saudi Arabia and

---

[402] According to author Dore Gold this funding was for non-Muslim countries alone. Gold, Dore (2003). Hatred's Kingdom :How Saudi Arabia Supports the New Global Terrorism. Regnery. p. 126.

[403] CNN Money US—ISIS soldiers earn between $400 and $1,200 a month, plus a $50 stipend for their wives and $25 for each child, according to the Congressional Research Service.

in "thousands of schools worldwide, funded by the Saudi Salafi Muslim charities. Indoctrination of students in Saudi Arabia, takes place in schools, through books and sermons of Saudi Salafi teachers and mosque preachers.[404]

Economic motivations: As described earlier, Jihadis earn $500-1500 per month- a salary, unheard of, in their own countries. A high salary gives a big incentive for youngsters who were struggling in their home countries. The Saudi government and Saudi charitable foundations, run by religious Saudi Salafis, directly aid terrorists and terrorist groups financially. Salaries of Jihadis come from funding provided by the sponsors in Saudi Arabia, Qatar, Kuwait, and UAE.[405]

U.S and Western Foreign Policy: the US and the western foreign policies about Muslims worldwide, are also strong proponents of terrorism by Muslim terrorists. According to Mm Eliza Buller, the former head of MI5, the security services warned Tony Blair, that launching the War on Terror, would increase the threat of terrorism. Robert Pape argued that terrorists, using suicide attacks, a particularly effective form of terrorism, are driven, not only by Islamic zeal but to compel the US and the west to withdraw from Muslim lands. Analysts like Martin Kramer, Michael Scheuer feel that US foreign policy regarding intrusions in the Middle East, Afghanistan, invasion of Iraq, and support of Israel triggered terrorism. Also, US support of aggressive regimes such as Egypt, Algeria, Morocco, Kuwait and Saudi Arabia, the presence of US Troops on Muslim Holy land in Saudi Arabia, and the Western World's religious discrimination against the Muslim immigrants have been other contributing factors. For decades, US Foreign Policy has revolved around their age-old politics of supporting allies, regardless of their current actions. For example, President Roosevelt, in 1945, signed an agreement of support and cooperation with the kingdom of Saudi Arabia, to serve US political goals in the Middle East, at that time. During the cold war, Saudis helped forestall Soviet influence in the region, and helped the downfall of the Soviet Union after

---

[404] Orthodox islam and violence are linked—says a Top Islamic Scholar—. *Time*. Retrieved 2017-12-27

[405] ISIS Paying Foreign Fighters $1,000 Per Month, Says King Abdullah of Jordan— Reported by Erin McClam with The Associated Press.

the Afghan Jihad, in which at least 25,000 Saudi Jihadis took part. But the World Situation today is different. The US is now the only superpower on the planet. The Soviet Union, which posed a challenge has been defeated and fragmented into smaller nation-states, just like the Ottoman Empire after World War 1. Still, the US is pursuing the old policy of siding with its allies, regardless of their policies and actions. Shia Genocide in the world, which has claimed millions of lives, since the 1979 Islamic Revolution of Iran, did not bother the US. Ignoring what has been happening in the world for decades, was not the solution to the problem. According to Richard Dearlove, Chief of MI6:" in the US, intelligence and facts are being fixed around the policy." The US, therefore, must respond to world events in a responsible manner, to address issues related to the infringement of human rights and the sanctity of human life, the rule of law, and justice in the world. Undue intrusions of the US and Europe, in internal affairs of Muslim countries, have been a factor that motivated the terrorists, in their atrocities against the United States, the West, and other countries.[406]

Democracy and Human Rights: The US and the Western countries have had democratic governments at home, but they opposed democracy abroad. They preferred dictators and autocratic setups in other countries. The ouster of a democratically elected President Mohammad Morsi of Egypt, by the Military, and cordial welcome of the new dictator El-Sisi by the US and Europe, is the modern-day example. Since 1979, Saudi-sponsored Jihadis had been engaged in a Shia Genocide in Iraq, Syria, Afghanistan, Pakistan, Russia, Africa, Yemen, and the Far East, killing millions of non-Saudi Salafis and fighting governments causing Worldwide instability, but the Shia Genocide in the world prompted no significant action by the US, UK, and the EU countries who claim to be strong proponents of human rights and sanctity of life. They all maintained their policy of 'turning a blind eye

---

[406] Scheuer (2004), p. 9—The focused and lethal threat posed to U.S. national security arises not from Muslims being offended by what America is, but rather from their plausible perception that the things they most love and value – God, Islam, their brethren, and Muslim lands – are being attacked by America."

'towards the policies and activities of Saudi Arabia and Gulf countries', who have been the proponents of the said Shia Genocide in the world.[407]

Terrorist Tactics

The terrorists used Various tactics, depending upon the terrorist's state of mind and motivation. The goal of martyrdom mostly drove them. A killed ISIS fighter's pocket contained a spoon, indicating that after suicide, he will be received by the prophet (pbuh) and dine with him in paradise, showing the extent of the indoctrination of terrorists. All these and other tactics are described in this section.

Suicide Bombings: Most terrorists, belonging to the Taliban, LeJ, Let, Boko Haram, AL Qaeda, ISIS, and Jihadis fighting in Iraq and Syria, used suicide attacks to maximize casualties of the enemies. Such attacks are against Islamic injunctions and have therefore been forbidden by Islamic Scholars except Saudi Ulama who supported the Jihadi groups. Groups which supported Suicide Attacks, referred to such attacks as "Martyrdom Operations" which by Islamic traditions carry rewards of Paradise for their actions.[408]

Hijackings: A very dreadful terrorist action which involves hijacking a passenger plane and blowing it up midair, killing hundreds of passengers, including women and children. Examples are the 9/11 attacks in New York, blowing up Air India Flight, bound for India from Canada, and ISIS

---

[407] Frontline: Al-Qaeda's new front Interviews ' Michael Scheuer—Retrieved March 8, 2008. ' Bin Laden has had success because he's focused on a limited number of U.S. foreign policies in the Muslim world, policies that are visible and are experienced by Muslims on a daily basis: our unqualified support for Israel; our ability to keep oil prices at a level that is more or less acceptable to Western consumers. Probably the most damaging of all is our 30-year support for police states across the Islamic world:—the Al Sauds and the Egyptians under [Hosni] Mubarak and his predecessors;—the Algerians; the Moroccans; the Kuwaitis. They're all police states.

[408] Casciani, Dominic (2 March 2010).—Muslim scholar condemns terrorism—. *BBC News*

blowing up a Russian airliner in the Sinai. Unlike the typical hijackings of land vehicles or ships, skyjacking is not usually committed for robbery or theft: most plane hijackers intend to use the passengers as hostages, either for monetary ransom or for some political or administrative concession, by the authorities. Various motives have driven such occurrences, including demanding the release of certain prisoners, highlighting the grievances of a community, or political asylum. Hijackers also have used plane as a weapon, to target locations, like the September 11 attacks. Hijackings for hostages, produce an armed standoff during a period of negotiation between hijackers and authorities, followed by some form of settlement. Settlements do not always meet the hijackers' original demands. If the hijackers' demands are considered too great and the perpetrators show no inclination to surrender, authorities sometimes employ armed Special Forces, to try a rescue of the hostages e.g. Lufthansa Flight 181 which was hijacked on 13 October 1977 by four members of the Palestinian Commandos, whose demand was, the release of some prisoners. However, security forces stormed the plane and all 86 passengers were rescued. Because hijacking is widely considered as an act of terrorism and how it can seriously endanger the lives of those upon the aircraft, and others on the ground, aircraft hijacking is often treated as an extremely serious crime. In most jurisdictions of the world, aircraft hijacking is punishable by life imprisonment or a lengthy prison sentence. In most jurisdictions where the death penalty is a legal punishment, aircraft hijacking is punished with a death sentence, as in India and the US states of Georgia and Mississippi.[409]

Kidnappings for Ransom: Militant groups like al-Qaeda, Boko Haram, ISIS and al-Nusra used kidnappings as a method of fundraising. al-Qaeda leader Nasir al-Wuhayshi describes kidnapping as "an easy spoil which I may describe as a profitable trade." Journalist Rukmini Maria Calimocho stated in a 2014 investigation, that the al-Qaeda received over $125 million from kidnappings in 2013 alone. The French government paid Boko Haram $3.15 million for release of 16 French hostages in 2013. Maria's article showed, that from a haphazard beginning in 2003, kidnapping grew into the Boko Haram group's main fundraising strategy, with targeted,

---

[409] *The Impact of 9/11 on Politics and War: The Day that Changed everything?* Palgrave Macmillan. p. 222

professional kidnapping of civilians from wealthy European countries—principally France, Spain, and Switzerland, willing to pay huge ransoms. US and UK nationals are less commonly targeted since these governments have shown an unwillingness to pay ransoms.[410]

Kidnapping Women: ISIS kidnapped girls and women for monetary gain, in Syria and Iraq, and sold them, in the markets of Mosul and in Raqqa, like cattle. The UN confirmed in 2014, that 5000-7000 Yazidi women and children, had been abducted and sold into slavery. On 15 April 2014, 276 girls were kidnapped from the Government Secondary School, in the town of Chibok, in Nigeria, by Boko Haram, the Islamic terrorist group, affiliated with al-Qaeda. 57 of the schoolchildren managed to escape over the next few months and some have described their capture, in appearances at international human rights conferences. Since then, hopes were raised on various occasions that the 219 remaining girls might also be released. Newspaper reports suggested that Boko Haram was hoping to use the girls, as a negotiating pawn, for exchange of some of their commanders in jail.[411]

Islamic Terrorist Groups

This section details the start, ideology, motivations, political support, and funding of the terrorist groups, whose members have been committing terrorist activities, in the name of Islam, although the religion does not sanction killing of any human being, as described in Chapter 1, on Islam, unless the killing is in retribution for another killing, ordered by an Islamic court. Teachings of Islam promote tolerance, harmony, and peace. Study shows that the Terrorist Groups, engaged in killing infidels (according to their interpretation of Islam) followed the religious

---

[410] Dreazen Yochi—ISIS uses mafia tactics to fund its operations—Foreign Policy. Archived on June 17, 2014. Retrieved September 4, 2014. 4=Rosen, Armin (Aug 20, 2014)—ISIS has been taking foreign hostages since the very beginning and getting paid for them—-—Business Insider—. Retrieved 4 September 2014.

[411] The Chibok Kidnappings in North-East Nigeria: A Military Analysis of Before and After. Small Wars Journal. Volume 13, No. 4, 11 April 2017. 2=Nigeria Chibok girls 'shown alive' in Boko Haram video—BBC News Africa. 14 April 2016. Retrieved 14 April 2016.

doctrine of Saudi Salafism, which declares all those who are different from them, as infidels whose killing and extermination is justified. It is this ideology of intolerance and violence which motivated them in their inhuman and abhorrent acts, against the Shias, Ahmadis, Jews, and Christians, in Muslim countries and elsewhere, including Europe and the United States. Main groups engaged in atrocious terrorist acts have been: Al Nusra Front, Al Qaeda, ISIS, and their associated Sunni groups, in Syria and Iraq; Tehrik-e-Taliban Pakistan (TTP), Lashkar-e-Jhangvi (LeJ), Jundullah, al-Qaeda, the East Turkestan Islamic Movement (ETIM), the Islamic Movement of Uzbekistan (IMU) and the Haqqani network in Pakistan; al-Qaeda-affiliated Jemaah Islamiyah in Indonesia; Boko Haram, another violent group, associated with ISIS, in Nigeria and other west African countries. All these groups have been supported and funded by charities and individuals in Saudi Arabia and other Gulf countries, with the tacit knowledge and approval of their governments. It has been a Global problem which needed to be addressed by the United States and its allies who encouraged and strengthened this extremism, in the first place, for political purposes - to contain and defeat the Soviet Union, and to counter socialist and nationalist movements in the world. This chapter describes the deception employed by the donors, to hide the funding mechanisms.US government agencies have been pointing out the deceptive activities of donors for decades, but no concrete actions have been taken, by the Arab governments so far. As a result, terrorism has been continuing, with no end in sight. It is only the King of Saudi Arabia who can discourage and isolate the terrorists, by abrogating the TAKFIR doctrine of Saudi Salafism, so that the Saudi religion accommodates all sects of Islam, other religions, and lifestyles. Abrogation of takfir will certainly demotivate the terrorists and delegitimize their actions which, at present, have a religious sanction. Without the King's direct and daring involvement, Islamic Terrorism cannot be stemmed. The terrorists mostly operate covertly. They are not always in the battlefield, like the Islamic State fighters, where they could all be killed. We will, now, look at the main terrorist groups in detail.

Al Qaeda: It is a militant Sunni Islamic organization, founded in 1988, by Osama bin Laden, Abdullah Azzam, and several other Arab volunteers, who fought against the Soviet Invasion of Afghanistan, in the 1980s. It works as a network, made up of Islamic extremists of Saudi /Salafi ideology. Al-Qaeda has carried out attacks on civilian and military targets in various countries. They are also involved in Sectarian Killings. Examples of sectarian attacks in Iraq, include the Yazidi bombings, Sadr city bombings, the Ashura Massacre and April 2007 Baghdad bombings. Tactics employed by al-Qaeda included Suicide Attacks and the simultaneous bombing of different targets. Al-Qaeda considered liberal Muslims, Shias, Sufis, and other sects as heretics and attacked their mosques and gatherings. Its ideologues envisioned a complete break from all foreign influences, in Muslim countries, and the creation of a new state, ruling over the entire Muslim world. Following the ideology of Sayyid Qutb, the Salafi Ideologue of Egypt, members of al-Qaeda believed that a Christian–Jewish alliance had been conspiring to destroy Islam and that the Muslims should fight the apostate regimes and populations, who did not follow the Islamic Law, and to this end, they believed that killing of non-combatants, including women and children, was religiously sanctioned . They were like the Khawarij of the seventh century of Islam, who ignored the injunctions of the Qur'an and Hadith, which forbids killing of any human except for the enforcement of the Rule of Law. Al-Qaeda opposed what it regarded as fabricated worldly laws and wanted to replace them with a strict form of Sharia Law.[412]

Organization: Al-Qaeda's leadership, following the "War on Terror," had "become geographically isolated," leading to the "emergence of decentralized leadership" of regional groups. described as "centralization of decision and decentralization of execution." Al-Qaeda had the direct affiliates in Iraq, Yemen, Somalia, Nigeria, Syria, India, Saudi Arabia, Lebanon, Bosnia, Mali, and Russia.[413]

Financing: Financing of al-Qaeda in the 1990s, initially, came from the personal wealth of Osama bin Laden. Other sources of income in 2001,

---

[412] Bill Moyers—a brief history of al-Qaeda—. PBS.com. July 27, 2007. Retrieved March 31, 2012

[413] al Qaeda ideology MI5.—Archived on February 28, 2009—. Retrieved May 19, 2012.

included the heroin trade and donations from supporters in Kuwait, Saudi Arabia, and other Gulf States. The Saudi government and Saudi charitable foundations, run by religious Saudi Salafis, directly aided the terrorists and terrorist groups financially. According to Anthony H. Cordesman, this flow of money from the Kingdom to extremists has "probably" had more effect than the kingdom's "religious thinking and missionary efforts." In addition to donations by believers in jihadism, money for terrorists also came as a form of payoff to terrorist groups by some members of the Saudi ruling class, in part, to keep the jihadists away from Saudi Arabia.[414] Some examples of funding are checks written by Princess Haifa bint Faisal, wife of Prince Bandar bin Sultan, Saudi ambassador to Washington, totaling as much as $73,000, ended up with Omar al-Bayoumi, a Saudi who hosted and otherwise helped two of the September 11 hijackers, when they reached America. A Wikileaks-released memo from the United States Secretary of State, sent in 2009, asserted that the primary source of funding of Sunni terrorist groups worldwide, was Saudi Arabia. Among the first pieces of evidence of Saudi Arabia's conspicuous support for al-Qaeda was the so-called "Golden Chain," a list of early al-Qaeda funders, seized during a 2002 raid, at the premises of the Benevolence International Foundation (BIF) in Sarajevo, by Bosnian police. The hand-written list, confirmed by al-Qaeda defector Jamal al-Fadl, included the names of both donors and beneficiaries. Osama bin-Laden's name appeared seven times, among the beneficiaries, while 20 Saudi and Gulf-based businesspeople and politicians were listed among the donors. Besides Osama bin Laden, among the most notable beneficiaries, were Adel Batterjee (founder of BIF and declared as a terror financier by the U.S. Department of the Treasury in 2004) and Wael Hamza Julaidan (U.S.- designated terrorist in 2002, as one of al-Qaeda's funders). The most prominent Saudi figures, among the donors, included Saudi billionaire Saleh Kamil (CEO of Dallah Al-Baraka, accused of funding and supporting al-Qaeda operations), Suleiman Abdul Aziz Al Rajhi (funder of SAAR Foundation, shut down within the framework of Operation Green Quest, and CEO of al-Rajhi Bank, investigated several times by U.S. authorities for his role in financing terrorism and al-Qaeda

---

[414] Eric Lichtblau and Eric Schmitt—cash flow to terrorists evades US Efforts—New York Times- December 5, 2010

especially), and Ahmad Turki Yamani (son of former Saudi chief Justice and former Saudi Minister of Petroleum). Saleh Kamil's case confirms Saudi Arabia's role as sponsor of al-Qaeda. For years, Omar al-Bayoumi, an associate of Khalid Al Mihdhar and Nawaf Alhazmi, two 9/11 hijackers, received a stipend from al-Baraka, the financial group Kamil directed. Kamil invested for several years, in a Sudanese bank that held accounts, under the names of senior al-Qaeda affiliates. According to the Wall Street Journal, the Jeddah-based al-Baraka Bank, one of the biggest subsidiaries of the financial group, was also suspected of giving banking services to al-Qaeda operatives.[415]

Qatar's Support of al-Qaeda: Qatar has been providing financial support to al-Qaeda as well. On December 18, 2013, the U.S. Treasury designated Abd Al-Rahman al-Nuaimi, a Qatari citizen, close to the al-Thani Ruling family and a human rights activist, who founded the Swiss-based NGO Akarma, as a global terrorist for his activities, in support of al-Qaeda. The U.S. Treasury claimed that Nuaimi, currently enjoying impunity in Qatar, "has facilitated significant financial support to al-Qaeda in Iraq and served as an intermediary between al-Qaeda in Iraq leaders and Qatar-based donors." Nuaimi was also accused of overseeing a $2 million monthly transfer to al-Qaeda in Iraq, for a period, as part of his role as mediator, between Iraq-based al Qaeda senior officers and Qatari citizens. He also allegedly entertained relationships with Abu-Khalid al-Suri, al-Qaeda's top envoy in Syria, who processed a $600,000 transfer to al-Qaeda in 2013. Moreover, Nuaimi and Mohammad 'Abd al-Rahman al-Humayqani, a Yemeni politician and founding member of Al-Karama, were listed as Specially Designated Global Terrorists (SDGT) by the U.S. Treasury in 2013.[416] Qatar Charity's record of terror financing includes, support to al-Qaeda terrorists in Chechnya, an accusation, vehemently denied by Hamad bin Nasser al-Thani, the ruling Emir of Qatar, from 1995 to 2013. In 1999, Qatar Charity funneled money to Chechnya-based al-Qaeda

---

[415] Simpson, Glenn R.; Wartzman, Rick (November 3, 2001)—US investigates saudi conglomerate for links to islamic militants—. Retrieved June 21, 2016 – via Wall Street Journal.

[416] treasury designates al-Qaeda supporters in Qatar and yemen—Retrieved June 21, 2016.

affiliates. Furthermore, Qatar Charity is among the NGOs, channeling funds to' Ansar Dine' in North Mali, a piece of information confirmed by French military intelligence reports, dating back to France's intervention in the country, in early 2013. The terrorist group has long been suspected of having ties with al-Qaeda.[417]

Al Qaeda Strategy: Al Qaeda's Strategy up to the Year 2020, published On March 11, 2005, by Al-Quds Al-Arabi, comprises five stages, to rid the Muslim Ummah from all forms of oppression: 1) Provoke the United States and the West, into invading a Muslim country, by staging a massive attack or string of attacks on US soil that result in massive civilian casualties. 2) Incite local resistance to occupying forces. 3) Expand the conflict to neighboring countries, and engage the US and its allies, in a long war of attrition. 4) Convert al-Qaeda into an ideology and set of operating principles that can be loosely franchised in other countries, without requiring direct command and control, and via these franchises, incite attacks against the US and countries allied with the US, until they withdraw from the conflict, as happened with the 2004 Madrid train bombings, but which did not have the same effect with the July 7,2005 London Bombings. 5) The US economy will finally collapse by the year 2020, under the strain of multiple engagements in numerous places, making the worldwide economic system, which is dependent on the US, also collapse, leading to global political instability, which in turn will lead to a global jihad, led by al-Qaeda, resulting in the installation of a Saudi Salafi Caliphate, across the world, following the collapse of the US and the rest of the Western world countries.[418]

Al-Nusra Front: Al-Nusra is a terrorist group, which had been engaged in fighting, against the Syrian Government forces, in the Syrian Civil War, with the aim of establishing an Islamist state in the country. It was the official Syrian branch of al-Qaeda, until July 2016. It did not have a global agenda. It was primarily made up of Syrian jihadis. Syrian members

---

[417] Reports, CATF.—Qatar charity—pioneer and master of terror finance—*stopterrorfinance.org*.—Retrieved June 6, 2017.

[418] Dreaming of a caliphate—The Economist. August 6, 2011. Retrieved May 19, 2012.

of the group claimed, that they were fighting only the Assad regime and would not attack Western states; while the official policy of the group was to regard the United States and Israel as enemies of Islam, and to warn against Western intervention in Syria. As of November 2013, there were five Americans fighting in Syria, three of whom were linked to al-Nusra. It was estimated that al-Nusra's fighting force was approximately 30% foreign fighters and 70% local Islamists.[419]

Nusra Front Support & Financing: The Nusra Front had been well-funded, since its inception in 2011. Funding for the group included private donations from wealthy individuals in Saudi Arabia, Qatar, and Kuwait, who provided funds through small money transfers, or by dispatching the money with individuals who crossed state borders into Nusra-held areas. The Nusra Front had received millions of dollars, through hostage exchanges, negotiated by the Qatari government. The group received $4 million, when it released four Greek Orthodox nuns in March 2014, and $25 million when it released 45 U.N. peacekeepers.[420] Saudi Arabia had accused Qatar of helping al-Nusra but, according to the Al-Ahram Weekly, the Saudis and Qataris provided funding to al-Nusra because it was the most in line with the Saudi/ Salafi Ideology. During 2012-2013, The US Government had been sending weapons to US-supported rebels in Syria, but they had been passed on to Al-Nusra by Ahrar ash-Sham.[421]

Sarin Gas Attack: Turkish newspapers reported that the Turkish police had arrested al-Nusra fighters, at the Syrian border, carrying 2 kg of Sarin Gas, which was confiscated. This proved that al-Nusra handled the Sarin Attacks on August 21,2013 at Ghouta, killing hundreds of people, and

---

[419] syrian Nusra Front announces split from al-qaeda—. 28 July 2016. Retrieved 28 July 2016. 2= Zawahiri disbands main al-Qaeda in syria—Global Post. 8 November 2013. Archived on 9 November 2013. Retrieved 15 November 2013.

[420] CATF Reports—Funding al-Nusra through ransoms by Qatar—consortium against terror financing—Stopterrorfinance.org. Retrieved 2016-07-28.

[421] Ernesto Londoño and Greg Miller (11 September 2013)—CIA begins weapons delivery to syrian rebels—. *The Washington Post*. Retrieved 18 August 2014. 2= US has secretly trained Syrian rebels since 2012—. *Los Angeles Times*. 21 June 2013. 3=Lisa Lundquist (27 April 2014)—shadowy flow of weapons into syria.—Longwarjournal.org. Retrieved 3 June 2015.

not the Syrian troops, as alleged by western media and politicians. Turkish MP Erdem explained the entire episode, in a testimony, to the Turkish parliament, alleging that the deadly gas was smuggled to Syrian opposition, with full knowledge of the Turkish government.

Turkish MP's Testimony: Addressing fellow members of the Turkish Parliament, Turkish MP Erdem from the opposition Republican People's Party directly confronted his government on a key issue. Waving a copy of "Criminal Case Number 2013/120," Erdem described official Turkish reports and electronic evidence, documenting a smuggling operation with Turkish government complicity. The General Prosecutor in the Turkish city of Adana opened a criminal case and a formal accusation stated, "chemical weapons components from Europe were to be shipped via a designated route through Turkey to militant labs in Syria." In an interview with RT four days later, Erdem said Turkish authorities had evidence of sarin gas-related shipments to anti-government rebels in Syria and did nothing to stop them. Erdem testified that the 13 suspects, who had been arrested in police raids on the plotters, were released just a week after they were indicted. The case was shut down abruptly by higher authority. Erdem told RT that the sarin attack at Ghouta took place shortly after the criminal case was closed. Coordination Meetings had taken place, just weeks before the sarin attack, at a Turkish military garrison in Antakya, some 15 miles from the border with Syria. These meetings were attended by CIA, Saudi Intelligence, ISIS, and Turkish Intelligence agents, who were said to be coordinating plans, with Western-sponsored rebels who were told to expect an imminent escalation in the fighting due to "a war-changing development." This, in turn, would lead to a U.S.-led bombing of Syria, and rebel commanders were ordered to prepare their forces quickly to exploit the bombing, march into Damascus, and remove the Assad government. Shortly after disclosing the Turkish government complicity, in transfer of deadly sarin gas to ISIS in Syria, in an interview with RT, treason charges were laid against MP Erdem, in December 2015.

It is hard to believe that a President of a major country calls the head diplomat of a rival state a "liar," but that is the label Russian President Putin chose for Kerry on the day, after his congressional testimony. Referring to Kerry, during a televised meeting of the Russian Presidential Human Rights Council on Sept. 4, Putin addressed the sarin issue in these words: "It is simply absurd to imagine that Assad used chemical weapons, given that he is gaining ground. This is a weapon of last resort." Putin claimed, correctly, that Assad had "encircled his adversaries in some places and was finishing them off." Putin continued: "I watched the congressional debates. A member of Congress asked Mr. Kerry, 'Is Al Qaeda present there? I've heard they have gained momentum.' He replied, 'No. I can tell you earnestly, they are not.'" Putin continued, "The main combat unit, the so-called Al-Nusra, is an Al-Qaeda subdivision. They [the Americans] know about this. This was very unpleasant and surprising for me. We talk with them, and we assume they are decent people. But he is lying, and he knows he is lying. That is sad. "We are currently focused on the fact that the U.S. Congress and Senate are discussing authorization for use of force in Syria. As you know, Syria is not attacking the U.S., so there is no question of self-defence; and anything else, lacking U.N. authorization, is an act of aggression. We are all glued to our televisions, waiting to see if they will get the approval of Congress. "On the following day, Sept. 5, Obama arrived in St. Petersburg, for a G20 summit, with ample reason to suspect that Putin was right about Kerry, lying about the sarin attack. President Obama, having been warned the previous week by National Intelligence Director James Clapper that there was no" slam-dunk" (irrefutable) evidence against the Assad regime. So, Obama agreed to Putin's offer, to get Syria to surrender its chemical weapons for destruction, and the war fever began to abate.[422]

ISIS (Islamic State of Iraq and Syria): ISIS follows Saudi Salafi doctrine of Sunni Islam, which sanctions killing of people who do not agree with them, such as the Shia Muslims, Jews, Christians, and people of other faiths and lifestyles, whom they consider apostates, who deserve to be killed. The self-declared "Islamic State" in Iraq and Syria, headed by Abu Bakr al-Baghdadi, had been described, as both more violent than al-Qaeda and more closely aligned with Saudi Salafism. For their guiding principles, the leaders of ISIS, were open and clear about their almost exclusive

---

[422] https://ahtribune.com/opinion/267-turke. 2= https://www.belfasttelegraph.co.uk/new 3=https://www.commondreams.org/views

commitment to the Saudi Salafi ideology. The group circulated images of Saudi Salafi religious textbooks from Saudi Arabia, in the schools it controlled. Videos from the group's territory, had shown Saudi Salafi texts, plastered on the sides of an official missionary van. ISIS eventually published its own books and, out of the twelve works by Muslim scholars, it re-published, seven were by Imam Mohammad ibn Abd al-Wahhab, the founder of Saudi Salafism. Sheikh Adil al-Kalbani, a former imam of the Grand Mosque of Mecca, told a television interviewer in January 2016, that the Islamic State leaders "draw their ideas from what is written in our own books, our own principles." According to former British intelligence officer Alastair Crooke, ISIS "is deeply Saudi Salafi ", but also "a corrective movement to the current Saudi Salafism." In Saudi Arabia itself, the ruling elite is divided. Some applaud that ISIS is fighting Iranian Shiite "fire" with Sunni "fire"; that a new Sunni state is taking shape at the very heart of what they regard as a historical Sunni patrimony. Former CIA director James Woolsey described Saudi as "the soil in which Al Qaeda and its sister terrorist organizations have been flourishing." However, the Saudi government strenuously denied these claims or that it exported religious or cultural extremism. ISIS gained global prominence in early 2014, when it captured key cities in Iraq. ISIS originated in 1999 when it pledged allegiance to al-Qaeda and participated in the Iraqi Insurgency, after the 2003 invasion of Iraq, by the US and Western forces. It claimed religious, political, and military authority over all Muslims worldwide. In Syria, the group conducted ground attacks against Syrian government forces and by December 2015, it held a large area in western Iraq and eastern Syria, containing an estimated 2.8 to 8 million people, where it enforced its interpretation of Sharia Law.[423] ISIS was then believed to be operational in 18 countries, including Afghanistan and Pakistan, with "aspiring branches" in Mali, Egypt, Somalia, Bangladesh, Indonesia, and the Philippines. As of 2015, ISIS was estimated to have an annual budget of more than US$1 billion and a force of more than 30,000 fighters. As

---

[423] Suadad Al-Salhy; Tim Arango (10 June 2014).—Sunni Militants drive Iraqi army out of Mosul—The New York Times. Retrieved 10 December 2015. 4=Arango, Tim (3 August 2014).—Sunni extremists in iraq seize 3 towns from Kurds and threaten maor dam—The New York Times. Retrieved 20 August 2014

of 2019, ISIS has been decisively defeated, in most countries, but sporadic attacks by ISIS, however, still exist. For example: In the Philippines, a cathedral was bombed by ISIS branch of Abu Sayyaf terror group, killing 22, and injuring 102. In Sri Lanka, on 21 April 2019 Christian churches were bombed killing 253, including 45 children, and 38 foreign nationals.[424]

ISIS Funding by Saudi Arabia and Qatar: Unregistered charity organizations, acted as fronts to pass funds to ISIS; they disguised funding for ISIS's operations as donations for "humanitarian charity". Private donors within Qatar, sympathetic to the aims of radical groups, such as al-Nusra and ISIS, supported these organizations. According to the US Treasury Department, several terrorist financiers from Qatar, such as Qatari citizen Abd al Rahman al Nuaimi facilitated funding from Qatari donors to the leaders of al-Qaeda in Iraq (AQI). He oversaw the transfer of US$2 million per month to AQI over a period. He was also one of several Qatar-based al-Qaeda financiers, sanctioned by the U.S. Treasury, in recent years. In August 2014, a German minister Gerd Mueller accused Qatar of having links to ISIS, saying "You must ask, who is arming, who is financing ISIS troops? The keyword there is Qatar". Richard Dearlove, former head of Britain's Secret Intelligence Service (MI6), said that the Saudis were "deeply attracted to any militancy that can effectively challenge the Shia version of Islam, Dearlove stated that, "For ISIS to be able to surge into the Sunni areas of Iraq in the way that it had done recently, had to be the consequence of substantial and sustained funding". In an August 2014 email, leaked by Wikileaks, which former US Secretary of State Hillary Clinton, sent to John Podesta (who was then a counsellor to Barack Obama), a memo saying that both Saudi Arabia and Qatar "are providing clandestine financial and logistic support to ISIS, and other radical Sunni groups in the region".[425] Julian Assange of Wikileaks, claimed in an interview, that Hillary Clinton's 'Clinton Foundation' and

---

[424] Philippines attack by Abu Sayyaf—. *Relief Web. Retrieved 17 June 2019*—. *Safi, Michael (25 April 2019)-Sri Lanka bombings death toll down to 253—The Guardian News—Retrieved 6 June 2019.*

[425] Cockburn, Patrick (14 October 2016).—We finally know what Hillary Clinton knew all along—US allies Saudi Arabia and Qatar are funding ISIS.—Independent.

ISIS, both receive funding from the same sources in the Middle East, namely the government of Saudi Arabia and Qatar.[426]

Turkish Support to ISIS: Turkey had been accused by experts, Syrian Kurds, and United States Vice-President Joe Biden, of supporting or colluding with ISIS A raid by US special forces on a compound housing the Islamic State's "chief financial officer," Abu Sayyaf in July 2015, produced evidence that Turkish officials dealt directly with ranking ISIS members. According to a senior Western official, documents and flash drives seized during the Sayyaf raid revealed links "so clear" and "undeniable" between Turkey and ISIS, "that they could end up having profound policy implications, for the relationship between US and Ankara." Journalist Patrick Cockburn wrote in November 2014 of "convincing evidence for a degree of collaboration" between the Turkish Intelligence and ISIS, although the "exact nature of the relationship remains cloudy" In July 2014, Cockburn said that "Saudi Arabia has created a Frankenstein Monster over which it is rapidly losing control." The same is true of its allies, such as Turkey which has been a vital back-base for ISIS and al Nusra by keeping the 820-kilometer long (510 mi) Turkish-Syrian border open. With many Islamist fighters passing through Turkey to fight in Syria, Turkey has been accused of becoming a transit country for such fighters and has been labelled the "Gateway to Jihad".[427]

Haqqani network: Haqqani Group is an Afghan guerilla group which has been fighting the NATO forces and the government of Afghanistan. It is led by Jalaluddin Haqqani and his son Sirajuddin. The Haqqani network's aims are nationalistic. They are ideologically aligned with the Taliban who have worked to eradicate Western influence and transform Afghanistan into a sharia-following state. Both groups have the common goal of disrupting the Western military and political efforts in Afghanistan and driving them away from the country permanently. Currently, the group demands that US and Coalition Forces, made up mostly of NATO

---

[426] German minister accuses Qatar of funding ISIS fighters—Reuters. 20 August 2014. Retrieved 8 May 2015

[427] Cockburn, Patrick—(6 November 2014).—Whose side is Turkey on ?—London Review of Books—Vol. 36 no. 21. pp. 8–10.

Nations, withdraw from Afghanistan and no longer interfere with the politics or educational systems of Islamic nations. CIA and Pakistani ISI supported the group, during the war in Afghanistan against the Soviet forces in the 1980's.[428]

Relations with Al-Qaeda and Bin Laden: Jalaluddin Haqqani commanded the Mujahideen Army from 1980-1992. He is credited with recruiting foreign fighters. Two well-known Arab jihadists, Abdullah Azzam and Osama bin Laden, both began their careers as volunteers, with Haqqani, who trained them to fight the Soviets. Al-Qaeda and the Haqqani network, in other words, evolved together, and they have remained connected throughout their history. The Haqqani network's relationship with Al-Qaeda dates to its founding. The significant difference between the two organizations is that AL-Qaeda goals are global and use global means; whereas Haqqani is solely interested in Afghanistan and the Pashtun Tribal regions. Jalaluddin Haqqani is more interested in the influence of Islamic Law, over Afghanistan, than the global Jihad. Foreign jihadists recognized the network as a distinct entity as early as 1994, but Haqqani was not affiliated with the Taliban until they captured Kabul and assumed control of Afghanistan in 1996. After the Taliban came to power, Haqqani accepted a cabinet-level appointment as Minister of Tribal Affairs. Following the U.S.-led invasion of Afghanistan in 2001 and the subsequent overthrow of the Taliban government, Haqqani fled to the bordering Pakistani tribal regions and regrouped to wage a guerrilla warfare against the coalition forces across the border. Many sources believe Jalaluddin Haqqani and his forces assisted with the escape of Al-Qaeda into safe-havens in Pakistan.[429] Considering how closely the two groups have been connected, it is well documented that the Haqqani network did help with the establishment of safe-havens for Al-Qaeda. Peter Bergen stresses this point in his book "The Battle for Tora Bora".[429]

---

[428] "Brown, V.; Rassler, D.; Fountainhead of Jihad: The Haqqani Network, 1973-2012." Columbia University Press 2013

[429] Smucker, Philip; Al-Qaeda's Great Escape: The military and media on Terror's" Dulles, Virginia, Bassey's 2004.

Haqqani Funding: Sirajuddin Haqqani brothers, traveled to Gulf countries to raise funds from wealthy donors. Also, they had tax offices, courts, madrasas, car dealerships and real estate activities in Miranshah, Pakistan, to raise funds. According to a tribal elder in Paktia, "Haqqani people asked for money from contractors working on road construction. They were asking for money or goods from shopkeepers. District elders and contractors were paying money to Afghan workers, but sometimes half of the money went to Haqqani people.[430]

Lashkar-e-Taiba (Let)[431]**:** It was the largest and most active militant organization in South Asia. It was founded by Hafiz Saeed, Abdullah Azzam and Zafar Iqbal in 1987, with funding from Osama bin Laden. Its headquarter was in Muridke, near Lahore, Pakistan. Its goal was to set up an Islamic State in South Asia and liberate Muslims of Indian Kashmir. Since 2015, it has been banned in Pakistan. The group was initially motivated by the 1992 demolition of Babri Mosque, by Hindu militants. Since then, its attacks had been directed against India. In January 2009, Let publicly declared that it would pursue a peaceful resolution of the Kashmir issue and that it did not have global jihadist aims, but the group was still believed to be active in several other spheres of anti-Indian terrorism. The disclosures of Jundal who was extradited to India by the Saudi Arabian government, revealed that Let was planning to revive militancy in Jammu and Kashmir and conducted major terror strikes in India.[432]

Funding of Let: Let assisted victims, after the 2005 Kashmir Earthquake. In many instances, they were the first to arrive on the scene, arriving even before the army or other civilians. A large amount of funds collected from the Pakistani expatriate community in Britain, to aid victims of the earthquake, were funneled for terrorist activities of Let, about which the donors were unaware. About 5 million pounds were collected, but more

---

[430] Gopal, Anand; Mansur Khan Mahsud; Brian Fishman (3 June 2010).—inside Haqqani Network—Foreign Policy. The Slate Group, LLC. Retrieved 23 November 2011.
[431] Lashkar-e-Taiba (Let)
[432] Deadly Embrace—Pakistan, US and future of Global Jihad—. Brookings.edu. Archived on 27 January 2012. Retrieved 28 October 2012.

than half of the funds were directed towards Let, rather than towards relief efforts. Intelligence officials stated that some of the funds were used to prepare for an attack on airliners. Other investigations also indicated the aid given for earthquake victims was directly involved, in expanding Lashkar-e-Taiba's activities within India.[433] The Let collected donations from the Pakistani immigrant community in the Persian Gulf and in the United Kingdom from Islamic Non-Governmental Organizations, Pakistani and Kashmiri businesspeople. Although a part of the funds collected went towards legitimate uses, e.g. factories and other businesses, a massive part was dedicated to military activities. According to US intelligence, the Let had a military budget of more than $5 million by 2009.[434]

Lashkar-e-Jhangvi: (LeJ) It is an offshoot of anti-Shia group Sipah-e Sahaba (SSP), Pakistan. It was founded by former SSP activists Riaz Basra, Malik Ishaq, Akram Lahori and Ghulam Rasool Shah who believed that SSP was not violent enough. The group killed about 600 Shias from 1999-2003.[435] About five hundred Shia doctors had fled Pakistan, in the space of a few years, after more than fifty of their colleagues were assassinated in Karachi. Terrorist groups like LeJ, consider not only the Shias but also, Sufi Muslims who venerate shrines of Sufi mystics, as infidels deserving death. In the summer of 2011, LeJ sent a letter to the Shia community in Quetta, the capital of Pakistan's Baluchistan province and home to around six hundred thousand Shias from the Hazara tribe. The letter, written in Urdu and signed by LeJ commander read: "All Shias are worthy of killing. We will rid Pakistan of [these] unclean people. Pakistan means land of the pure, and the Shias have no right to be here. We will make Pakistan their

---

[433] Partlow, Joshua; Kamran Khan (15 August 2006).—charity funds said to provide clues to alleged terrorist plot—. The Washington Post. Retrieved 21 January 2009. 7= Quake came as a boon for Lashkar leadership—The Hindu, November 17, 2005.

[434] Kate Clark—(5 October 2006).—UN quake aid went to extremists—BBC News. Retrieved 28 February 2012. 5=McGurk, Jan (October 2005).—Jihadis in Kashmir—politics of Earthquake—. Qantara. Retrieved 5 December 2008.

[435] Roul, Animesh (2 June 2005)—sectarian violence in Pakistan and ties to international terrorism—. *Terrorism Monitor.* Jamestown Foundation. 3 (11). Retrieved 24 September 2013.

graveyard— bombs and suicide bombers will destroy their houses". The LeJ is responsible for many Shia Massacres in Pakistan, including killing of over 200 Hazara Shias in Quetta in 2013; the abduction of Daniel Pearl in 2002 and an attack on Sri Lanka Cricket Team in Lahore in 2009.[436] Basra, the first Leader of LeJ, was killed by police in 2002; the second leader Malik Ishaq, along with Ghulam Rasool Shah, were also killed by police, in 2015. LeJ (of Pakistan) follows a Saudi Salafi-influenced version of the Deobandi movement and seeks to set up a Sunni state in Pakistan. LeJ is virulently anti-Shiite, declaring Shiites infidels and directing most of its attacks against them. It also advocates the destruction of other religions, including Judaism, Christianity, and Hinduism. In the 2000s, it began to work toward an additional goal of driving Western influences from the region.

Funding of LeJ: LeJ gets most of its funding from wealthy donors in Saudi Arabia and the broader Middle East. The group also engages in extortion, to fund its operations. Most of its members are recruited from Sunni madrassas in Pakistan. A testament of Saudi funding of LeJ is the following episode: "After a meal of chicken, curry, and spinach, Ludhianvi, an official of LeJ, (Head of the group) and his aides stood up to warmly welcome a visitor: A Saudi Arabia-based cleric Abdul Haq al-Mekki. A Pakistani cleric, knowledgeable about Sunni groups, described Mekki as a middleman between Saudi donors, intelligence agencies and the LeJ, the SSP and other groups."[437] "Of course, Saudi Arabia supports these groups. They want to keep Iranian influence in check in Pakistan, so they pay," the Pakistani cleric said. His account tallied with that of a Pakistani intelligence agent, who said jailed militants had confessed that LeJ received Saudi funding.[438] A Stanford University study also said that, "LeJ receives money from several Persian Gulf countries, including Saudi

---

[436] Pakistan Shias killed in Gilgit in sectarian violence—BBC News. 16 August 2012. Retrieved 11 December 2012. A predominantly Punjabi group, Lashkar-e-Jhangvi is linked with the 2002 murder of US reporter Daniel Pearl and other militant attacks, particularly in the southern city of Karachi.

[437] https://www.reuters.com/article/us-pak—Special Report—under" Saudi Connection"

[438] http://web.stanford.edu/group/mapping

Arabia and the United Arab Emirates. These countries fund LeJ and other Sunni militant groups, primarily to counter the rising influence of Iran's revolutionary Shiism. This is especially relevant now, that LeJ attacks on Shias are becoming more frequent and lethal. They just killed 81 people in Quetta and another 100-people last month.[439]

Jundullah: It was set up in 2003, as a Baluch militant group in Sistan and Baluchistan province of Iran. It has about 2000 members. As of December 2014, it is said to handle killing of 154 and injuring 320 Iranian citizens, since 2003, while Jundullah commanders claim the group has killed up to 400 Iranian soldiers. Its founder, Abdolmalek Rigi, was radicalized in a Pakistani madrassa in the 1990s. Its goals are to fight for Sunni rights and improve economic conditions, in their province.[440] The Iranian government characterizes Jundullah as, a radical separatist movement. Since 2005, it has carried out attacks on both government and civilian targets, including kidnappings, ambushes, and bombings. In 2005, it ambushed President Mahmoud Ahmadinejad's motorcade near Zabul, killing one of his bodyguards.[441] In October 2009, 40 people were killed in a bombing in Pishin; 15 were Revolutionary Guards, including veteran commander Noor Ali Shooshtari.[442] Jundullah is also, reportedly, involved in narcotics and oil smuggling. Like many terrorist groups, Jundullah has an extreme ideology of Saudi / Salafism. It kidnaps and beheads civilian targets.[443] Most fighters are recruited from religious seminaries in both Iran and Pakistan. Rigi has claimed that between 20 and 50 operatives

---

[439] SATP. 2015. "Lashkar-E-Jhangvi." Research Group. South Asia Terrorism Portal. Accessed May 14. www.satp.org/satporgtp/contries/pakistan/terroristoutfits/lej.html

[440] Spencer, Richard; Osborn, Andrew; Waterfield, Bruno (2010-02-23).—Iran arrests most wanted man after police board civilian flight—The Daily Telegraph. London. Retrieved 2010-05-07. 6=.Iran-Jundullah leader claims US military support—BBC News. 2010-02-26. Retrieved 2015-08-19.

[441] Fathi, Nazila (2007-02-15).—car bomb in Iran destroys a bus carrying revolutionary guards—. The New York Times. Retrieved 2010-05-07.

[442] Middle east—Iranian commanders assassinated—BBC News. 2009-10-18. Retrieved 2009-10-20.

[443] 11 guards killed in Iran bomb blast—archived—2007-09-27 at the way back machine—. Gulf Times

are trained each month, in its mountain bases, in Sistan/ Baluchistan. The majority are then sent into the field. Some 200 members maintain mountain bases. The Islamic Republic has been aggressive in combating Jundullah. It has assassinated members as well as arrested, tortured and executed leaders. In 2010, Iran captured Rigi in a commando operation. His trial and execution, at Evin Prison were highly publicized.[444]

Funding: Mossad agents posing as CIA officers met with, and recruited, members of Jundullah in cities such as London to carry out attacks against Iran. After Rigi was arrested on 23 February 2010, Iran's intelligence minister Heyder Moslehi, at a press conference in Tehran, claimed that Rigi had been at a US base in Afghanistan, 24 hours before his arrest. On February 25, Iranian state television broadcast a statement by Rigi stating he had had American support and that "The Americans said Iran was going its own way and they said our problem at the present is Iran, not al-Qaeda and not the Taliban. They [Americans] promised to help us, and they said that they would cooperate with us, free our prisoners and would give us [Jundullah] military equipment, bombs, machine guns, and they would give us a base."[445] Iran considers Jundullah as a group connected to Taliban and their Opium revenues, getting financial as well as ideological support, directly from Saudi Arabia, in collusion with other hardline elements within Pakistan and Afghanistan. Others alleged that United States has long supported, low intensity conflicts and assassinations, with Saudi money, especially against nationalists, socialists, and Shias.

Jaish ul Adl: Jaish ul Adl, or "Army of Justice," is another Baluch Sunni Islamist group in Sistan / Baluchistan. It is one of many splinter organizations that arose, after Rigi was executed. Since 2013, it has become one of the most active movements. The group has ties to al Qaeda cells in Pakistan. It has voiced support for the Sunni opposition in Syria's civil war, as well as, for Iranian Kurdish separatists. In April 26, 2017, the group claimed killing at least nine Iranian border guards, in an ambush. Two

---

[444] Iran executes insurgent leader—accused of ties with American intelligence—CNS News. Retrieved 15 December 2014

[445] Iran—Jundullah leader claims US military support—BBC News. 2010-02-26. Retrieved 2015-08-19.

others were injured, while patrolling at the Pakistan-Iran border. Jaish ul-Adl claimed responsibility for the attack.[446]

Harakat Ansar Iran: Harakat Ansar Iran, or "Movement for the Partisans of Iran," is a third Baluch Sunni Islamist militant group in Sistan and Baluchistan. It is a follower of Jundullah, propagating Salafist ideology. It was primarily active from 2012 to 2013, until it merged with another Baluch militant group, Hizb ul Furqan. The organization received funding from Gulf states, where it operated websites appealing for patronage. Other reports claim, it had received patronage from the Pakistani Sunni extremist group Sipah-e-Sahaba Pakistan, which had supported Sunni extremist and anti-Shiite groups, such as Lashkar-e Jhangvi and the Tehrik-e-Taliban Pakistan (the Pakistani Taliban).[447]

Ansar al Furqan: It is another Baluch militant group working in Sistan and Baluchistan. It is the merger, in 2013, between Harakat Ansar Iran and Hizb ul Furqan. Iran reported that its leader, Hesham Azizi, was killed by Iranian security forces in 2015.[448] Abu Hafs al Baluchi took over afterwards. Iranian sources charge that Ansar al Furqan is receiving support, primarily, from the Gulf States. According to terrorism research and analysis consortium—it had ties to al-Nusra of Syria and Jaish ul-Adl.[449]

Jemaah Islamiyah: It was a Southeast Asian militant extremist Islamic terror group, dedicated to the establishment of an Islamic state in Southeast Asia. On October 25, 2002, after the Bali bombing, JI was declared to be a terrorist group by the UN and the NATO countries. JI had cells in Thailand, Singapore, Malaysia, and the Philippines. The war on terrorism had continued in Southeast Asia, and governments in the region deserve credit for the arrests of more than 200 Jemaah Islamiyah (JI) members,

---

[446] Iran's Sunni Baluch extremists operating from areas in Pakistan—Jamestown foundation—20 March 2014. Retrieved 11 November 2014.
[447] (in Persian). Mashregh News—. Retrieved 15 April 2015. What is Qatar up to, in south of Iran?
[448] Head of Ansar al Furqan killed in Iran—Press TV. 22 April 2015. Retrieved 23 April 2015
[449] Ansar al-Furqan—terrorism research and analysis consortium—28 March 2014. Retrieved 20 October 2014

through September 2003, including more than 30 in Singapore, 80 in Malaysia, 80 in Indonesia, about 12 in the Philippines, and 8 in Thailand and Cambodia.[450] Several members of JI's regional shura, its leadership body, were arrested, including operations chief Rizwan Isamuddin (Hambali), Mohammed Iqbal Rahman (Abu Jibril), Agus Dwikarna, and Faiz bin Abu Bakar Bafana, while its spiritual leader, Abu Bakar Ba'asyir was tried in Indonesia for treason. These arrests were significant, especially as JI was not a large organization, with 500 to 1,000 members. The fact, that it focused on soft targets, such as tourist venues, showed institutional weaknesses—the result of two years of intensive investigations and arrests— and it was less able to plan and execute terrorist attacks against hardened targets such as U.S. embassies.[451]

Bali Bombing: The most atrocious terrorist act committed by Jemaah Islamiyah, was the Bali Bombing, on 12 October 2002, in the tourist district of Kuta, on the Indonesian island of Bali. The attack killed 202 people (including 88 Australians, 38 Indonesians, and people from more than 20 other nationalities). A further 209 people were injured. Various members of Jemaah Islamiyah, were convicted in relation to the bombings, including three individuals who were sentenced to death.[452]

Boko Haram: It is an Islamic terror group, follower of Saudi/Salafi ideology of takfir, by which it sanctions killing of non-Saudi Salafis, including Shias, Sufis, Jews, Christians, and other lifestyles. It is allied with ISIS and is intent on setting up an Islamic State.[453] Since 2009, it has killed 20,000 and displaced 2.3 million from their homes. It was ranked

---

[450] NBR Analysis (Dec 2003) Funding Terrorism in Southeast Asia: The Financial Network of Al Qaeda and Jemaah Islamiyah

[451] Zachary Abuza—Contemporary Southeast Asia Vol. 25, No. 2 (August 2003), pp. 169-199

[452] Bali deathtoll set at 202—BBC News. 19 February 2003. Retrieved 14 July 2010. .3= Bali Bombing mastermind Dulmatin killed by police—9 March 2010. Archived—on 14 June 2017. Retrieved 5 April 2011.

[453] Global Terrorism Index(PDF). Institute for Economics and Peace. November 2015. p. 41. Retrieved 23 March 2016.

as the world's deadliest terror group by the Global Terrorism Index 2015.[454] After its founding in 2002, Boko Haram's increasing radicalization, led to a violent uprising in July 2009, in which its leader was executed. Its unexpected resurgence, following a mass prison break in September 2010, was accompanied by increasingly deadly attacks, including suicide bombings of police buildings and the UN office in Abuja. Of the 2.3 million people displaced by the conflict, since May 2013, at least 250,000 have left Nigeria and have fled to Cameroon, Chad, and Niger. Boko Haram killed over 6,600 in 2014. The group carried out mass abductions, including the kidnapping of 276 schoolgirls in April 2014.[455] In mid-2014, the militants gained control of territory, in and around their home state of Bornu, estimated at 50,000 square kilometers (20,000 sq. miles). In September 2015, the Director of Information at the Defense Headquarters of Nigeria, announced that all Boko Haram camps had been destroyed.[456]

Financing of Boko Haram: Ransom for kidnappings, is the most lucrative means of funding for the group, as it makes $1 million for each wealthy Nigerian or foreigner kidnapped. In 2013, Boko Haram kidnapped a family of seven French tourists on vacation in Cameroon and, two months later, released the hostages along with 16 others, in exchange for a ransom of $3.15 million The group also receives money from local governments. For example, Governors of Kano and Bauchi States, pay them monthly. Funding from other sources, like AQIM (al-Qaeda in Maghreb) is nothing compared to income from kidnapping. Other sources of income are bank robberies, drug trade and extortion.[457]

Al-Shabaab: It is an Islamic militant group, based in East Africa, that claims to be waging Jihad against the enemies of Islam. It follows the

---

[454] Abduction of girls—an act, not even al-Qaeda can condone—The New York Times. 8 May 2014. Retrieved 21 May 2016
[455] Abduction of girls—an act, not even al-Qaeda can condone—The New York Times. 8 May 2014. Retrieved 21 May 2016
[456] Nnenna Ibeh (9 September 2015).—Boko Haram camps wiped out-Nigerian Military—Premium Times. Retrieved 10 September 2015.
[457] Ogundipe, Taiwo (29 January 2012).—tracking the sect's cash flow—The Nation. Archived on 13 June 2012. Retrieved 20 March 2012.

Saudi/Salafi Jihadi ideology and is engaged in a combat against the Somalian Government and the African Union Mission forces in Somalia. Al-Shabaab has 7000-9000 militants, at its disposal. Al-Shabaab saw some success in its attacks, against the weak Federal Government, capturing Baidoo, the base of the Transitional Federal Parliament, on January 26, 2009, and killing three ministers of the government in a December 3, 2009 suicide bomb attack, at a medical school graduation ceremony. The group is strong and dangerous, and has been responsible for exceptionally deadly terrorist attacks, such as the 21 September 2013, attack on Westgate Shopping Mall, in Nairobi, in which 67 people died and more than 175 were wounded. Also, On 14 October 2017, a truck bombing in Mogadishu, the capital of Somalia, killed at least 512 people and injured 316. [458]

---

[458] death toll from Mogadishu truck bombing rises to 512—BNO News. Retrieved 2 December 2017. 3= Somalia declares 3 days of mourning—Bloomberg. Retrieved 15 October 2017

CHAPTER 8

Saudi-inspired Conflicts in the World

In recent decades, there have been several regional conflicts, which were inspired or encouraged by Saudi Arabia, to delegitimize and stamp out the Shia religion in general, and to crush the Shia-led 1979 Islamic revolution of Iran, which challenged the Saudi hegemony in the Gulf region. Iraq was encouraged to invade Iran by promising to fund the war. Iran/Iraq war lasted 8 years, 1980 to 1988, and ended in a stalemate, resulting in the strengthening of Iran's revolutionary regime. After Iran/Iraq War, disgruntled Iraq, with formidable military arsenal, turned on its benefactors, invading Saudi Arabia, and occupying Kuwait. Saudi Arabia invited the US to defend it against Iraq, leading to the 1990 Iraq War, waged by the US coalition, which did not topple Iraq's Saddam government. In the meantime, the Afghan Jihad in which about 25,000 Saudi Jihadis took part, ended in defeat and withdrawal of Soviet forces from Afghanistan, in 1989. On September 11, 2001, members of al-Qaeda, most of whom were Saudi nationals, attacked the US, killing about 3000 Americans. The US demanded from the Taliban government of Afghanistan that it hand over Al-Qaeda chief Osama bin Laden, the organizer of the 9/11 attacks. Failure to follow the US request, led to the US attack on Afghanistan, in December 2001. In 2003, the US attacked Iraq, on suspicion of developing Weapons of Mass Destruction, to remove Saddam from power because he posed a danger to Israel and the neighboring Arab countries, who were US allies. Saud Arabia opposed this war because they disliked an expected

Shia-led government in Iraq. They stealthily started strengthening the Iraqi Sunnis, during and after the 2003 Iraq War, thus launching an insurgency, through their proxies, the Al-Qaeda, and the ISIS, against the Shias in general, and the US and the Shia Iraqi government forces. Over time, the insurgency turned into a full-fledged civil War in Iraq, between the Saudi-supported Sunnis, and the Iraqi government forces, supported by Shia militias. The Iraqi civil war had been going on, since 2003, resulting in thousands of deaths in Iraq, of security forces, and civilians, including women and children. In 2011, the Jihadi groups of ISIS, al-Qaeda, and their affiliates were assigned another Jihad, of fighting the Shia-led Syrian government, to topple it. This turned into the Syrian Civil War, in which the Syrian government had been supported by Hezbollah of Lebanon, Iran, and Russia, and the Syrian opposition had been supported by the US, and the European countries, along with the Sunni governments of the middle east. In this chapter, we will discuss all the conflicts mentioned above.

Saudi Policy of Shia Genocide: Terrorists fighting their governments, to set-up Islamic States in their countries were:—ISIS, al-Qaeda, in Iraq, Syria-LeJ (Lashkar-e-Jhangvi), Let (Lashkar-e-Tayyiba) and Taliban in Afghanistan, and Pakistan.—Jemaah Islamiyah in Indonesia.—al-Shabaab and Boko Haram in Somalia and Nigeria. Shia Genocide consisted of mass killings of Shia Muslims in the Muslim majority countries, conducted through the following conflicts which targeted mainly the Shia Muslims: Iran/Iraq War of 1980-88, targeted the Iranian Shias. Iraqi wars of 1990 and 2003, followed by insurgencies in Iraq and Syria, targeted the Shia Muslims of Iraq and Syria. The Yemen War started in 2015, persecuted the Houthi Shias of Yemen. These conflicts were all parts of a broader policy of a Shia Genocide in the world, spearheaded by Saudi Arabia, with emphasis on the Muslim majority countries. The crusades were aimed at, either voluntary or forcible conversion of the populace of these countries, to the extremist ideology of Saudi Salafism. Jihadists were initially influenced by Saudi Ulama, to fight against the Soviet apostate forces in Afghanistan but, after the Soviet defeat and withdrawal, the radicalized Jihadists were encouraged to operate in their home countries, to replace the secular governments, with the Islamic States, based on the Saudi Salafi doctrine. Jihadists were provided with unlimited funding and war materials, by individuals and Charities in Saudi Arabia, Qatar, Kuwait, UAE, with the tacit knowledge and approval of their governments. These Jihadi groups were all adherents of Saudi Salafi/ Jihadi ideology, following a Worldwide policy of Shia Genocide, which was being implemented covertly, by the Saudi Government, since the 1979 Islamic Revolution of Iran. This policy was initially aimed at, countering the effects of the Islamic Revolution of Iran, but later developed into a full-fledged Genocide of the Shia Muslims, all over the world. The following conflicts were instigated, primarily, by the followers of Saudi Salafism (i.e., the Kingdom of Saudi Arabia), to fight and kill the Shia Muslims, whom they consider to be apostates, who deserve to be killed. These conflicts, summarized below, have so far, caused thousands of American, European, Muslim, and non-Muslim deaths of security personnel, civilians, women, and children worldwide:

List of Conflicts:

No.	Period	Conflict	Casualties
1)	1980-88	Iran/Iraq War-	Iran: 400,000 killed Iraq -500,000 Killed & 6000 Iraqis taken prisoners by Iran.

This war started when Iraq invaded Iran, encouraged by the Saudis, with the tacit approval of the United States, to crush the Iranian Revolutionary Government, because the instigators feared export of the revolution, into other countries, and possible disruption of Oil supplies to the US and the West.

2)	1990-91	Gulf War	US & Allied -292 killed-780 wounded 35000 Iraqis killed, 75000 wounded. 4200 Kuwaitis killed, 12000 captured.

This war started after Iran/Iraq War, when Iraq, equipped and funded by the Saudis, Kuwait, and the U.S., turned into a rogue nation, with a formidable military power, attacked and occupied Kuwait, along with a

Saudi border town, Khafji. US coalition attacked to free Kuwait and the Saudi Territory, but Saddam was not removed from power.

3) 11 Sept.2001— 2996 killed
   9/11 Attacks- 1000 died later by debris exposure.
   6000 injured.

Numerous Studies, carried out in the wake of the 9/11 attacks, concluded Saudi connections to the terrorists. Some such studies are described in this book.

4) Afghan War— US Soldiers killed 2300.
   US Allied killed 1100—
   civilians killed 26000—
   civilians injured 20000.
   2002-todate 60,000–65,000+ Taliban killed
   13,700-16,013 US Coalition& Afghan govt. forces killed

Taliban of Afghanistan had been fighting the Afghan Government and the U.S. Coalition. They were followers of Saudi Salafi Ideology and were struggling to topple the Afghan Government. Taliban have always been openly supported by Saudi Arabia.

5) 2001-14: Pakistan Terrorism 6000 soldiers killed-
   30000 Taliban killed.
   21000 civilians killed

Saudi Arabia and other Sunni Arab countries financially supported the Taliban and other terror groups affiliated with them such as LeJ, Let, Jundullah, ISIS, and Al-Qaeda who were followers of Saudi Salafi Ideology, funded lavishly by Saudi Charities, Saudi Princes, with approval of the Saudi government, along with other Sunni Arab countries of the region. They had been fighting the Government of Pakistan, to impose the Saudi/Salafi version of SHARIA law in the country.

6) 2003-2018:   Iraq War   US troops killed: 4500
                            US Allies   "   4800
                            Iraqis killed: 500,000

The rationale for invading Iraq, was a response to 9/11, and allegations of a connection between Saddam Hussein and al-Qaeda 'and that Iraq was building weapons of mass destruction, and hiding a vast chemical and biological weapons arsenal, posing a threat to US allies such as Israel, and the Arab countries of the region. CIA documents, declassified in March 2015, showed that the CIA misled the US government to pass a resolution in Congress, authorizing the use of military force in Iraq, to remove Saddam from power. Saudis opposed this war because they feared the possibility of a Shia-led government in Iraq and did not join the US coalition. Soon after the US attack on Iraq in 2003, Saudis launched an insurgency in Iraq by supporting the Iraqi Sunnis with arms, money, and Saudi jihadis, resulting in the formation of ISIS and other terrorist groups to fight Iraqi Shia civilians and government forces, along with their allied US coalition personnel.

7) 2001-11:   Terrorism in Pakistan   35000 killed
                                        $68 billion
                                        economic loss

Taliban and their associated terrorist groups in Pakistan, have been carrying out suicide bombings and other atrocities, since 2001. They are followers of extremist Saudi Salafi ideology of Islam. Their victims have been mainly Shia Muslims who are considered apostates by them and, therefore (in their opinion) deserve to be killed.

8) 2001-9   Indonesia   500-1000 killed-

Jemaah Islamiyah, an al Qaeda affiliate in Indonesia carried out most of the terrorist attacks in Indonesia. As of 2017, the leaders of the organization have all been captured and killed by Indonesian security forces, and the Jemaah Islamiyah has been disbanded.

9) 2014-15:   Africa   About 9000 killed

Terrorist groups Al Shabab in East Africa, and Boko Haram in west Africa (Nigeria) both have been adherents of Saudi Salafi ideology. As of June 2019, Boko Haram is still active in Nigeria.

10) 2015-to date   Yemen War   over 17000 killed
500 killed in Saudi Arabia
3,154,572 displaced

A Saudi-led coalition, consisting of UAE/Kuwait/Sudan/Egypt have been targeting the Houthi Shia of Yemen, causing loss of life, and major destruction of Yemen's infrastructure, including airports, schools, hospitals, homes. The main instigator of the war has been Saudi Arabia which is supported by the US, Britain, and some European countries, with the most modern weapons of war. Even internationally forbidden weapons such as Cluster munitions are being used against the defenseless civilian populations

11) 2011-2017: Syrian Civil War   Syrians killed 470,000
86000 civilians
6.6 million displaced
4.8 million fled to Turkey, Jordan, Lebanon, Egypt, and Iraq over 1 million sought refuge in Europe-

This war was aimed at replacing the Shia-led government of Bashar Assad of Syria, with an Islamic state of Saudi/Salafi ideology. Saudi proxies consisted of ISIS, al-Qaeda, and their associated groups such as al-Nusra and others. They all aimed at marginalizing and annihilating the Shia populace of Syria. All Groups, fighting against the Syrian Government, were Sunni Muslims, who followed the Saudi/Salafi ideology, including the so-called moderate opposition, and were all supported, directly or indirectly, by the Saudis and/or Gulf donors. There was no such thing as moderates, evidenced by the war events. It was merely a misconception of the western countries, to consider them moderate rebels. President Putin of Russia was allied with the Syrian Government because there were 2000 to 3000 Chechen (Russian) fighters among the ISIS, fighting the Syrian government, and because Russians have had a defense pact with Syria since 1948.

Detail of Conflicts:

Iran/Iraq War: (22 September 1980 to August 1988): Saudi Arabia encouraged Iraq to attack, promising to fund the war, to undermine the 1979 Islamic revolution of Iran, which was so well received, even by the Sunnis of the region and the world. After eight years of a devastating war, the conflict ended on 20 August 1988, after a UN-brokered ceasefire. About a million Iraqi and Iranian soldiers, along with, over 100,000 civilians, were killed in the war, with thousands injured. About 100,000 Iranians, including women and children, died from Chemical Weapons, used by Iraq, during the war, and thousands more maimed for life. The US blocked all efforts, by the UN, to condemn Iraq, for the use of chemical weapons. The war, however, brought neither reparations nor punitive measures or changes in borders. To recoup damage, caused by the Iran/Iraq war, Iraq invaded Kuwait in 1990 but was repulsed by a US-led coalition in the Gulf War of 1990. [459]

Saudi Instigation of Iran/Iraq War: The Shia–Sunni Divide, between Iran and Saudi Arabia, played a pivotal role in the Iran/Iraq War. According to Karen Armstrong, the United States, and the West provided a tacit approval and support to Iraq, for an attack on Iran. The world powers, the United States, Soviet Union, all Arab countries, and the Western powers provided support for Iraq, while Iran was isolated.[460]

The US and Other Support to Iraq: The French sold weapons to Iraq equal to US$5 billion, which included well over a quarter of Iraq's total

---

[459] Molavi, Afshin (2005). The Soul of Iran: A Nation's Journey to Freedom (Revised ed.). England: W. W. Norton & Company. p.152
[460] Bowen Wayne H—the history of Saudi Arabia—Greenwood Press 2008—p.120

arms stockpile.⁴⁶¹ Aid to Iraq, included several billion dollars of economic aid, non-U.S. origin weaponry, military intelligence, and special operations training. While there was, sometimes, direct combat between Iran and the United States, the fighting between the US and Iran was not, specifically, to benefit Iraq. The US and the UK blocked UN resolution to condemn Iraq for using chemical weapons.⁴⁶² The UN did not come to repel Iraqi aggression and the Iranians, therefore, considered the UN as biased, in favor of Iraq.⁴⁶³

Financial Support to Iraq and US Policy: Iraq's principal financial backers were the oil-rich Persian Gulf states. Saudi Arabia gave $30.9 billion, Kuwait $8.2 billion, and the United Arab Emirates $8 billion, in aid to Iraq. Also, Iraq received $35 billion, in loans, from the West, and the Gulf states. During the war, Iraq was considered, by the West and the Soviet Union, as a counterbalance to post-revolutionary Iran.⁴⁶⁴

Jordan's Support to Iraq: King Hussein of Jordan, persuaded the Reagan Administration, to help Iraq.⁴⁶⁵

Support to Iran from Israel and Others: North Korea was a significant arms supplier to Iran. It also facilitated Iran's deals with communist countries. Other suppliers of Iran included Libya and China. Syria, breaking Arab solidarity, supported Iran with arms, rhetoric, and diplomacy. Israel sold US$75 million worth of arms to Iran in 1981. Material included 150

---

461 SIPRI database Indicates that of $29,079 million of arms exported to Iraq from 1980 to 1988 the Soviet Union accounted for $16,808 million, France $4,591 million, and China $5,004 million.
462 Annex D: Iraq Economic Data (1989–2003)"—comprehensive report of special advisor to the director of intelligence on Iraq's WMD—. 1 of 3. Central Intelligence Agency. 27 April 2007
463 United Nations Special Commission-UNSCOM comprehensive review—James Martin Center for Non-proliferation Studies. Archived on 3 January 2013.
464 McCarthy, Andrew C. (3 March 2012).—it is a pity somebody has to win—National Review Online. Retrieved 7 November 2012.
465 David B. Ottaway—the Washington Post, Feb.1,1982—Iranian Virus spurred Jordan's Aid to Iraq. 2= Rami G. Khouri January 29, 1982—Washington Post—Jordan's aid to Iraq

M-40 anti-tank guns with 24,000 shells for each weapon, spare parts for tanks and plane engines, 106 mm, 130 mm, 203 mm and 175mm grenades and TOW missiles. According to Trita Parsi, arms sales to Iran totaled an estimated $500 million from 1981 to 1983.[466] According to Ahmad Haidari, "roughly 80% of the weaponry bought by Tehran", immediately after the start of the war, originated in Israel. Also, Israel facilitated arms shipments from the US to Iran in the Iran-Contra Affair. Israel attacked Iraq's Osirak Nuclear Reactor on June 7, 1981, inflicting severe damage to Iraq's nuclear program. In fact, Iran bombed it first, back in 1980, but the attack only damaged secondary buildings. Israel supplied instructors, and non-armaments help to Iran, for the war effort, according to Trita Parsi.[467] According to Mark Pythian, the Reagan administration allowed Israel to channel arms of US origin to Iran, to prevent an easy and early Iraqi victory, resulting in Iran's ability to revive its air force, which was grounded due to lack of spare parts. Israeli arms dealer Yaakov Nimrud signed a deal with Iran's Ministry of National Defense, to sell arms worth $135,842,000, including Lane Missiles, Copperhead Shells and Hawk Missiles.[468] The volume of arms sale was so great that an office was set up in Cyprus, to help the arms transfers to Iran. The most well-known of the intermediaries, helping the arms deals, was Saudi billionaire Adnan Khashoggi.

Osirak Nuclear Reactor of Iraq: On 7 June 1981, a squadron of Israeli Air Force F-16 fighter aircraft, with an escort of F-15's, bombed Osirak Nuclear Reactor of Iraq, severely damaging it, The reactor was part of Iraq's Weapons Program, as had been reported, on September 8, 1975, by, then-Vice President Saddam Hussein, who declared publicly that the acquisition of the French Reactor, was the first step towards atomic weapons program.[469]

---

[466] Parsi, Trita Treacherous Alliance: The secret dealings of Israel, Iran and the United States, by Trita Parsi, Yale University Press, 2007.
[467] Parsi, Trita Treacherous Alliance: The secret dealings of Israel, Iran and the United States, by Trita Parsi, Yale University Press, 2007.
[468] Scott, Peter Dale, The Iran-Contra Connection: Secret Teams and Covert Operations in Reagan Era, 1987, South End Press,p.169-174
[469] preventive attacks against Iraq nuclear programs—Dan Reiter-Success at Osirak

1990 Gulf War (17 January – 28 February 1991)

Background: Iraq considered Kuwait as Iraqi territory, as Kuwait had been a part of the Ottoman Empire, as 'Basra Province. After world war 1, the UK drew the border between the two countries in 1922, making Iraq landlocked. Iraq accused Kuwait of exceeding its OPEC quota, by overproducing oil, which brought the price down to $10 a barrel, from $15. This resulted in Iraq losing, about $ 7 billion a year, in oil revenues.[470] Iraq also accused Kuwait of slant drilling at Iraq/Kuwait border, depriving Iraq of oil of its Ramallah oil fields.[471] Also, by the end of the Iran/Iraq war in 1988, Iraq had turned into a rogue nation, due to massive funding from the US and the Gulf states. Iraq' army consisted of 955,000 standing soldiers and 650,000 paramilitary forces.[472] Iraq wanted to lease Umm Qasr, a port on the Persian Gulf, from Kuwait, but its request was rejected by Kuwait. All these factors played a role in Iraq's decision to invade Kuwait.

Iraq's Invasion of Kuwait: At the Jeddah talks, held to negotiate a settlement of Iraq's grievances, Iraq demanded $10 billion to cover the lost revenues from Rumaila Oil Field. Kuwait offered $9 billion. Iraq responded by the invasion of Kuwait, which started on 2 August 1990, with the bombing of Kuwait's capital. The commander of a Kuwaiti armored battalion put up a good defense, west of Kuwait City. Kuwaiti planes scrambled to meet the invading force, but most were lost or captured. The Iraqis attacked the ruler's palace, which was defended by the Emiri Guard, supported by M-84 tanks. In the process, the Iraqis killed Fahd Al-Sabah, the ruler's youngest brother. Within 12 hours, Kuwaiti resistance ended, and Iraqi forces took control of Kuwait City and were then redeployed on

---

[470] Youssef M. Ibrahim, -Iraq threatens UAE and Kuwait on Oil Glut—New York Times, 18 July 1990.
[471] Stork, Joe; Lesch, Ann M. "Background to the Crisis: Why War?" *Middle East Report.* Middle East Research and Information Project (MERIP) (167, November–December 1990): 11–18.
[472] Youssef M. Ibrahim,—Iraq threatens UAE and Kuwait on Oil Glut—New York Times, 18 July 1990.

the Saudi border. [473]UN Security Council Condemned the Occupation of Kuwait, resulting in immediate sanctions by the member countries.

1990 Gulf War Details: A remarkable feature of the 1990 Gulf War was that it was telecast live by CNN from the front lines of battle, with cameras fitted, on the US bombers.[474] The war started with aerial and naval bombardment from the aircraft carriers, lasting for five weeks. The coalition carried out over 100,000 air attacks, dropping 88,500 tons of bombs, destroying the military and civilian infrastructure of Iraq. Air attacks were launched from Saudi bases and US aircraft carriers. Iraqi command and communication facilities were targeted, along with Truck-Mounted Scud Missiles. Special ground forces were covertly sent into western Iraq, to locate the scud launchers.[475] Iraq fired many Scud missiles on Israel, killing 74 Israelis, injuring 230, and damaging general property in Israel, consisting of 1,302 houses, 6,142 apartments, 23 public buildings, 200 shops, and 50 cars.[476] By attacking Israel, Iraq hoped to provoke a military response from Israel, resulting in many Arab states withdrawing from the Coalition, as they would be reluctant to fight alongside Israel. Following the first attacks, Israeli Air Force was ready to retaliate, but President Bush persuaded Israel not to, promising to deploy Patriot missiles for the protection of Israel. Iraq also fired scud missiles on Saudi Arabia. A scud missile hit the US Army barracks in Dhahran, Saudi Arabia, killing 28 soldiers and injuring over 100. The allied forces used massive artillery fire.[477] Both sides suffered casualties, although Iraqi forces suffered more than the allied forces. Iraqis lost over 3000 tanks and over 2000 other combat vehicles, during the battles against the coalition. Iraqis were expelled after four days of fighting. And while retreating, the

---

[473] Cooper, Tom; Sadik, Ahmed (16 September 2003)—Iraqi Invasion of Kuwait 1990—Air Combat Information Group.- Retrieved 17 April 2010

[474] CNN.com—Gulf War via Internet archive—Archived—on 12 June 2008. Retrieved 23 March 2008.

[475] Rick Atkinson (1994).—Crusade: The Untold Story of the Persian Gulf War. Houghton Mifflin Harcourt, p. 47.

[476] 3 Israelis killed as scud missiles hit Tel Aviv—the Tech- 1991. Retrieved 11 January 2009.

[477] DOD—Information Paper—Iraq's Scud Ballistic Missiles—Iraqwatch.org. Retrieved 18 March 2010.

Iraqis set fire to about 700 Oil Wells, and placed landmines around them, to make fire extinguishing difficult.[478]

Casualties: Coalition—292 killed (147 killed by enemy action, 145 non-hostile deaths.) 467 wounded in action. Iraq—20,000–35,000 killed, 75,000+ wounded. About 3,664 Iraqi civilians killed. Kuwaiti Civilian Losses—Over 1,000 killed.

2003 Invasion of Iraq: The 2003 Iraq War was meant to topple the government of Saddam Hussein, suspecting his involvement with al-Qaeda and having weapons of mass destruction. Saddam Hussein was captured in December, and executed 3 years later, after trial by a military court, for the killing of Iraqis. Allied forces withdrew in December. After the invasion, no evidence was found to support the initial claims about WMDs. Also, claims of Iraqi collaboration with al-Qaeda were proven false. The rationale and misrepresentation of US pre-war intelligence, therefore, faced heavy criticism both domestically and internationally.[479]

War Details: The US Invasion of Iraq was preceded by an airstrike on the Presidential Palace in Baghdad on 20 March 2003. The following day, coalition forces launched an attack into Basra Province, from their assembly point near the Iraq-Kuwait border. Special Forces attacked Basra and the surrounding petroleum fields, from the Persian Gulf.[480] Casualties of 2003 Iraq War: Coalition: Total Killed =196 (US—139, UK—33, Kurds—24) Coalition Wounded= 551. Iraqi Soldiers Killed = about 30,000 (according to General Tommy Franks) Iraqi Civilians Killed= 7269.[481]

---

[478] Holsti Ole R—(2011-11-07).—the US and Iraq before Iraq War—"The United States and Iraq before the Iraq War" American Public Opinion on the Iraq War—. p. 20.—. Air attacks inflicted heavy casualties on retreating forces along what became known as 'the highway of death.' American, British, and French units pursued the Iraqis to within 150 miles of Baghdad.

[479] US hardliners search for a saddam connection—Gulf States Newsletter—Middle East Insider (9). September 2001.

[480] John Pike.—on point—US Army in operation iraqi freedom—Globalsecurity.org. Retrieved 7 September 2010.

[481] Iraq Body Count—2003-2005—. Retrieved 2 May 2007

Iraqi Insurgency: Saudi Arabia opposed, 2003 Invasion of Iraq, by the US-led coalition and did not join the alliance because it feared formation of a Shia-led government, if Saddam Hussein was toppled, a scenario unacceptable for the Saudis who, then, covertly sent Saudi Jihadis into Iraq to embolden the Sunnis and to fight the US and Iraqi Shia forces, resulting in Iraqi Insurgency, which later turned into a dreadful Civil War. The insurgency led to widespread Shia/Sunni violence. The insurgent forces, consisting of al-Qaeda, and ISIS who then targeted the US-led coalition, which included the US and Shia Iraqi Government Forces. All the Insurgent groups were propped up by the Saudis who supplied them with funds and war materials.[482] The real cause of this support was the intense dislike and hatred of Saudis for the Shias whom they considered apostates who deserved to be killed. Saudis started, covertly, supporting, Al-Qaeda in Iraq in 2004, later assisting the ISIS in 2006, 2013, and 2014 in Iraq and Syria. Bush administration officials voiced concern over the counterproductive role of Saudi Arabia, in the Iraq War. Half of the foreign fighters, who were fighting in Iraq, were Saudi nationals who came across the border from Saudi Arabia, with the tacit approval of the Saudi Government.[483]

Saudi Policy of Shia Genocide: For decades, Saudi policy had been aimed at GENOCIDE of the SHIA Muslims worldwide because of their hatred for Shias whom they consider apostates and non-Muslims. This approach towards Shia Muslims was part of their Saudi Salafi religion. The genocide had been conducted, since the 1979 Iranian Revolution, initially to counter the revolution, culminating into an ongoing Genocide of Shia Muslims worldwide, particularly in Iraq, Syria, Yemen, Pakistan, Afghanistan, Africa, Russia, and other countries wherever the Saudi Salafi religion got a foothold. Warnings by the US Strategists and Government officials failed to convince the US administrations of President Reagan, Bush, and Obama that any action different from candid discussions with Saudi Leaders, was required. Shia Lives probably did not matter much

---

[482] Norton-Taylor, Richard (23 November 2009).—five key questions to be answered—via The Guardian

[483] Saudi Role in Iraq Insurgency—LA Times—July 2007—July 2007. Archived on 23 February 2009.

to them, ignoring Human Rights and regard for the sanctity of human life. The US policy of not alienating their age-old ally, Saudi Arabia, was kept at all costs. All US actions revolved around this policy. According to Sir Richard Dearlove. the boss of M16, intelligence, and facts had always been geared towards the US Policy.[459] Time and again, the Saudi leaders announced their genocidal policy, to the US on several occasions, ever since the Shia-led 1979 Islamic Revolution in Iran. According to US government documents, armed groups of Saudi Salafi ideology, like al-Qaeda, ISIS and al Nusra were formed, supported, and funded by the Saudis and Qataris, as their proxies, to fight and kill the Shia Muslims, and to replace the Shia-led governments with their form of caliphate, based on Saudi Salafi version of Sharia. Other armed groups, and organizations following the Saudi Salafi ideology, have been the Taliban in Afghanistan and Pakistan; Jamaat e Islami in Indonesia; al Shabab in Somalia; Boko Haram in Nigeria; Let(Lashkar-e-Tayyiba) and LeJ (Lashkar-e-Jhangvi) in Pakistan - all of them, funded by individuals and charities in Saudi Arabia, Qatar, UAE, and Kuwait with the tacit approval of their governments.[484]

Iraq Insurgency and the Saudi Role: In 2003, Saudi King Abdullah spelled out the Saudi policy, while talking to US Vice President Dick Cheney That: "Saudi Arabia will give funds to Iraqi Sunnis if there was a conflict with the Shias. "American and Arab diplomats said. King Abdullah condemned the US presence in Iraq as an illegal foreign occupation. The former head of M16, Richard Dearlove, revealed that Saudi Arabia was involved in the ISIS-led Sunni rebellion in Iraq, referring to Prince Bandar's statement.[459] In 2014, former Prime Minister of Iraq Nouri al-Maliki said Qatar and Saudi Arabia incited and encouraged terrorist movements, like ISIS and al-Qaeda, supporting them politically, in the media, with money and, by buying weapons for them.[485]

Foreign fighters in Iraq Insurgency: In May 2003, after the defeat and disbanding of Iraqi forces, the US military noticed increasing attacks on

---

[484] Terror Alliance In Iraq Targets U.S. Force—14 June 2003—FDD {foundation for defense of democracies)

[485] Hashim, A.S., 2003, The Insurgency in Iraq, Small Wars and Insurgencies, Volume 14(3), pp 1-22.

US troops in Sunni areas of Tikrit, Baghdad, Fallujah, and Ramadi. The insurgency was made up of elements of Saddam government, army and intelligence personnel, Saudi Salafi/ Salafi Muslims, Shia militia like the Mehdi Army, followers of Muqtada al-Sadr, and volunteers from other countries.[486]

Syrian Civil War: Syrian War had also been a very devastating war, started in 2011, against the Shia-led Syrian government, by the Sunni countries of the Middle East, supported by the US and European countries. It was like the Iraqi Civil War, against the Syrian Shia Muslims in general, and against the Shia-led government of Syria, to replace it with an Islamic State, like Saudi Arabia.[487] Most parties involved in the war in Syria, received various types of support from foreign countries. Iran, Russia, and Hezbollah of Lebanon supported the Syrian Government while the Opposition was supported by Saudi Arabia and the Sunni Gulf States, backed by the US and some European countries, who were keen to topple the Syrian government. Iran supported Syria because it has had a longstanding cooperation agreement with Syria, since 1956 and the Iranian Forces were there, at the request of the Syrian Government. Syria was the only country in the middle east that supported Iran, during the Iran/Iraq War of 1980-88. Russia had been supporting the Syrian government because it also has had a defense pact with Syria, since 1980 and a cooperation agreement, since 1946. Russia also has a Naval Military Base at Tartus, in Syria, since 1970.[488] Furthermore, Russia got involved in Syria, at the request of the Syrian government, and because it was concerned about 2500 Russian Jihadis who had been fighting alongside ISIS, against the Syrian government. The Syrian opposition consisted of Jihadi groups, such as ISIS, al-Qaeda, and al-Nusra, which had been heavily funded and armed, covertly, by Saudi Arabia, Qatar, Kuwait, UAE, Jordan, Turkey,

---

[486] the national origins of foreign fighters in Iraq—by Alan B. Krueger, Princeton University and NBER, 30 December 2006.
[487] Syria—the story of conflict—11 March 2016 – via www.bbc.com.
[488] O'Connor, Tom (31 March 2017).—Iran's military leader tells US to get out of Persian gulf—. Newsweek. The Gulf Arab faction, especially Saudi Arabia, has been engaged in a proxy war of regional influence with Iran.

and several non-state groups, individuals, and organizations from these countries.[489]

Casualties of the Syrian war: Total killed- over 475,000 (July 2017 Estimate). Over 7,600,000 internally displaced. Refugees—5,116,097 (July 2015 estimate by UNHCR.)

UAE Support for Syrian Opposition: UAE had been less aggressive, in supporting Syrian rebels, than Saudi Arabia and Qatar, and had supported Russian involvement in the conflict. However, it had been funding the moderate rebels and democratic forces of Syria. In July 2012, Switzerland ceased arms exports, to the UAE, after it came to know that Swiss weapons were finding their way to opposition fighters.[490]

Qatari Support to Al-Qaeda: According to Ron Proforma, Israeli diplomat, Qatar is the most two-faced nation in the world. It ignores terrorist financiers, operating in Qatar, with impunity, and also supports the US-led coalition in Syria. One of the leaked emails, in August 2014, addressed to John Podesta, named Qatar and Saudi Arabia as financers of ISIS and other radical Sunni groups, although Qatari Emir denied these accusations on American television on September 25, 2014. A diplomat in Qatar told the media that 8-12 "key figures in Qatar" were raising millions of pounds for Jihadi fighters in Syria. On June 9, 2017, during a press conference, US President Trump blamed Qatar for funding terrorism.[491]

Qatar's Support to Al-Nusra Front in Syria: Qatar sponsored al-Qaeda's affiliate in Syria, al -Nusra, since 2013, through ransom payments and fundraising campaigns. Qatar mediated release of 45 UN

---

[489] Syria allies—why Russia, Iran, and china are standing by the regime—CNN, 30 August 2013.
[490] UAE reaffirms support for Syria—*Gulf News*. 25 September 2013. Retrieved 25 September 2013. 8= UAE ready to commit troops to fight syria jihadists—*Defense News*. 30 November 2015. Retrieved 23 December 2015.
[491] Doha's dangerous Dalliance—issue 27—fall/winter 2014—journal of international Security Affairs. Retrieved 10 August 2017. 13= Sigurd Neubauer (8 August 2017).—rift between Qatar and GCC could threaten Trump's foreign policy—The National Interest. Retrieved 10 August 2017.

Fijian peacekeepers kidnapped in August 2014. Also, Qataris sponsored fundraising campaigns to ask for help in the procurement of weapons, food, and supplies for al-Nusra in Syria.[492]

Kuwaiti Support of Terrorism: According to journalist Andrew Gilligan, in 2013, Jihadis openly appealed for donations for weapons and troops on TV, websites and social media in Kuwait and Qatar. The Taliban and the Haqqani groups earned "significant funds" through Kuwait -based businesses.[493]

Yemeni Civil War (2015–present): Since April 2015, a Saudi-led coalition of nine Sunni countries, consisting of Egypt, Morocco, Jordan, Sudan, UAE, Kuwait, Qatar, Bahrain, and mercenaries from other countries, had been taking part in the military offensive, causing over 100,000 casualties by 01 November 2019, according to a report by the US-based Armed Conflict Location and Event Data Project (ACLED) and widespread damage to Yemen's infrastructure.[494] The United States had been giving intelligence and logistical support, in addition to accelerated sales of weapons, to coalition countries. Pakistan was invited by Saudi Arabia, to join the coalition, but its parliament voted to keep neutrality.[495] 78% (20 million) of the Yemeni population was in urgent need of food, water, and medical aid. Aid ships were permitted, but the bulk of commercial shipping, on which the country relied, was blocked. On one occasion, coalition jets prevented an Iranian Red Crescent plane from landing, by bombing the Sana'a airport's runway, which blocked aid delivery via air. As of 10 December, the fighting had internally displaced more than

---

[492] al-Nusra and ts gulf financiers—the political cost of along-running alliance—**consortium** against terrorist finance—*Stopterrorfinance.org*. Retrieved 2016-09-04.
[493] Walsh, Declan (December 5, 2010)-Wikileaks cables portray Saudi Arabia as a cash machine for terrorists—the Guardian—. London. 24=US embassy cables—Afghan Taliban and Haqqani Network using United Arab Emirates as funding base—the Guardian—December 5, 2010
[494] Background Note-Yemen- US Department of State, January 2006
[495] (editor) Herbert-Burns, Rupert; (editor) Bateman, Sam; (editor) Lehr, Peter (September 2008).—Lloyd's MIU handbook of maritime security—. Boca Raton: CRC Press. p. 60.—. Retrieved 27 September 2016.

2,500,000 people. Many countries evacuated their citizens from Yemen. More than 1,000,000 people left Yemen for Saudi Arabia, Djibouti, Somalia, Ethiopia, Sudan, and Oman. 17 million people were facing famine, due to a shortage of food, and thousands infected by cholera. The Saudi coalition had been using the banned UK and US-made cluster munitions on Sana'a.[496] On 8 October 2016, a Saudi-led airstrike on a funeral ceremony, killed 100 people and injured 500, including children

Use of White Phosphorus in Yemen: Under US regulations, white phosphorus is only used to signal troop movements in low visibility. If used on humans, it burns human flesh down to the bone. Saudi coalition used white phosphorus in the Yemen war, a callous practice.[497]

Targeting of wounded and medical personnel: The United Nations alleged that the Saudi-led coalition had committed a war crime because the coalition attacked the wounded, aid workers and medical personnel, who were attending the wounded.[498]

The Taliban: They are a by-product of the Afghan Jihad, which was led by about 25,000 Saudi Jihadists, in the 1970s and 1980s. Taliban had always been supported, by Saudi Arabia and its allied Gulf Sunni countries. Taliban means students of Madrasas (Islamic religious schools). Madrasas for Afghan refugees in Pakistan, appeared in the 1980s, near the Afghan-Pakistan border. They were initially funded by zakat donations in Pakistan, through the religious parties and later started receiving money from charities and individuals in Saudi Arabia and other Gulf countries. Most of these madrasas, follow Deobandi ideology, which is like the religion of Saudi Arabia. There are now over 15000 madrasas with over a million students, in South-East Asia. Many graduates of these

---

[496] On 27 May 2016, the United States suspended transfer of cluster munitions to Saudi Arabia in the wake of harm caused to civilians in Yemen—CMC—June 2016

[497] Saudi Arabia appears to be using US supplied white phosphorus in its war in Yemen—. *The Washington Post.* 19 September 2016.

[498] www.un.org/press/en/2016/sc12536.doc.htm. Evidence of attacks against the sick and wounded, as well as medical personnel and facilities, underscored the grim reality that international humanitarian law

madrasas later joined the Taliban, and many fought in Kashmir. At the Haqqani School near Peshawar, Taliban leader Mullah Omar and eight future ministers of the Taliban government learned the Deobandi Sect's rigidly anti-modern teachings. After the Soviets departed, Afghanistan descended into anarchy, as warlords and ethnic armies, competed for power. The head of Saudi intelligence Prince Turki al-Faisal tried but could not get the warring factions to work together. Then, in 1994, the Afghan refugee students who had developed into a religious-political-military force, intervened and whenever they entered a town, implored the warlords, to put down their weapons, for God's sake. If the warlords refused, the Taliban killed them. By the end of 1995, the Taliban had taken control of all the southern and western Afghanistan. In 1996, they moved east and took Kabul in September. The first reaction of the people, toward the Taliban, was relief that order had finally replaced chaos.[499] While in power, the Taliban implemented the "strictest interpretation of Sharia Law "like Saudi Arabia. They outlawed television, music, singing, fashion magazines, cigarettes, alcohol, use of the toothbrush, and being clean-shaven. In soccer stadiums, the Taliban whipped drunkards, cut hands of thieves, and let families of murder victims kill the killers of their loved ones. The Taliban's most oppressive laws dealt with the women and the Shia Muslims. Women could not work, teach, go to school or anywhere outside, without a relative and had to wear a head to toe abaya or burqa, outside the home.[500] Saudis and the clerics liked what they saw. The Taliban reminded them of their own pre-oil past, of the early Saudi Salafis of the eighteenth century and the Ikhwan warriors, in the 1910s and 1920's. Saudi Arabia, Pakistan, and UAE recognized the Taliban as the official government of Afghanistan, before the 9/11 attacks, (after 9/11 no country recognized it). Saudi officials gave them money, vehicles, weapons, and gasoline tankers to capture Kabul. They helped the Taliban to form religious police like Saudi Arabia. Osama bin Laden admired the Taliban and supported them with financial and paramilitary help and, in 1997, he moved to Kandahar, the Taliban stronghold. During their rule, the

---

[499] the Taliban—Mapping Militant Organizations. Stanford University. Retrieved June 5, 2016.

[500] Skain, Rosemarie (2002). The women of Afghanistan under the Taliban. McFarland. p. 41.

Taliban killed thousands of civilians mercilessly, denied food to 160,000 starving civilians, burnt large areas of fertile land, and destroyed thousands of homes, as reported by the UN, which also said Taliban were responsible for 76% of all afghan deaths in 2010, and 80% in 2011and 2012.[501] Many accuse the Pakistani ISI and military to support the Taliban during their reign and their continued support during the insurgency, but the official Pakistani position is that it dropped all support for the group, after the 9/11 attacks. Al-Qaeda also supported the Taliban, with fighters from Arab countries and Central Asia. Saudi Arabia had been giving financial support to the Taliban all along, during its government and during the insurgency. Thousands of Afghans fled to northern Afghanistan, the United Front-controlled territory, Pakistan, and Iran, during the Taliban's reign. The group is named as a terrorist organization, by some governments, but not by the United Kingdom, the US, France, Russia, and China.

Shia Killings in Pakistan: Since 2008, "thousands of Shias Muslims," had been killed in Pakistan and Afghanistan, by Sunni extremists of Saudi Salafi Ideology. Terrorists often attacked Shia mosques to maximize fatalities, and to "emphasize the religious dimensions of their attack."[502] In 2011 and 2012, Pakistan minority groups Hindus, Ahmadis, and Christians, also faced insecurity and persecution in the country. Attacks on Sufi shrines have also taken place.[503] Among those blamed for the sectarian violence in the country have been Sunni militant groups of Saudi/Salafi Ideology, such as the Lashkar-e-Jhangvi, Sipah-e-Sahaba, Tehrik-e-Taliban Pakistan, and Jundullah, against the Shias, according to Human Rights Watch. These Sunni militant groups have also been attacking the fellow Sunnis, Barelvis, and Sufis.[504]

---

[501] UN says Taliban starving hungry people for military agenda—Associated Press, 1998-01-07

[502] Pakistan—Rampant killings of Shias by extremists—Human Rights Watch. 30 June 2014. Retrieved 16 November 2014.

[503] Charlotte Buchen—Sufism under attack in Pakistan——(video). The New York Times. Retrieved 21 May 2012.

[504] Sunni Ittehad Council-Sunni/Barelvi activism against Deobandi/Wahhabi terrorism in Pakistan—by Aarish U.Khan—Retrieved 12 December 2013.

ISIS and Taliban's Shia Killings in Afghanistan: In February 1993, the Taliban government, allied with Abdul Rasul Sayyaf of Saudi Salafi-supported Etihad-e-Islami, attacked Afshar district, west of Kabul, killing 70 people on the street and abducting 700-750 people of Hazara Shias, who were never returned, and probably died in captivity.[505] In July 1998, the Taliban, aided by several hundred Afghan Arab fighters, sent by Osama bin Laden, attacked Mazar-e-Sharif. They used the trucks mounted with machine guns, donated by Saudi Arabia, to capture Mazar-e-Sharif and slaughtered 6000 to 8000 Shia men, women, and children, slitting their throats and bleeding them to death, halal-style, and baking hundreds of victims in shipping containers, without water, to be baked alive, in the desert sun.[506] At that time, 10 Iranian diplomats were also killed, prompting Iran to mobilize its forces and 250,000 Iranian troops were stationed, along Iran Afghan border. Pakistan mediated to diffuse tensions and bodies of Iranians, were returned to Tehran. The similar massacre was repeated later, in 1999, in Bamiyan, where hundreds of men, women, children were executed. This reminded the author Dr. Dore Gold, of the Saudi Salafi Attack on Shia shrines in Karbala and Najaf in Iraq, in 1802 by Saudi King Abdul Aziz, in which over 5000 Shia civilians, including women and children, were massacred.[507] On January 8-10,2001, another massacre took place in the town of Yakawlang, Bamiyan province, where over 300 people, including many aid agency personnel and a UN Official, were killed.[508] On January 5-14, 2000, a mass murder, was carried out at Robatak Pass, killing 31 people, of which 26 were Ismaili Shias. The victims were detained for 4 months before their execution, on January 5-14, 2000, by Taliban troops. In June 2000: 9 Hazara Shias, were killed in Khas Uruzgan district.[509] In November 2015: 4 men, 2 women and an

---

[505] massacre at Robatak Pass—may 2000—2006. Retrieved 2012-04-12
[506] Gutman, Roy (2008). *How We Missed the Story: Osama Bin Laden, the Taliban, and the Hijacking of Afghanistan.* Institute of Peace Press. p. 142
[507] Armajani, Jon (2012). *Modern Islamist Movements: History, Religion, and Politics.* Wiley-Blackwell. p. 207
[508] Maley, William (2002). *The Afghanistan wars.* Palgrave Macmillan. p. 240.
[509] massacre at Robatak Pass—may 2000—2006. Retrieved 2012-04-12— Urzogan: Alissa J. Rubin (June 26, 2010).—Taliban kill 9 members of minority in ambush—New York Times—. p. A6.

8-year girl from Hazara Shias, were beheaded, by the Taliban, in Zabul. Their throats were cut with metal wire. On July 23,2016: Two ISIS suicide bombers, blew themselves up in a Kabul street, killing 160 and wounding over 200. Again, in July 2016, Shooters wearing police uniforms, attacked Sakhi Shrine in Kabul, killing 18 and injuring 54, on the eve of Ashura, the Shia Mourning Day. The next morning, at least 15 Hazara Shias, were killed by an IED, claimed by the ISIS. In Hov.2016, a Shia mosque of Baqir-ul-Uloom was attacked, killing 27, and wounding dozens.[510] On July 24,2017, A bus carrying government workers was bombed, killing 30 when the Shia gathered to mark the first anniversary of bombing by ISIS that had killed 80. On October 19, 2017, Taliban militants attacked an army base in Maiwand while the soldiers there slept—reported Glass. "A suicide bomber blew up an armored vehicle, and then, the fighters went in.10 Taliban fighters were also killed, and Six soldiers from the base were reported missing. This brought the week's toll to more than 120 people killed, by the militant group".[511]

U.S. War in Afghanistan: The US War in Afghanistan was in response to the 9/11 Al-Qaeda attacks in the United States. Although Saudi Arabia was not involved directly or indirectly in this war, it did give support, at some stage, to the main planner of 9/11 attacks, the founder of Al-Qaeda, Osama bin Laden, who had turned against Saudi Arabia but chose to target the United States, instead of the kingdom itself. Also, the Taliban and their government have always been supported by Saudi Arabia. Even if the Saudi government denies direct support, support from the members of the Saudi Royal family cannot be denied. For example, when Osama bin Laden was under the sanctions of the Saudi government and returned to Afghanistan from Sudan, a midlevel Saudi prince visited him and gave him $100 million. This has already been described while discussing Osama in another section. After the 9/11 attacks, the US demanded that

---

[510] Kabul explosion—IS admits attack on Hazara protesters—BBC Asia. 23 July 2016. Retrieved 24 July 2016.-2=Sakhi shrine: Shuja, Ahmad-Afghanistan's Shia hazaras suffer latest atrocity—hrw.org. Retrieved November 3, 2017

[511] Kandahar: www.spokesman.com/stories/2017/oct/19—/taliban-attacks-kill-58-nearly-wipe-out-afghan-arm/—Taliban attacks kill 58, nearly wipe out Afghan army camp. UPDATED: Thu., Oct. 19, 2017, 12:06 p.m.

the Taliban Government hand over Osama bin Laden and expel al-Qaeda from Afghanistan.[512] As a result, on 7 October 2001, the U.S. and the United Kingdom attacked Afghanistan. The northern alliance, led by Ahmad Shah Masood, later, joined the coalition, to fight the Taliban. After the Taliban Government, was toppled by the US coalition, Mullah Omar launched an insurgency in 2003, against the US-backed Afghan Government and the US coalition. Though outgunned and outnumbered, Taliban insurgents waged a Guerrilla Warfare, against the coalition forces.[513] ISAF (International Security Assistance Force) responded in 2006, by increasing troops. Violence sharply increased from 2007 to 2009. In May 2012, NATO started withdrawing their forces. In May 2014, the United States announced that its major combat operations would end in December 2014 and that it would leave a token force in the country. In October 2014, British forces handed over the last bases to the Afghan Military, officially ending their combat operations in the war. On 28 December 2014, NATO formally ended combat operations in Afghanistan and transferred full security responsibility to the Afghan government.[514] Since early 2017, thousands of American and other NATO troops stayed in Afghanistan, as military advisors, and for the counterterrorism operations, without any formal plans to withdraw.

Fatalities of Afghan War: Fatalities of this war included over 4000 ISAF (US and Allied forces) soldiers and civilians, over 15,000 Afghan Government forces as well as 20,000 civilians. The Taliban suffered about 25,500-40,500 killed, along with 31,000 civilian deaths, and 15000 wounded.[515]

---

[512] Bush rejects Taliban offer to hand over Bin Laden—The Guardian. Retrieved 24 January 2015. 2=Vulliamy, Ed; Wintour, Patrick; Traynor, Ian; Ahmed, Kamal (7 October 2001).—after 9/11 attacks—'it is tie for war—Bush and Blair tell Taliban'—the Guardian.

[513] Taliban Resurgence in Afghanistan—Archived—on 27 September 2006 6= Starkey, Jerome (30 September 2010).—Karzai/Taliban talks raise spectre of civil war—warns former spy chief—. The Scotsman. Edinburgh

[514] US formally ends war in Afghanistan—(online). CBA News. Associated Press. 28 December 2014. Retrieved 28 December 2014.

[515] Crawford, Neta (August 2016).—update on the human costs of war for Afghanistan and Pakistan—2001 to mid-2016 (PDF). brown.edu.

CONCLUSION

From the preceding chapters, the reader has, most probably, noticed that Saudi Salafism, is a deviation from the teachings of Islam, as evidenced from the clear injunctions of the Quran and the teachings of the Prophet (pbuh), outlined in Chapter1, which emphasize the sanctity of human life regardless of religious affiliation, tolerance of other faiths, choice of lifestyle, resistance to cruelty and injustice in society, freedom of worship, respect for women, and other traits necessary for a successful life. Saudi Salafism, the extremist ideology of Sunni Islam, which formed the ideological basis of Global Terrorism, was propagated throughout the world, at a phenomenal cost of over 70 billion dollars in the 1970's and 1980's by Saudi Arabia, with the tacit approval and support of the U.S and the Western nations, for political purposes. Saudi Arabia's goal was, initially, to undermine Shia Islam of Iran whose 1979 Islamic Revolution, seemed to threaten the Gulf Monarchies and autocratic regimes, although Imam Khomeini, the revolutionary leader of Iran, called for Shia/Sunni unity and brotherhood, but encouraged the replacement of aggressive regimes, like the Shah of Iran, with republican governments, representing the people, rather than a dynasty or a family. The U.S., and the West, encouraged the Saudi Extremism, as they foresaw fundamentalist Islam as a powerful tool, to defeat the Ottoman Empire, to counter the Soviet expansionism, and to counter nationalist and socialist movements, like the Nasserism of Egypt. However, the Jihadis fighting the Soviets in Afghanistan were radicalized, during the Afghan Jihad. After the withdrawal of Soviet forces from Afghanistan, the Jihadis returned to their home countries, with a radical agenda, to replace their governments with an Islamic State, following the Salafi Jihadi ideology of Sayyid Qutb of Egypt. Osama bin Laden was a follower of this ideology that sanctioned the killing of civilians, including women and children, along with the apostate Muslims, Jews, and Christians. In their quest for Muslim World Domination, through their Jihadi proxies and unique financial resources, the Saudis had been engaged in a Shia Genocide, in the Muslim countries, since the end of Iran/ Iraq war of 1980-88, and committing terrorism in Europe to kill the Jews, Christians, and non-Saudi Salafi Muslims. When confronted, they said, they were themselves, victims of terrorism, although the terror attacks in Saudi Arabia, targeted only foreigners or Shias or, at the most, the Saudi Security forces. None of the over 20,000 Saudi Princes, had ever been attacked or suffered any property loss, in Saudi Arabia or abroad, although they have had sprawling mansions and businesses, within the kingdom and in all the major cities of the world. When King Abdullah told Dick Cheney, the US Vice President in 2003, that they would support Iraqi Sunnis, in any war against the Shias in Iraq, if the US pulled its troops out of Iraq, what did the US do in response? The US did nothing, and the Shia Genocide had continued, unabated all over the world, since 2003, particularly, in Iraq, Afghanistan, Pakistan, Africa, and Syria. Prince Bandar bin Sultan confirmed the Saudi Policy of Shia genocide while talking to the M16 boss, Sir Richard Dearlove, sometime before the 9/11 attacks, saying "time is not far off in the Middle East when it will be hell for the Shias." The Iran/Iraq War of 1980-88, the Gulf Wars of 1990 and 2003, the 2001 Afghan War, and Iraqi/Syrian Civil Wars, had cost the US and its allies, about 20,000 lives of security personnel. In these conflicts: 1,035,000 Iraqis, 500,000 Iranians, 475,000 Syrians, 100,000 Pakistanis, and about 10,000 Africans had lost their lives, including civilians, women, and children. The total number of fatalities of these wars is estimated at 2,200,000 human lives. (see chapter 8) Unfortunately, these wars were instigated and funded primarily by Saudi Arabia and supported by the US and its allies, either overtly or covertly. The only person who could stem the Jihadi violence in the world, is the King of Saudi Arabia, by abrogating the Saudi / Salafi doctrine of TAKFIR (the doctrine of terror), which motivated the Jihadis, to kill apostates (according to their interpretation of Islam), including Shias, Sufis, Jews, and Christians. The Saudi Religion must be reformed to accommodate all non-Saudi Salafis, including mainstream

Muslims, Shias, Jews, Christians, and other lifestyles, through preachers of all the mosques in the world, particularly through pronouncements in the holy mosques of Mecca and Medina. This action would pave the way for World Peace, but the edict of the King, would need to be supplemented, by his daring announcement of renouncing all the Jihadi groups and an immediate halt to their funding by organizations, governments, and individuals in the Arab World, and finally committing Saudi forces, to fight those who persisted in terrorism. May God Bless the King of Saudi Arabia, for His Help, in Stemming the Violence against the oppressed and marginalized Shia Muslims and Others. The present King Salman, and the Crown Prince Mohammad bin Salman (the future King), in November 2017, expressed their resolve, to return Saudi Arabia to Moderate Islam. This is, no doubt, a daunting commitment on the part of the Crown Prince, Mohammad bin Salman, and the King, which they could surely accomplish, with determination and courage. By tradition, The Saudi Salafi clergy, are subservient to the King of Saudi Arabia. The ancestor of the Saudi Royals, and father of King Salman, King Abdul Aziz bin Saud (r.a), in 1929, crushed the Saudi Salafi Extremist Ikhwan, who did not agree with his friendship of the British and Americans and opposed his desire to use modern technology of automobiles and telegraph. The king called a meeting of all Muslim leaders, including the Shias, to discuss ways of combating socialist and nationalist movements, in the Muslim world. Against the wishes of the religious establishment, the king allowed Shias to come for Hajj and pilgrimages and forbade forced conversions of Shias to Saudi Salafism. However, as of June 2019, nothing concrete has been done by the King and the crown prince to soften their religion. Executions of critics, journalists, and Shia Muslims have recently been done by Saudi Arabia despite their promise to moderate the religion. The recent killing of famous journalist and critic of Saudi policies Khashoggi, in the Saudi consulate in Turkey, is the modern-day example.

ADDENDUM

Eu Study On "The Involvement of Salafism/Saudi Salafism in Support of Rebel Groups in the World"

Policy Department DG External Policies of EU—STUDY—"THE INVOLVEMENT OF SALAFISM/Saudi Salafism IN THE SUPPORT AND SUPPLY OF ARMS TO REBEL GROUPS AROUND THE WORLD." The European Parliament's Committee on Foreign Affairs requested this study. AUTHOR(S): Claude MONIQUET, CEO, European Strategic Intelligence and Security Center (ES ISC), Belgium.

ABSTRACT OF STUDY

The war in Afghanistan is undoubtedly a key moment in the emergence of an armed rebellion in the Muslim world. The impact of this conflict quickly exceeded the borders of Afghanistan to extend to Pakistan. Since then, the Iraq war, the civil war that engulfed Syria and the armed conflict in the Sahel have helped to increase guerrillas in the Muslim world. This study aims to analyze the role of the Salafi / Saudi Salafi networks in financing and arming rebel groups. Note: This study names Saudi Arabia and Qatar as the main proponents of Global Islamic Terrorism in the form of Global Jihad against infidels namely non-Saudi/Salafi Muslims, Shia Muslims, Jews, and Christians, in the world by supporting and funding the terrorist groups.

FURTHER READING

-Prophets and Princes --Mark Weston
-Muqtada --Patrick Cockburn
-Out of the Ashes -- " ----
-Rise of the Islamic State -- " ----
-Siege of Mecca --Yaroslava Trofimov
-On Saudi Arabia --Karen Elliott House
-Saudi Arabia --James Wynbrandt
-Princes of Darkness --Laurent Murawiec
-Syria is Burning --Charles Glass
-Hatred's Kingdom --Dore Gold
-Brilliant Unmasking of the Destructive Saudi Policies by A.E. Moutet Nov 24, 2005
-Saudi Salafi War on the West by Shalom Freedman Oct 9, 2005
-A Factual Analysis of Saudi Arabia by George Murray Feb. 19, 2006
-A Convincing Rant by P. Wilson April 4, 2006
-'Saudis Backed Terror' by Patricia Sullivan Washington Post Staff Writer October 14, 2009-

A FERVENT APPEAL TO THE KING OF SAUDI ARABIA

O' the Mighty Prince Mohammad ibn Salman (the Future King)—Being the youngest King in the History of Saudi Arabia, with belief in the sanctity of God-given life, exceptional courage, drive and ability, unlike your predecessors, there are high hopes and expectations from you, for humankind in general, and the marginalized communities like the Shias, the Sufism, Christians, Jews, and the people of other lifestyles. The Shia Muslims have been facing severe persecution, all over the world, for last 4 decades, resulting in thousands of deaths. Your sympathetic direct intervention can end the violence, being committed by armed Muslim groups. The people of the World, and the Scholars of the West expect that you will reform Islam to make it more accommodating and tolerant towards other beliefs, like the Prophet (pbuh). It is expected that you rule like your grandfather, King Abdul Aziz (r.a), who was tolerant towards all branches of Islam, and about whom, Sir Percy Cox, Britain's Political Resident in the Middle East, at the time, once said "he never knew Ibn Saud to make a wrong move." May God bless you and your kingdom.